TOWARDS A PEACE ECONOMY IN THE UNITED STATES

TOWARDS A PEACE ECONOMY IN THE UNITED STATES

Essays on Military Industry, Disarmament and Economic Conversion

Edited by Gregory A. Bischak
Introduction by Seymour Melman

St. Martin's Press   New York

First published in the United States of America in 1991

Printed in Hong Kong

ISBN 0–312–04731–2

Library of Congress Cataloging-in-Publication Data

Towards a peace economy in the United States: essays on military
industry, disarmament, and economic conversion / edited by Gregory
A. Bischak; introduction by Seymour Melman.
p.   cm.
Includes bibliographical references.
ISBN 0–312–04731–2
1. Economic conversion–United States.   2. Disarmament–Economic
aspects–United States.   3. Defense industries–United States.
I. Bischak, Gregory A., 1950– / .
HC110.D4T68   1990
338.973–dc20   90–32034
                                                                CIP

Contents

List of Tables

List of Figures

Notes on the Contributors

J. Davidson Alexander is Associate Professor of Political Economy at Fitchburg State College, Fitchburg, Massachusetts. He has written on economic conversion policy and the effects of military spending on the economy.

Gregory A. Bischak is Senior Economist at Employment Research Associates, Lansing, Michigan. He has written on industrial policy, environmental and energy economics, disarmament and economic conversion issues. He has taught as an assistant professor of economics, and has particular expertise in nuclear power economics.

Michael Black is a San Francisco-based policy analyst who writes on the social impact of science and technology, state economic planning and development, and the environment. He is also a Visiting Assistant Professor of Government at Mills College, Oakland, California.

Anthony DiFilippo is Associate Professor of Sociology at Lincoln University, Pennsylvania. He is the author of several articles on military research and development policy and its effects on industrial competence, and a book *Military Spending and Industrial Decline: A Study of the American Machine Tool Industry* (1986).

Lloyd J. Dumas is Professor of Political Economy and Economics at the University of Texas at Dallas. He is the author of several books, the most recent of which is *The Overburdened Economy*, 1986, which examines the causes of unemployment and inflation, and the economic effects of the military economy.

Jonathan Feldman is Program Director at the National Commission for Economic Conversion and Disarmament in Washington, DC. He is the author of *Universities in the Business of Repression*, 1989, which examines the role of the academic–military–industrial complex in shaping US Central American policy.

Nance Goldstein is Associate Professor of Economics at the University of Southern Maine, Portland, Maine. She has written on military–industrial research policy and the computer software industry, and has served as an economic adviser on defense, employment and technology issues for a Member of Parliament, House of Commons, London.

Seymour Melman is Professor Emeritus of Industrial Engineering at Columbia University in New York. He is the author of eight books. The most recent of these are *The Demilitarized Society*, 1988 and *Profits Without Production*, 1983 and 1988.

Joel Yudken is a policy analyst in Technology Policy and Industrial Alternatives, Stanford, California. He is a National Science Foundation, Studies in Science and Technology & Society Fellow at the Tremont Research Institute, San Francisco, California, 1989–90.

Preface

As the citizens and political leaders of the United States begin to debate the character of a post-Cold War military and security policy, it is evident that the economic legacy of the Cold War must be examined in order to chart a path toward a peace economy. The contributions in this volume attempt to shed light on the complex economic effects of what has been deemed 'the permanent war economy'. Further, they seek to identify alternatives to the current militarily-dominated industrial, security, and science and technology policies.

While some may be tempted to view this book as consisting of contributions holding to a singular standpoint, namely, the so-called depletionist school, it would be a mistake to ascribe such a view to each contributor. Nevertheless, each of the chapters present new and interesting ideas and findings about the effects of the military on the economy, industry and society.

In the introductory chapter, Seymour Melman presents a compelling analysis of the economic and ideological heritage of the Cold War, and argues that democratic conversion planning is an essential step in the economic and political renewal of the United States. The chapters in Part I analyze the effects of military high-technology policy on innovation and economic performance. In the first chapter, Anthony DiFilippo examines the different approaches to high-technology policies in four advanced capitalist countries, and the comparative effects of these policies on each nation's performance and industrial base. Chapter 2, by Nance Goldstein, analyzes the contradictory effects of military-sponsored research and development on the computer software industry in the United States, an industry of growing importance for the vitality of the high-technology sectors of the economy.

In Part II, a theoretical and empirical analysis of the effects of military resource use is presented in two complementary chapters. In the chapter by Lloyd J. Dumas, a theoretical framework is advanced for understanding and analyzing the economic implications of different types of resource use in the economy, with particular consideration given to the non-contributive nature of military activities in the economy. J. Davidson Alexander develops a detailed empirical analysis of the effects of military spending and resource use on US manufacturing productivity, in an attempt to evaluate many of the hypotheses about the depletionary effects of the military on the economy.

Part III attempts to identify alternatives to the current military–industrial policy and advance proposals for disarmament, economic conversion and a more democratic approach to using and developing the nation's science and technology resources. Alternative security policies are examined in a chapter by Gregory A. Bischak, with the aim of showing the political-economic function of the arms race and the prospects for real disarmament and security, as opposed to another round of 'arms control' as usual. In the chapter by Joel Yudken and Michael Black, a National Needs Agenda is advanced for defining and developing a civilian-oriented science and technology policy which could replace the current militarily-oriented policy. The concluding chapter by Jonathan Feldman seeks to identify the political and economic constituencies which could forge a post-Cold War coalition to begin the process of social, economic and environmental reconstruction.

It is hoped that this book can contribute to the task of redefining the terms of the debate over the future of the United States' social, economic and security policies.

Gregory A. Bischak

Introduction

Seymour Melman

ECONOMIC CONVERSION AND ECONOMIC RENEWAL

The close of the Cold War and possible wind-down of major military budgets draws attention to alternative civilian uses of the resources of military economy. For this purpose, having accurate information on the micro and macro nature and scale of military economy becomes a matter of direct policy importance.

The Great Depression and the Second World War were experiences that decisively shaped political–economic policy in the United States for the remainder of the twentieth century. The Great Depression led to a consensus understanding of 'the economic problem' as primarily one of fluctuation in market demand – especially for capital goods. Thereby the main problem of public policy was how to control this fluctuation within acceptable limits. The Second World War seemed to demonstrate that the United States could produce both a torrent of military materiel and more consumer goods at the same time. Indeed, average American consumption expenditures rose during the Second World War. From that four-year experience economists and politicians drew a set of inferences that had fateful consequences for the US economy for the remainder of the century. It was assumed that this country could have guns and butter for an indefinite period, that the economic experience of the Second World War could continue during forty years of further cold and hot war. Economists further assumed that government spending, particularly military spending, was an appropriate method for regulating market demand. That role of government has been agreed by every President, every federal administration in the United States from the Second World War to the present day.

The name of that policy system is 'military Keynesianism'. Keynesianism is the use of government spending to regulate market demand and thereby income and employment. Military Keynesianism is therefore accomplishing those ends primarily through military expenditures, which are assumed to be as effective as any other for regulating market demand.

xiii

Indeed, the confidence in this policy-orientation has been so thoroughgoing that American textbooks of economics, with only one exception,[1] do not identify military economy as a separate entity. Accordingly the military economy, set in permanent motion after the Second World War, is treated in US textbooks as an undifferentiated part of the rest of the economy.

The orientation to military Keynesianism was a unified orientation from political right to left. Thus, *U.S. News and World Report*, a conservative journal, wrote in 1950, 'business won't go to pot so long as war is a threat, so long as every alarm can step up spending for defense at home and aid abroad. Cold War is almost a guarantee against a bad depression.' In the liberal center Jerome Weisner, science adviser to Presidents Kennedy and Johnson, judged that, 'the armaments industry has provided a sort of automatic stabilizer for the whole economy'. And on the left among the neo-marxists, Herbert Gintis, Professor of Economics and contributor to the *Review of Radical Political Economics*, noted in an evaluation of American Keynesianism, 'the military industrial complex has eliminated the specter of secular stagnation'.[2]

This consensus has formed an important part of the ideology to which Americans have been trained. The ideology was bolstered after the Second World War by the manifest productive competence of the US industrial system – really the only major one left intact, not bombed, not destroyed. That confidence was furthered by the way the rest of the world looked to the United States as a model to be emulated. The 'productivity teams' came to the United States from all parts of the world to learn how to be an industrial country, how to be efficient.

In keeping with this confidence and in pursuit of the use of military power as a worldwide political instrument, the government of the United States expended from 1947 to 1987 $7.6 trillion (in 1982 dollars) in its military budgets. This immense capital fund exceeded the value of all US industrial plant and equipment, plus all US infrastructure, by 1982.

I am wary of understating the role of ideology (especially the elements pertaining to US–USSR relations) as a factor in driving the Cold War and its arms race. That is why I wish to supplement the summary of US mainstream ideology that I have given above with a brief but authoritative assessment of the role of ideology given by Mr Eduard A. Shevardnadze, the Minister of Foreign Affairs of the

USSR (at the Foreign Policy Association, New York City, 2 October 1989). He stated in part:

> Let me recall historical precedents and draw some parallels between, for example, the current situation in our economy and the Great American Depression.
>
> In 1929, a powerful and confident state took an economic nosedive. There were bread lines in New York's Times Square and tents of the jobless huddled along Riverside Drive. In Washington troops were fighting the Bonus Army that had invaded the capital. People were dying in demonstrations, strikes and riots.
>
> On 7 October 1931 *Business Week* magazine reported that Amtorg had received 100,000 requests from Americans who wanted to emigrate to work and live in the Soviet Union.
>
> It is well known that in those years there were wide-spread expectations in left-wing circles that the severe crisis of the world capitalist system would finally bring about the world revolution. And long after that it was still believed that only the World War helped that system to stand up and survive.
>
> On a theoretical level, critics of imperialism made two conclusions which left an imprint on subsequent relations between the two social systems.
>
> Number one. In this development capitalism had reached the last stage; it was doomed and could prolong its existence only through militarization.
>
> Number two. Recurring economic crises would inevitably push it toward aggression and war for it would have no other option.
>
> Critics of communism took a similar view of the Soviet Union's development. They too made gloomy assumptions that communism could survive only through militarization and aggression.
>
> The result was that both systems launched a massive effort to arm themselves.

Quite apart from ideological formulation, the permanent war economy has had consequences that are readily defined, with respect to characteristics of product, resources used, and effects on productivity.

The military product, whatever usefulness it may have in military or political matters, nevertheless has no use value of an ordinary consumer sort. You cannot eat, wear, live in or use as public transportation a nuclear-powered submarine. Neither can it be used for any further production. Hence the military product is, from an economic standpoint, essentially parasitic.

But American ideology on the feasibility of a permanent guns-and-butter economy gave rise to beliefs and expectations about the US as a post-industrial society – an economy with wealth-producing capability so large as to render further production competence unimportant. American knowledge and hi-tech products would be easily traded for the ordinary goods whose production could be left to less fortunate, foreign underclasses. But post-industrial society ideology crashed against reality as American industry, not only of the smokestack but also of the high-tech variety, became altogether incapable of holding position in the world economy. So even the high-tech industries, which were in favorable balance of trade in 1980, went into negative balance of payments by 1986–87. American industry could not escape the cumulative effect of draining civilian capital via the tax system in favor of financing the permanent war economy.

The permanent military economy also engendered, unexpectedly, a characteristic effect of altering the internal mode of operation of the military industry firms and facilities. Compared to the classic civilian industrial profit-maximizing firm the military-serving firms do not strive for cost-minimizing, trying to be more efficient, mechanizing work, being more systematic in the organization of work. Those were the ways by which the productivity of US industry was once constantly improved, making it possible to pay high wages while producing goods at low prices.

In military economy, the internal *modus operandi* is one of *cost-maximizing*, steady cost and price escalation within generous budget limits. The cost-maximizing effect results from merely following the ordinary rules and regulations prescribed by the central office in the Pentagon. It is the ordinariness of the $600 toilet-seat, of the $8000 pulley-puller, of the fact that the B–2 Bomber cost more than its equivalent weight in gold – that makes the nature of cost-maximizing hard to see.[3] After all, from the vantage-point of military Keynesianism, the wellbeing of economy is gauged decisively by the volume of money-valued transactions, regardless of the nature of the product. This detracts attention from the special nature of military products, from their costs and prices, and from the efficiency or inefficiency by which they are produced. Inefficiency is made into a national purpose by the directorate of the war economists who turn to the logic of military Keynesianism to justify ever-larger expenditures on military account.

The military economy also generates a large core of engineers with a trained orientation to produce according to the requirements of the military: complexity rather than the simplicity most desired in civilian products; high-maintenance requirements rather than the durability desirable for civilian purposes. In consequence there is now a core of engineers in the United States with a trained incapacity for functioning in the civilian economy. The same applies on the management side. The senior managers of military economy are skilled for dealing with the Pentagon, but they couldn't design, oversee production, or sell civilian products to ordinary department stores to save their lives.

Ideologues of military Keynesianism led themselves into an unexpected trap by their focus on short-term effects. Military spending certainly does generate immediate income and employment among the recipients. However, it has escaped the attention of most economists that repeated application of the military-Keynesian economic medicine produces the unplanned but major effect of poisoning the cost-minimizing process of production decision-making – with the result of slowing productivity growth.[4]

These consequences of war economy are now visible in the condition of US industry. Half the machine tools bought in the United States must be imported. Eighty-six per cent of the shoes on our feet are imported. The consumer electronics industry has all but disappeared from the United States.[5]

Military economy has the further effect of reallocating claims on goods and services produced in this country. That transfer takes place by the concentration of military expenditures in particular industries and regions, all paid for by the extraction of tax revenue in excess of expenditures from other industries and regions. This pattern of internal imperialism, the exploitation of parts of the society and the enrichment of other parts, is a characteristic feature of military economy.[6]

These features of military economy are not unique to the United States. They are visible in the Soviet Union as well, for they are specific to military economy, not to any particular ideology. The economic ruin now visible in the Soviet Union is the consequence of priority to military economy on a very small civilian industrial base, an industrial base that was largely wrecked by the experience of the Second World War. Principal ideological rationalizations for military economy are widely prevalent in the Soviet Union as well. Soviet economists recite the litany that the Soviet Union has a high-tech industry only because of military economy. Indeed, the military economy is the high-tech industry. The absurdity of the spinoff thesis is independent of culture.

There is no theory or body of experience from which to assume that the rest of the world is going to keep supplying the United States with the consumer and producer goods needed in a modern industrial economy as a continuing gift. That gift now takes place as those goods are shipped here in return for greenbacks or bank credits. But there is less and less confidence in the potential usefulness of the greenbacks to buy goods manufactured in the United States, so the use of these funds by foreigners to purchase capital assets here is on the rise. An ultimate outcome of this process is illustrated by a report in the *New York Times* of 19 February 1989.

The formidable Chairman of Nomura Securities International, Masaki Kurokawa, was expressing skepticism in a conversation about whether American political leaders would take action on the trade and budget deficits. The badly needed solutions, he said, might have to come from Japan. What did he have in mind?

Stressing that he was just brainstorming out loud, Mr. Kurokawa proposed allowing the yen to strengthen to one hundred to the dollar, making it difficult for Japanese companies to export profitably to the American Market.

Then came the *quid pro quo*. California would be turned into a joint economic zone to be shared by both countries. Millions of Japanese workers would be relocated to the new high-tech factories of this brave new state, built on land dirt cheap by the standards of Japan's astronomical real estate market. If the plan worked, the whole West Coast could be turned into a Japanese-American condominium.

In a word, what is left to be sold by the United States, is the United States.

Growing industrial incompetence is paralleled by breakdown in the infrastructure of the society. Competent industrial systems require competent transportation, power supply, communication, the education of the labor force, clean water, allied facilities for coping with industrial and other wastes, and the like. By 1990 no special studies or learned monographs are needed to deliver the evidence that the infrastructure of the United States is in gross disrepair. You find the evidence by walking out into the streets of any city or travelling the highways between cities.

At this writing there is a 19 000-mile electrified railway system being constructed in Western Europe, with trains to operate inter-city and inter-country at 185 miles per hour.[7] This contrasts with the rattletrap Toonerville Trolley-type railroad transportation to be found throughout the United States. Confidence in the airways is abridged as there is a growing recognition that the planes are getting old, the air traffic control systems are inadequate, that airports are overcrowded. The condition of health care is manifestly incompetent, as emergency medical services, for example, are overwhelmed, notably in big cities. Condition of school buildings, from public schools to universities from coast to coast reflect disrepair and technical backwardness.

In consequence of these conditions the essential economic problem of the United States has been transformed. Competence in production and allocation of resources has in fact displaced fluctuation in market demand as the economic issue commanding central attention.

A first-rate economy is characterized by these points: the ability of the industrial system to offset cost increases of every sort by productivity growth; the ability to pay high and rising wages while producing marketable goods; vigorous research in basic science and in the technologies; the availability of an increasingly competent production support base, infrastructure; having the use of a currency of stable, that is predictable, value; having the capability for organizing people for productive work; and finally, as a result of all this, enjoying a rising level of living.

These were, in fact, conditions of American industrial economy until the 1970s. None of this is to say that the US was without its well-known class barriers, inequities, and brutalities. It is to say that there was a developing production capability that could, if turned to productive account, be the basis for a great transforming improvement in the material qualities of life.

That potential was checkmated as the US lost the qualities of a first-rate industrial economy. The collapse of productivity growth played a central role in this transformation to a second-class industrial country. The development, however, is ongoing. A third-class industrial country is one characterized by the absence of, or the inability to produce, the means of production needed to repair the damage. The means to repair the damage rests fundamentally on the competence of the machinery-producing industries – industries that produce the means for further production. Results of the Census of Manufactures of 1987 shows that in the machinery-producing industries of the United States from 1977 to 1987 there was a dramatic downturn in production capacity. In the vital machine tool industry, the core unit of an industrial system, the labor force of production workers was cut by more than half from 1977 to 1987. This was not the consequence of productivity growth. Rather, there was a net closing of manufacturing firms. The same decay appears in the industries producing heavy electrical machinery, turbines and generators, textile machinery, construction machinery, farm machinery, mining machinery, etc.

The United States is thereby *en route* to becoming a third-rate industrial country. In industrial terms this means that to repair the damaged industrial base it becomes necessary either to bring in complete production systems from abroad, or to send persons abroad to be trained-up where the work is done competently. This is the fashion of an unindustrialized country, seeking to move into industrialism. (These are the options currently being pursued by the Soviet economy, within the limits of their capability.) These are the options that the US will also have to consider if the movement toward third-rate economy continues.

In the United States, as demonstrated by the detailed studies of David Noble[8] and Anthony DiFilippo,[9] the Pentagon's control over the American machine tool industry through subsidies for R&D and market control encouraged computer-controlled product design that was viable only within the framework of cost-maximizing operations. The result was that twenty years after the 1950s and availability of the Pentagon-sponsored computer-controlled machine tools, only three per cent of the machine tools installed in US industry were using this technology. Expansion in the utilization of numerical control came only as the Japanese and German machine tool industries simplified product design, and undertook production with cost-minimizing methods that reduced the price of computer-controlled machine tools and made them more accessible to a wider number of US metalworking firms. This experience left the US machine tool industry in a second-rate position with respect to the newest class of machine tool technology and thereby played an important part in the decline of the US industry. By the 1980s about half of the machine tools purchased in the United States were imported, and the imports featured the more sophisticated high-tech range of machine tools. So the Pentagon's preference for cost-maximizing modes of operation disabled the US machine tool industry as a primary supplier of basic equipment to US industry.

ON THE SOVIET MACHINE TOOL INDUSTRY

In 1959, in a report to the European Productivity Agency on the productivity of the machine tool industry of Western Europe, I presented a series of recommendations by which the productivity of that industry could be improved by fifty per cent and more. Following completion of this study in Western Europe I visited machine tool factories in the Soviet Union. In a postscript to the report on Western Europe I stated that, 'The main recommendations of the present report (1959) and of the report published by the Anglo-American Council on Productivity (1953) are being implemented in the machine tool industry of the U.S.S.R. This comment is based on first-hand observation of several leading machine tool factories in that country.'

This analysis of Soviet trends was followed by numerous articles that called attention to the prospect of a major Soviet political–economic success as a world supplier of good machine tools at modest prices. This would be based upon wide application of quality production methods with stable (hence, optimally-productive) industrial systems.

In the years following the publication and wide discussion of this report I found no evidence of the development of the Soviet machine tool industry along the lines that I had judged to be imminently possible. The matter remained a mystery until recently, when I obtained reliable evidence to the following effect. Soon after 1959 the Soviet government embarked on priority development of military aerospace technology. In pursuit of this priority the most capable electrical and other engineers were plucked from the graduating rosters of Soviet engineering schools and directed to the military aerospace field. This limited the size and quality of the talent pool that was available to develop not only computer control of machine tools but also the machine tool industry's product design and production systems. By the 1980s, the machine tool industry of the USSR was clearly backward.

Hence the military ministries of both the United States and the Soviet Union, through their respective pursuit of priority in military products and related research, each checkmated the development of their respective machine tool industries and thereby contributed mightily to retarding industrial development in both countries. In the Soviet Union the primary route for reaching this result was through the preemption of prime technical talent, while in the United States the depletion of the machine tool industry was achieved primarily by influencing product design and production methods in a cost-maximizing direction.

CONCLUSION

From available evidence, neither private nor state capitalism can survive the predations of a permanent war economy. There is no available way to secure exemption from the decay of production competence and infrastructure that is the necessary effect of the preemption of resources for military enterprise, and from implementing cost-maximizing modes of industrial decision-making.

That is why deliberate conversion of production facilities from military to civilian economy is an indispensable component of policy for offsetting the production and infrastructure decay from permanent war economies. For this purpose it is vital to have a competent set of ideas that account for the main operating characteristics and effects of military economies. Such knowledge is a valuable tool for designing and implementing the demilitarization of economy.

Notes

1. D. Fusfeld, *Economics* (San Francisco: Scott Foresman Co., 1988).
2. See S. Melman, 'Limits of Military Power', *International Security*, Vol. II, No. 1, Summer 1986.
3. E. Fitzgerald, *The Pentagonists* (New York: Houghton Mifflin, 1989), Chapters 4, 9, 10.
4. S. Melman, *Profits Without Production* (New York: Alfred A. Knopf, 1983; University of Pennsylvania Press, 1987), Chapter 9.
5. Ibid., Chapters 9 and 10.
6. James R. Anderson, *Bankrupting America* (Lansing, Michigan: Employment Research Associates, 1989).
7. *The Wall Street Journal*, 6 November 1989.
8. David F. Noble, *Forces of Production: A Social History of Industrial Automation* (New York: Alfred A. Knopf, 1984).
9. Anthony DiFilippo, *Military Spending and Industrial Decline: A Study of the American Machine Tool Industry* (Westport, Connecticut: Greenwood Press, 1986).

Part I
Effects of Military-Oriented High-Technology Policies

1 Military Spending and Government High-Technology Policy: A Comparative Analysis of the US, West Germany, Japan and Great Britain

Anthony DiFilippo

By the early 1970s it was widely proclaimed that the US was becoming a post-industrial society. One of the major arguments of the post-industrial thesis was that it envisioned the coming dominance of science-based or high-technology industries. The post-industrial thesis also suggested that the US economy was making the transition from traditional manufacturing to more service-oriented production.[1] Thus the post-industrial thesis rightly predicted, and indeed encouraged, the abandonment of traditional manufacturing production by US corporate managers. Although the post-industrial thesis did foresee the continued growth of scientists and technical personnel in the US as necessary for improving high-tech process and product technologies,[2] it did not anticipate the preemption of many of these workers and much of the nation's technological expenditures by the military, nor did it anticipate the impact of these problems relative to the advantages gained from civilian industrial development policies of Japan and West Germany.[3] As this chapter will show, Great Britain, another major Western military power, has experienced military-related problems similar to those adversely affecting many US high-technology industries.

3

PROBLEMS IN US HIGH TECHNOLOGY

The continued deterioration of the US high-technology trade balance over the years indicates clearly that American manufacturers have been encountering major competitive problems both in domestic and foreign markets.[4] Measured in constant 1982 dollars, the US high-technology trade balance in 1986 registered its first deficit ever, plummeting to −$2.3 billion dollars from a nearly $20 billion surplus a decade earlier.[5] By the end of 1987 the US trade deficit in high technology products had disappeared, though the surplus was barely visible at $510 million in real 1982 dollars.[6]

Ironically, at the same time the US was supposedly making the transition to a post-industrial society, the nation's share of the international high-technology export market was already in decline. Between 1965 and 1980 the US share of the high-technology exports of fourteen industrial nations declined in seven out of ten markets.[7] In this same period, the percentage change in the US share of the technology-intensive world export market of twenty-four countries decreased by almost 17 per cent, while Japan's share grew by nearly 100 per cent.[8] During this time the West German share of this export market remained about the same. Between 1980 and 1985 the US share of the technology-intensive world export market moderately improved, though the percentage change in its market share still fell by over 10 per cent between 1970 and 1985. Japan's share of this market continued to grow rapidly in the first half of the 1980s, from 14.3 per cent in 1980 to 19.4 per cent in 1985. The West German share of this export market, however, declined during the 1980–85 period.

But one should not draw the hasty conclusion that West German high-technology manufactured goods are no longer in strong demand. West Germany exports many of its high-technology goods to countries other than its chief competitors, the US, Japan and, until recently, France. After excluding these three countries, West German high-tech exports grew substantially from the mid-1960s to 1980.[9] In 1984 West Germany's trade balance in technology-intensive products was $10.6 billion, including surpluses of $1.6 billion with Italy, $900 million with Great Britain and even a $1.8 billion surplus with France.[10] High-tech exports are very important to the West German economy. In 1984 high-tech exports came to 5.5 per cent of the West German GNP. This is higher than the figure for the UK which stands at 4.8 per cent, with much of this due to aircraft and

Percentage

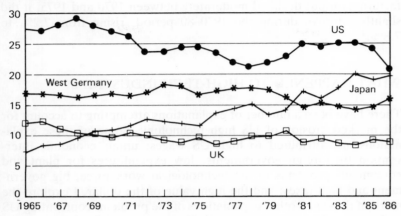

Figure 1.1 Shares of technology-intensive world export market for the
US, UK, Japan and West Germany, 1965–86
Source: National Science Foundation, *International Science and Technology
Data Update, 1988* Washington, DC (NSF 89–307), p. 93.

related industries, Japan at 4.3 per cent, and the US with a 1.7 per
cent high-technology share of GNP.[11]

While West Germany's share of the technology-intensive world
export market improved in 1986, recovering to about where it had
been in 1980, Japan is now seriously challenging the US leadership
position of this market. By the end of 1986 the US held 20.9 per cent
of the technology-intensive world export market compared to 19.8
per cent controlled by Japan. Actually, what Japan has gained in the
technology-intensive world export market since 1965 has been earned
at the expense of the US and, to a lesser extent, Great Britain. As
Figure 1.1 shows, while the West German share of the technology-
intensive world export market was about the same in 1965 and 1986,
both the US and the UK have been the biggest losers. Post-
industrialism has backfired in these two countries.

The strong performance by both Japan and West Germany in
high-tech world exports is based on their increasing production
shares. Between 1970 and 1980 the Japanese share of the total high
R&D manufacturing output in eleven advanced capitalist nations
increased from 15.8% to 21.7%, while the West German share grew
from 8.8% to 10.8%. The US share, however, declined precipitously

from 57.7% to 38.4%. Although the UK share of high R&D manufacturing output declined moderately between 1970 and 1975, it did
slightly improve during the 1970–80 period, rising from 7.2% to
7.8%.[12]

WHAT HAPPENED TO HIGH-TECH INDUSTRIES?

There have been a number of explanations attempting to account for
the marked erosion of US high technology. Some of these explanations are attributed to high US wages; unfair economic intervention by foreign governments; low expenditures for plant and
equipment; problems in the technological work force; big government and high taxes; and the high value of the dollar. I explore the
merit of these and other explanations of the problems confronting US
high-tech industries elsewhere.[13] However, in this chapter, it is
important to point out that none of the aforementioned explanations
adequately addresses the foremost problem of commercial high-
technology production, namely, the direct and long-term appropriation of national technological resources by government. This
appropriation of high-technology resource is taking place in an international environment where some foreign governments are providing
industrial support through a comprehensive civilian policy. Beyond
this, it is important to say a few words here about the effects of the
high value of the dollar on the US high-tech trade balance because
this is both the official and the most popularized recent account.[14]

The rapid appreciation of the dollar in the early 1980s only intensified the relative deterioration in US high-technology trade which
had been going on for more than a decade. Moreover, fluctuations in
the relative value of the dollar do not correspond with US high-tech
trade performance. Between 1969 and 1973 the value of the dollar
depreciated, but the US share of the high-tech world export market
continued to decline. Accompanying the rapid appreciation of the
dollar in the first half of the 1980s, as we have seen, was a slight
improvement in the US share of the international technology-
intensive export market. If exchange rates were so important, no
improvement would have taken place in the US share of this market
in the early 1980s, and a significant improvement should have
occurred in the 1969–73 period. While the increase in the value of the
dollar helps to explain the deterioration of the US position in high-
tech trade, it is not as important as maintained by many, nor is it the

only factor. Indeed, even a recent report prepared for the Joint Economic Committee of Congress does not consider the rapid appreciation of the dollar during the early 1980s as the only factor explaining the erosion of American high-tech trade.[15] It is noteworthy that the relative fall in the multilateral trade-weighted real value of the dollar between 1985 and 1986 corresponded with a 13.6 per cent decline in the US share of the technology-intensive world export market.

In contrast to the role of the dollar, other factors have adversely affected US high-tech industries, particularly the form of managerialism which places too much emphasis on near-term profitmaking rather than improving production competence, the relative inadequacy of capital investments, and the shortage of technical personnel. An especially important factor which is often overlooked by conventional analysts, is the appropriation of the nation's technological resources – both personnel and capital – by the US military. Intensifying this problem is the fact that Japan and West Germany use the majority of their technical resources for civilian purposes. Moreover, both of these nations have industrial policies specifically aimed at assisting the development of their high-tech industries.

MILITARY VS. CIVILIAN TECHNOLOGIES

By 1970 US high-technology industries were beginning to encounter very strong competition in international trade. While it was inevitable that some 'technological catching-up' would occur by other advanced capitalist nations,[16] the major problems affecting many US high-technology industries suggests that the causes were more structural than this phrase suggests. Indeed, an international comparison can illuminate the structural aspects of these problems.

Great Britain's marked competitive decline in world high-tech markets began at about the same time as that of the US. Although UK high-tech industries never collectively dominated international markets as did the US, their slippage over the last two-and-a-half decades suggests some conditions similar to those existing in the US. Like the US, the British government promotes a government science policy that is not directly beneficial to civilian-oriented high-tech industries.

The high-tech, military-oriented science policies emphasized by the American and British governments depend upon abundant technological resources, including an adequate number of technical personnel. Two recent estimates indicate that almost a third of the scientists and engineers in the US are dependent on military spending for their livelihoods.[17] The US Department of Defense (DoD) employed over one-half of all scientists, engineers and computer scientists working for the federal government in 1986.[18] According to the National Science Foundation (NSF), by 1987 nearly 60 per cent of the nation's aeronautical/astronautical engineers and 22 per cent of the mechanical engineering technicians are expected to be performing military-related activities.[19] Indeed, in order to perform work on the $18.9 billion awarded to military R&D prime contractors in fiscal year 1987, required a large number of technical personnel. For the UK, it has been estimated that over 30 per cent of British scientists and engineers are dependent on military work.[20]

The drain of qualified scientific and engineering personnel is especially problematic in this age of advanced technology. In the US this drain has contributed to reported shortages of scientists and other technical personnel. Given the increased government interest in improving the US defense apparatus, it is not surprising that sizeable shortages of scientific, engineering and technical personnel have been reported in areas indispensable to a technological military buildup. For example, in 1984 almost 20 per cent of the firms surveyed for the NSF reported shortages of electrical engineers, 15 per cent reported shortages of computer engineers and 12 per cent reported shortages of electronics and nuclear engineers.[21]

Since 1973 the number of full-time scientists and engineers actively involved in R&D has increased steadily in the US. Despite consistent increases in more recent years amounting to an average growth rate of 3 per cent per annum during the 1980–87 period, there have been constant shortages of scientific and engineering personnel in industry. The demand for these workers is especially great in high-technology industries.[22]

Here an important question arises. Why is it that the supply of scientists and engineers has been growing at the same time that US control of international markets has been eroding? One would expect, *ceteris paribus*, that the increase in technical personnel would improve the competitive capability of the many US high-technology industries experiencing decline. At the very least one would expect that these US high-tech industries would be able to stabilize world market shares.

The answer to this question is not as complex as it might first appear. While both the supply and demand of scientists and engineers has been growing, demand has been greater in military-serving firms than in non-military serving companies.[23] Government economists have estimated that a larger number of technical and professional personnel are found in defense-related jobs than in manufacturing as a whole. The strong demand for these workers is reflected in the fact that employment of professional and technical personnel performing military work in industry increased by 41 per cent between 1980 and 1985.[24] Moreover, according to the NSF, firms doing technology-intensive military work reported higher shortages of scientists, engineers and computer specialists than companies not performing military work. Thus, all things are not equal. Although reported shortages of scientific and engineering personnel exist in the same areas for military and non-military serving companies, both demand and shortages are greater in the military-serving firms.[25]

Simply stated, the answer to the question posed above is that consistently heavy doses of military R&D spending have been absorbing a growing proportion of technical personnel in the US industrial economy. These personnel, along with others in academia and government, cannot simultaneously pursue both military and civilian work. While the supply of US technical personnel has been steadily increasing, it has not been great enough to offset the strong demand stemming from military-related R&D and still permit the nation to compete effectively in high-tech markets with a nation like Japan.[26] Thus, while Japan devotes most of its national technical resources to civilian production, US high-tech firms are at a comparative disadvantage in domestic and international markets.

Thus the problem is really not that the supply of R&D personnel in the US is not growing, for the data clearly show that it is. Rather, the heavy and increasing demand placed on this supply by the needs of the military is a major source of America's technical personnel problem. This problem is currently more critical, for by 1986 the number of scientists and engineers per 10 000 in the US labor force was below that reported for Japan.[27] The kind of work being performed by 'post-industrial' personnel has to affect the competitive capabilities of a nation's high-tech industries and ultimately impact on its standard of living.

The situation in Great Britain is even more disturbing. Because the UK devotes a relatively large amount of government R&D to military work (see Figure 1.2), like the US, its scientific, engineering and other technical personnel are being diverted from the civilian sector.

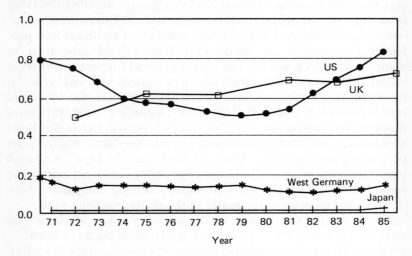

Figure 1.2   Military R&D as a percentage of Gross National Product (GNP) for the US, Japan, West Germany and the UK, 1971–85
Source: Calculated from the National Science Board, *Science & Engineering Indicators, 1987* (Washington, DC: US Government Printing Office, 1987), pp. 236–7.

The really disturbing fact is that on a comparative basis with Japan, West Germany, the US and even France, Great Britain has a shortage of scientific and engineering personnel. For example, in 1986 the figures indicating the number of scientists and engineers per 10 000 in the labor force for Japan (67.4), the US (66.2), West Germany (52.3), and France (43.8) were markedly higher than the figure for Great Britain (35.5).[28] This relative shortage of technical personnel adversely affects both innovation and the diffusion of technology in Great Britain. Compounding this relative shortage is the military factor, which puts Great Britain's civilian technology base at a disadvantage *vis-à-vis* Japan and West Germany.

Table 1.1 shows that in the US and the UK military expenditures per scientist and engineer performing R&D work on a full-time basis were noticeably higher than in either Japan or West Germany in 1987. These figures relate directly to the distribution of national R&D funds for military purposes. In 1987 almost 80 per cent of federal R&D expenditures in the US was for military-related

Table 1.1   Estimated military and civilian spending (in constant 1982 dollars) per scientist and engineer actively involved in R&D work in the US, Japan, West Germany and the UK, 1987

Country	Military spending per scientist & engineer (dollars)	Civilian spending per scientist & engineer (dollars)
US	41 305	83 726
Japan	717	92 756
West Germany	6 601	121 452
UK[a]	35 461	104 357

a. The figures for the United Kingdom are for 1986.
Source: Calculated from National Science Foundation, *International Science & Technology Data Update: 1988* (NSF89–307), pp. 4, 8 and 36.

purposes.[29] In the UK expenditures for the military also took 50.3 per cent of the government's total R&D budget in 1987. In contrast, the governments of Japan and West Germany assigned considerably less to military R&D, 4.5 per cent and 12.5 per cent respectively.[30] Between 1971 and 1985 military R&D averaged nearly 27 per cent of the US's *total* technological effort, compared to 0.6 per cent for Japan and 5.5 per cent for West Germany. Though the data for Great Britain are incomplete, what is available indicates an average of about 28 per cent during this period.[31] Figure 1.2 makes clear that the technological impact of military R&D is much more significant in the US and the UK than in West Germany and Japan. In Japan military R&D has a negligible effect on its economy.[32]

Table 1.1 also shows that in 1987 civilian spending per scientist and engineer was lower in the US than in either Japan or West Germany. The high civilian figure for the UK relates to the relatively smaller number of full-time scientists and engineers in this country. For example, though the British and West German populations are of comparable size, in 1986 the UK had only 67 per cent of the full-time scientists and engineers working in West Germany. (If Great Britain had a share of scientists and engineers from its total population similar to West Germany's share, the civilian R&D estimate for the UK would be $73 835, well below all the other countries listed in Table 1.1. However, using this adjusted denominator on the UK's total military R&D expenditure still results in a substantially higher estimate for Britain ($25 090) than either Japan or West Germany.) As shown in Figure 1.3, civilian-oriented R&D is markedly lower in

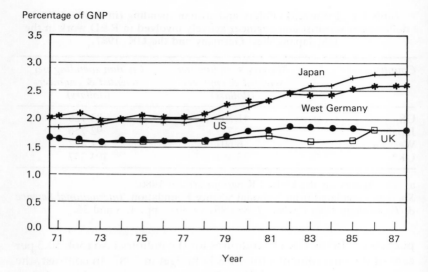

Percentage of GNP

Figure 1.3   Civilian R&D as a percentage of GNP for the US, Japan, West Germany and the UK, 1971–87
Source: National Science Board, *Science & Engineering Indicators, 1987*, p. 237; and National Science Foundation, *International Science and Technology Data Update*, 1988, p. 8.

the US and the UK compared to either West Germany or Japan. The combination of a relatively lower impact from civilian R&D and a relatively higher impact from military R&D in the US has meant that catching up technologically has been much easier for the Japanese and the West Germans. Meanwhile, catching up to the UK in technology-intensive markets was not nearly as big a problem for Japan, and West Germany already held a lead over Great Britain by the mid-1960s. Thus, it seems that the outcome of too much military R&D and too little civilian R&D has hobbled British high-tech industries.

The technical requirements of modern warfare, whether in the US, the UK or anywhere else, draw heavily on the technological resources of the electronics industry. For example, the UK electronics industry, like that in the US, is heavily involved in military work. Not surprisingly, both nations' electronics sectors have had huge trade deficits.[33] A military-oriented electronics industry finds it exceedingly difficult to compete effectively against producers in Japan, where, assisted by government, electronics research is almost totally devoted to civilian concerns.

The relationship between government expenditures appropriated by the military and the concomitant preemption of scientific and engineering personnel should be clear enough. Especially in more recent years, a nation that spends heavily on a sophisticated military apparatus will utilize its technical resources on projects largely, if not completely unrelated to civilian work.

LITTLE COMPENSATION FOR MILITARY R&D

The massive diversion of technological resources in the US and the UK could be mitigated somewhat in three ways. Government could take a more active part in supporting financially civilian industrial development in both a direct and indirect manner. Companies could spend much more money on commercially applicable R&D. Finally, if the spin-off effect from the military to the civilian sector were significant enough, then the existence of huge defense R&D budgets would have some justification.

Government-supported civilian R&D

Because the majority of federal R&D spending going to industry is for military purposes in the US, government expenditures for commercial production and supporting civilian technological advancement get relatively little attention. For example, in 1983 only about 19 per cent of federal expenditures for industrial R&D was for civilian work.[34] The contrast between the US and West Germany and Japan concerning government R&D spending for industrial growth and development is noteworthy. In 1987 only 0.2 per cent of federal R&D spending in the US was for industrial growth and development; in West Germany and Japan these figures were 15.3 per cent and 4.8 per cent respectively.[35] The Organization for Economic Co-operation and Development remarks that: 'It is against the fundamental principles of the US science policy to give direct aid to industrial technological development.' But this does not mean that the US government 'does not support industrial R&D, only that it prefers to do so via other objectives – especially Defence and Aerospace'.[36] While the UK allocates more than the US and even Japan to industrial development (8.7 per cent of government R&D funds in 1987), what it spends on this objective is clearly not sufficient to improve the competitiveness of British high-tech industries.

Authorizing a large proportion of government R&D funds for military R&D work, moreover, prevents the US and the UK from spending more on scientific and technological areas that help to support industry. In the US only 3.6 per cent of federal R&D money in 1987 was for the advancement of knowledge, a category which includes the advancement of research and general university funds. Although the British government spends a higher proportion of its R&D budget on the advancement of knowledge than the US (20.2 per cent in 1987), it still devotes a substantially smaller proportion to this objective than either Japan or West Germany.

What Japan lacks in funds for industrial development it makes up in expenditures earmarked for the advancement of knowledge. In 1987 the Japanese government spent over 50 per cent of its R&D funds on the advancement of knowledge. Besides spending heavily on industrial growth and development, West Germany also devotes a significant proportion of public R&D funds to the advancement of knowledge, almost 44 per cent of federal government R&D funds in 1987.[37]

In 1985 two public organizations in Japan were authorized to spend 74 per cent of all government R&D funds. The Ministry of Education, Science and Culture (Monbusho) controls almost half of the government's R&D budget and supports Japan's 95 national universities, as well as research institutions connected to them. One recent example of Monbusho's funds supporting industrial research is the 1986 award to the Tokyo Institute of Technology to perform laser engineering work in the area of semiconductor technology.

The Science and Technology Agency is the second largest R&D organization in the Japanese government. Connected to this agency are a number of research institutes and public corporations. The Research and Development Corporation of Japan is one of the public corporations which is very beneficial to industry, since its primary purpose is to promote research work performed at national universities and research institutions that is thought most applicable to commercial use. The Research and Development Corporation of Japan is responsible for the Exploratory Research for Advanced Technology (ERATO) projects. Some recent ERATO projects have been implemented specifically to be useful to industry.[38]

As noted, the West German government also spends heavily on the objective of the advancement of knowledge. About 75 per cent of this objective goes to general university funds, which make up about

33 per cent of total government R&D spending in West Germany. Together the two objectives, industrial growth and development and the advancement of knowledge, account for about three-fifths of the West German government's R&D budget.[39]

Company support of R&D

If companies spent significantly more of their own money on R&D they could counteract some of the adverse impact of military spending. But US industry has maintained a relatively constant level of R&D funding over the years. R&D funding provided by industry came to about 1 per cent of GNP in 1970, and in 1980 this figure was about the same. Although US industry funding increased slightly by 0.2 per cent of GNP between 1980 and 1986, the new R&D investment tax credit apparently has made it easier for companies to write-off, at the public's expense, costs other than purely R&D expenditures.[40] Even many high-tech companies are reluctant to invest too much of their capital in R&D, particularly in basic research, because it is risky and the return on investment is frequently long-term rather than immediate.

Mainly because of the comprehensive industrial policies found in Japan and West Germany, industries in both of these countries have substantially increased R&D funding. In West Germany during the period 1975 to 1986 industry's proportion of total national R&D increased from 50 per cent to 62 per cent; during this same interval, industry's share in Japan grew from 55 per cent to 69 per cent. Given what has just been said about American industry, however, it is not surprising that this trend did not occur in the US. During the period 1975 to 1986 industry's contribution to total R&D expended in the US increased very modestly from 45 per cent to 48 per cent. While it is true that in the UK, industry's share of the total increased from 41 per cent to 50 per cent during the same period, this growth cannot be attributed entirely to British companies. Great Britain receives a larger proportion of foreign R&D funds than do the US, Japan and West Germany. This makes the data for the UK a less genuine indication of the R&D effort of British industry.[41]

Military R&D and spin-off

Many of the problems related to high levels of defense R&D spending could be minimized by a large amount of spin-off from the military sector. Indeed, most supporters of the military argue that a significant amount of spin-off regularly occurs. Moving well beyond the military-spending-creates-jobs argument, today's supporters of huge military budgets allege that the technologies of war are not at all incompatible with the technologies useful in the civilian sector. The nub of this deeply-flawed argument is that what is good for the military is good for the commercial economy since 'there is really no such thing as pure "defense technology".'[42] According to this argument, not only are there spillovers from the military to the civilian sector, but the growing emphasis on technological warfare, which requires the increased use of national technical resources, has helped to popularize the term 'dual-use technology'. So, as the argument supporting high(er) military research and development budgets goes, because there is 'no pure defense technology, then neither is [there] any pure defense R&D'.[43]

Have the many supporters of big military R&D budgets explained how the Advanced Technology Stealth Bomber (a new strategic bomber designed to avoid enemy radar, and which in 1987 rated as 'the Pentagon's most expensive weapon ever')[44] is not a defense technology? What practical civilian use would there be for such an advanced military-designed technology? More specifically, why would a civilian airliner want to remain undetectable to radar? Have they explained to the 32-plus million people in the US who officially live in poverty, and the large number of homeless, and the many unemployed, how the billions of dollars already expended on stealth technology has improved their standard of living or, for that matter, the standard of living of the average person? Or take the billions spent on R&D for ballistic, anti-ballistic and anti-satellite weapons systems. Are the civilian uses of these technologies readily accessible? Below in the ocean depths, large and rapidly increasing R&D expenditures for anti-submarine warfare designed, for example, to locate quieter enemy submarines, offer no pragmatic civilian use.

Though nearly $7 billion had been spent by mid-1988 on Star Wars – the nation's largest research project ever – no important spin-off has yet to materialize from this program, now more than six years old. Significantly, an important question has been raised among computer experts concerning support by the Defense Advanced Research Projects Agency (DARPA) for supercomputers, which could be used for space warfare. There is grave concern that DARPA's generous support for supercomputer development with specific military applications will create problems for civilian technologies in this market.[45] In view of the fact that the Japanese government helps support two major long-term civilian efforts involving supercomputers – the Fifth Generation Computer Project receiving $63 million a year and directed by the newly established Institute for New Generation Computer Technology, and the $15 million per year Supercomputer Project – it should not be surprising to learn that the Japanese have quickly become the leading rivals to US producers in this rapidly growing world market.[46]

While it has been argued that the examination of the spin-off issue is problematic because it has not been sufficiently defined and conceptualized and because there are measurement difficulties,[47] this methodological problem can be at least partly overcome by identifying a key military technology area, such as supercomputers, and comparing it with the results of civilian work being performed in other countries. As we have already seen, in the US and the UK the electronics industries perform a large amount of military work. Because this is not true in Japan and West Germany, we have a better understanding of why the US and the UK currently hold so little of the world radio and TV reception equipment market. In 1986, while the US and the UK *together* held 3.8 per cent (0.5 per cent for the US and 3.3 per cent for the UK) of this market, the Japanese controlled 69.1 per cent and the West Germans 12.5 per cent of it.[48] The technology connected to the Strategic Defense Initiative's X-ray laser weapon, which is powered by a nuclear explosion, is not easily integrated into the commercial sector and stands in stark contrast to the advancements stemming from work on civilian laser technology being performed in Japan.[49] In short, much more so than in the past, contemporary warfare is largely dependent on sophisticated technologies which have minimal or no direct benefit to most civilian industries. Such results occur because the continued demand for specific military weapons systems and supporting equipment tends to bifurcate defense and civilian technologies.

Compounding the 'if' in the spin-off issue is the 'when' associated with it. The tight security restrictions surrounding military R&D can make any identifiable spin-off from the defense sector meaningless in today's quickly-changing and very competitive high-tech markets. So *if* a defense technology supported by the DoD has commercial potential, the delays connected with performing military R&D work make the matter of *when*, if ever, it can be introduced to the market a big problem for US commercial manufacturers who must compete with foreign producers not facing such restrictions. An example of this is the DoD's Very High Speed Integrated Circuit Program, which places strict security restrictions on the diffusion of semiconductor technology, compared to projects in this general area supported by the Japanese government, which promote the diffusion of knowledge. Thus civilian spin-offs that have occurred from the DoD's program have not made a dent on Japan's majority control of the semiconductor market. Then there are the highly-specialized technologies developed for military use alone. Again the DoD's Very High Speed Integrated Circuit Program provides a good example because the development of military-designed technologies and the specific military requirements are not beneficial to civilian business practices.[50]

For these reasons, military R&D frequently offers little or no compensation to most civilian high-technology industries. Spending $50 billion a year on military R&D as the US is now doing, or devoting a nearly proportionate amount of GNP for this purpose as the British do, severely restricts the use of government funds for civilian uses. While heavy spending on military R&D may eventually produce some spin-off, applying national technological resources directly to the civilian sector, is the most expedient way to produce commercial results.

As we have seen, the direct application of technological resources to the civilian industrial sector is not the preference of the US government, nor the British government. While the US government currently supports about a third and the British government a quarter of the industrial research performed in their respective countries – which is substantially higher than the proportion funded by the Japanese (2 per cent) and the West German (15 per cent) governments – a very large part of these state expenditures in America and Great Britain is for military-related purposes.[51] Specifically, military-related industrial R&D financed by the American and British governments is mainly directed toward the high-tech electronics, computer and aerospace industries.[52] The combined appropriation of R&D funds and personnel for military purposes puts US and UK high-tech industries in a very disadvantageous position relative to Japanese and West German producers. Assisted by their respective governments, high-tech producers in Japan and West Germany directly apply most national technological resources to civilian efforts, while in the US and the UK manufacturers must rely mainly on company funds and the indirect spin-off effects of the defense apparatus.

While West Germany presently controls the world export market in the areas of electrical machinery and equipment, drugs, and plastics and synthetics, Japanese dominance extends to radio and TV reception products, communications equipment, and professional and scientific instruments. Reflecting the massive infusion of state expenditures to the aerospace industry, which receives the majority of its R&D funds from military-related sources, US manufacturers control almost half of the aircraft and parts market worldwide, followed by British producers.[53] Although the spin-off spigot is still flowing in the aerospace industry, it is very costly to keep US manufacturers in the lead in this market. In 1985 the US government supplied the aircraft and missiles industry with $13.4 billion in R&D funds,[54] most of which was for military and related purposes.

Indeed, it is possible that the continued divergence of the military and civilian aerospace markets, will have adverse effects on the industry as a whole. Excessive military spending has already intensified the competitive problems of the semiconductor, machine tool and robotics industries. Also, in spite of the fact that early funding for the development of computer technology came from the DoD (and that the computer industry still receives much R&D financial support from the Pentagon) imports of computer products make up a large part of US consumption. Although the value of the dollar declined from earlier in the 1980s, in 1988 imports of computer equipment and parts, mainly from Japan, made up 39 per cent of the approximately $51 billion US market.[55]

Numerical controlled (NC) machine tools, developed in the early 1950s with funds from the Air Force, are now overwhelmingly produced by the Japanese. American users of NC tools import far more of this equipment from Japan than US producers export there.[56] Moreover, US users of NC and other machine tools are very dependent on foreign-built equipment, especially from Japan. By 1988, 55 cents out of every dollar spent by machine tool consumers in the US was for foreign-built merchandise, up 6 cents from the previous year. In 1988, Japanese producers exported to the US 67 per cent of the over 11 000 high-tech NC machine tools imported by US customers.[57]

Like NC technology, early semiconductor research was supported by the military in the US, though defense subsidies were not as directly beneficial to the industry. Today while this support continues – for example, through DoD funds going to Sematech, a consortium of US semiconductor producers – Japanese manufacturers have the lead in the vast majority of semiconductor technologies.[58] In robotics, despite the fact that the industrial robot was first developed in the US, the DoD's interest in process and product technology in this area has not forestalled the influx of imports into the US, principally from Japan and West Germany.[59]

IS THERE AN ALTERNATIVE?

Although much disagreement exists concerning exactly how government should use national technological resources, it is difficult to dispute the argument that their direct application to the civilian economy would produce more salutary results than relying on indirect effects through spin-offs from military work. Because economic conversion is the planned transfer of financial and technical resources from military to civilian use, it therefore promotes their direct commercial application. Economic conversion would free technological resources from the constraints connected to a military economy. These include not only the technological constraints specified above, but also the controls imposed by the DoD on the export of products and technologies to foreign countries. Short of implementing conversion from a military to a civilian economy in the US and the UK, the proof of the viability of very low levels of military spending can be observed in Japan and West Germany, where technological resources are mainly used in the civilian sector.

Conversion would not idle technical personnel, since there are presently many areas in the civilian economy where, once properly trained and retrained, these workers could apply their valuable talents and skills. Many more engineers working on the badly-damaged infrastructure in the US would be a very worthwhile activity and add much-needed support to the weakened industrial economy. More engineers and other technical personnel working in commercial high-tech industries, such as consumer electronics in the US and UK, would also be advantageous to the economies of these countries. Instead of performing military work, engineers, scientists and computer specialists could help to rejuvenate the technological base of militarily-dependent industrial economies now showing clear signs of industrial decay. As conditions now exist, many high-tech industries in both the US and the UK are operating at a relative disadvantage to rival commercial industries in Japan and West Germany.

In order for conversion to be feasible, militarized nations must want to make this transformation. Ideally, this means that a disarmament process must be implemented and accompany economic conversion.[60] Though disarmament has been a long-neglected issue, currently conversion legislation exists in the US.[61] The existence of conversion legislation suggests that at least some policymakers recognize it as a viable alternative to military economy. The problem is garnering sufficient congressional and popular support for the passage of conversion legislation. A large part of the solution to this problem is to explain the economic damage linked to excessive military spending.

CIVILIAN INDUSTRIAL POLICIES

While conversion is essential for a military economy like the US, since it redirects finite financial and technical resources to the civilian sector, the implementation of this policy alone would have only limited success. Conversion leaves too much of the management of the economy in the hands of business executives, who, as they do now, opt for high short-term profits rather than long-term economic growth accompanied by an improvement in the general standard of living. Conversion, in short, will not correct the myopic business perspective currently held by many executives in the US who manage firms to turn a quick profit at the expense of almost everything else.

Because US and UK high-tech companies must compete with increasingly competent Japanese and West German firms that receive structured government assistance, the relative disadvantage they experience in domestic and international markets has a major source other than lower national commitment to military R&D spending. Besides relatively low levels of military R&D spending in West Germany and Japan, many high-tech industries in these nations receive important technical and financial assistance, including tax breaks, from their governments through their comprehensive civilian industrial policies.[62]

Though its highly-coordinated science and technology network promotes a formidable national effort, Japan's industrial policy functions principally through the Ministry of International Trade and Industry (MITI), which is the third-largest R&D-spending organization in the government. Assisted by its affiliated organizations, such as the Agency of Industrial Science and Technology (AIST) and the Electrotechnical Laboratory, MITI targets and subsidizes innovative civilian research. Other government organizations also assist high-tech industries by making low-interest investment capital available to companies.

As in Japan, the West German government works closely with high-tech industries to promote their growth through low-interest loans and R&D subsidies. The most important government organization in West Germany responsible for implementing its industrial policy is the Ministry for Research and Technology. The federal government of West Germany also helps to support important research institutes, such as the Max Planck Society, the Fraunhofer Society and the thirteen 'big science' national laboratories, all of which in turn, directly or indirectly assist high-technology industry-related research.

Undergirding the Japanese and West German industrial policies is the generous financial assistance by government to universities and national research institutes. Reflecting this critically important support for a national science and technology policy is the relatively high percentage of government R&D funds for the advancement of knowledge, as noted earlier, in Japan and West Germany. Moreover, Japan and West Germany have highly-coordinated domestic science policies. By working closely and cooperatively with high-tech industry, the governments of Japan and West Germany have strengthened this sector of their economies. The Japanese government has targeted a number of high-tech industries, including microelectronics, lasers, robotics and many others, while the West German government recently has concentrated on computers, microelectronics and the electronic office equipment industries.[63]

A good example of the cooperative work evident in Japan's industrial policy is the Large-Scale Project. This AIST-supported program has been responsible for twenty-four different projects – eight of which were operating in 1987 – since it began in 1966. The research work connected to the Large-Scale Project involves companies which receive contract money from AIST and technical support from Japanese universities and national laboratories.[64] Similarly, in West Germany university work often benefits industry. For example, in the mid-1980s the government-financed German Research Society was supporting cooperative electronics work, specifically semiconductor research, at Aachen University, then involved in a number of other industry-related projects.[65]

In contrast, in the US and UK government industrial policy revolves around advancing the military apparatus. Apart from the collaborative network known as the military–industrial complex, the US government has no comprehensively organized plan for advancing civilian industry. Industrial technologies emphasized for development by the US government for military purposes, while often in the same broad technology areas, nonetheless are strikingly different than those targeted by the Japanese and West German governments.

British industrial policy has been described as 'reactive' and 'ad hoc'.[66] Although badly organized, to varying degrees British industrial policy has been consistently interventionist, despite the presence of Conservative or Labour governments. Because of the weak performance of UK industry, government's policy has been to react to a steady flow of competitive crises. Given the poor performance of UK high-technology industries in international markets, it is fair to say that the British industrial policy has been largely unsuccessful.

A large part of the reason for this lack of success relates to the UK's strong commitment to bolstering military industry. A recent study analyzing the impact of the military sector on the British economy shows that during a ten-year period beginning in 1975 the Ministry of Defence allocated a proportionally growing share of its R&D funds to industry, from 55 per cent to 65 per cent. This study also notes that in 1983–84 more than 40 per cent of the R&D expenditures of the UK's engineering industries (mechanical engineering, electronics, aerospace, auto and shipbuilding) came from the Ministry of Defence, and that the aerospace and the electronics industries receive considerable military support.[67] Spurred by the July 1987 White Paper, there has been recent talk by British ministers about cutting military R&D and shifting some national funds to civilian uses.[68] However, the implementation of such a policy change remains to be seen. Given the substantial and long-term commitment of the British government to military R&D, there would need to be a big shift of expenditures away from defence in order for the civilian sector to realize major benefits.[69]

CONCLUSIONS

The major problems many US and UK high-technology industries have been confronting from losing domestic and foreign market shares are strongly related to excessive military R&D spending and the accompanying preemption of technical talent which has taken place over the last few decades. Among other factors, high levels of military R&D spending have contributed to the deteriorating competitive positions of these industries, meaning fewer jobs than if they had remained strong. Moreover, the preclusion from development of civilian-oriented process technologies that would improve productivity growth has played an important part in the reduced standard of living evident in the US over the last decade.[70] Similarly to the US, in the UK excessive expenditures for military R&D and a crisis-oriented government policy have not prevented the erosion of high, medium and low R&D manufacturing industries in world markets over the years.[71] Because Japan and West Germany spend proportionally less national resources on military R&D and have comprehensive civilian industrial policies fully assisting industrial high technology, market advantages have accrued to manufacturers in these countries, as US and UK firms have suffered from the consequences of an opposite government policy.

Notes

1. Daniel Bell, *The Coming of Post-Industrial Society* (New York: Basic Books, 1976), p. 344.
2. Ibid., pp. 198 and 232.
3. Seymour Melman, *Profits Without Production* (New York: Alfred A. Knopf, 1983), pp. 65–8.
4. There are at least three different official definitions of high technology currently in use. See US Department of Commerce, *An Assessment of U.S. Competitiveness in High Technology Industries* (Washington, DC: US Government Printing Office, February 1983), pp. 33–7; and Organization for Economic Co-operation and Development (OECD), *OECD Science and Technology Indicators, No 2 R&D, Invention and Competitiveness* (Paris: OECD, 1986), pp. 58–60. Because the classifications of products and industries considered to be high technology and technology-intensive can change from one period to the next, these terms are arbitrary. In this paper our concern is with the general high-technology/ technology-intensive category which identifies products and industries that rely heavily on research and development. Technology-intensive products are those that have R&D costs that are more than 2.36 per cent of the value added and include the following product groups: aircraft and parts; office, computing and accounting machines; electrical equipment; optical and medical instruments; drugs and medicines; plastics and synthetics; engines and turbines; agricultural chemicals; professional, scientific and measuring instruments; industrial chemicals; and TV and radio reception equipment. See *International Science and Technology Data Update, 1988*, National Science Foundation (NSF 89–307), p. 92–4.

5. National Science Board (NSB), *Science & Engineering Indicators, 1987* (Washington, DC: US Government Printing Office, 1987), p. 313.
6. Calculated from National Science Foundation (NSF), *International Science and Technology Data Update: 1988* (NSF 89–307), p. 88 and *Economic Report of the President* (Washington, DC: US Government Printing Office, 1989), p. 312.
7. See US Department of Commerce, *An Assessment*, p. 50.
8. NSF, *International Science and Technology Update: 1988*, p. 92.
9. US Department of Commerce, *An Assessment*, p. 49.
10. NSF, *The Science and Technology Resources of West Germany: A Comparison with the United States* (NSF 86–310), p. 37.
11. Calculated from NSB, *Science & Engineering Indicators, 1987*, pp. 236 and 324 and the *Economic Report of the President, 1989*, p. 431. The military-related aircraft and parts industry is responsible for a large part of British exports. On this see Victoria Hatter, *U.S. High Technology Trade and Competitiveness*, Office of Trade Administration, US Department of Commerce, February 1985, p. 30.
12. OECD, *Science and Technology Indicators* (1986), p. 115.
13. This work is currently being written and is tentatively titled *From Industry to Arms: The Political Economy of High Technology*.
14. *Economic Report of the President* (Washington, DC: US Government Printing Office, 1984), p. 45.
15. See the report prepared by William Finan, Perry Quick and Karen Sandberg for the Joint Economic Committee of Congress, *The U.S. Trade Position in High Technology: 1980–1986* (October 1986). For a discussion of trade problems in manufacturing and the effects of the appreciation and depreciation of the dollar see, The Report of the President's Committee on Industrial Competitiveness, *Global Competition: The New Reality*, Vol. II (Washington, DC: US Government Printing Office, January 1985), pp. 14–15.
16. Nathan Rosenberg, *Inside the Black Box: Technology and Economics* (Cambridge: Cambridge University Press, 1982), pp. 280–83.
17. See Lloyd Dumas, *The Overburdened Economy* (Berkeley: University of California Press, 1986, p. 211; also see Gregory A. Bischak, cited in Michael Dee Oden, *A Military Dollar Really Is Different* (Lansing, MI: Employment Research Associates, 1988), p. 50n.
18. NSF, *Federal Scientists and Engineers: 1986* (NSF 87–320), p. 8.
19. These estimates can be found in NSF, *Projected Responses of the Science, Engineering, and Technical Labor Market to Defense and Nondefense Needs: 1982–87* (NSF 84–304), p. 7.
20. Mary Kaldor, Margaret Sharp and William Walker, 'Industrial Competitiveness and Britain's Defence', *Lloyds Bank Review* (October 1986), p. 39.
21. NSF, *Shortages Increase for Engineering Personnel in Industry*, (NSF 85–309).
22. NSF, *National Patterns of Science and Technology Resources: 1987* (NSF 88–305), p. 21.
23. NSF, *Shortages Increase for Engineering Personnel in Industry*.
24. See David Henry and Richard Oliver, 'The Defense Buildup, 1977–85:

Effects on Production and Employment', *Monthly Labor Review* (August 1987), p. 10, from which the 41 per cent figure was calculated.

25. NSF, *Shortages Increase for Engineering Personnel in Industry*.
26. This is a critical mistake made by those who take a neutralist position concerning the effects of military spending on the economy. See Gordon Adams and David Gold, 'Recasting the Military Spending Debate', *Bulletin of the Atomic Scientists*, (October 1986), p. 31.
27. NSF, *International Science and Technology Data Update: 1988*, p. 38. .
28. Ibid.
29. U.S. Bureau of the Census, *Statistical Abstract of the United States: 1988* (108th Edition) (Washington, DC, 1987), p. 557.
30. NSF, *International Science and Technology Data Update: 1988*, p. 10.
31. Calculated from NSB, *Science & Engineering Indicators, 1987*, pp. 236–7.
32. In 1986 the official Japanese ceiling on total defense spending changed to 'about 1% of GNP' from the previous one of 'less than 1% of GNP'. See *Japan Economic Almanac 1988* (Tokyo: The Japan Economic Journal, 1988), p. 146.
33. Kaldor, et al., 'Industrial Competitiveness and Britain's Defence', p. 41.
34. Calculated from NSF, *Research and Development in Industry, 1983* (NSF 85-325), p. 29.
35. NSF, *International Science and Technology Data Update: 1988*, p. 10.
36. OECD, *OECD Science and Technology Indicators* (Paris: OECD, 1984), p. 98.
37. NSF, *International Science and Technology Data Update: 1988*, p. 10.
38. See NSF, *The Science and Technology Resources of Japan: A Comparison with the United States* (NSF 88-318), pp. 12–13 and 65–9 for information in this and the preceding paragraph.
39. See NSF, *The Science and Technology Resources of West Germany: A Comparison with the United States*, p. 49.
40. Perry Quick, 'Businesses: Reagan's Industrial Policy', *The Reagan Record*, eds John Palmer and Isabel Sawhill (Cambridge, MA: Ballinger, 1984), pp. 302–3.
41. See NSF, *International Science and Technology Data Update: 1988*, pp. 12–13.
42. See Bruce Berkowitz, 'Reviewing Defense R&D', *Issues in Science and Technology* (Winter 1988–9), p. 60.
43. Ibid.
44. Quoted in Center for Defense Information, 'The Pentagon Prepares for Nuclear War', *The Defense Monitor*, Vol. XVI, no. 4 (1987) p. 6.
45. For more details concerning this controversy see Nancy Miller, 'Supercomputers and Artificial Intelligence: Recent Federal Initiatives', in *Hearing Before the Subcommittee on Energy Development and Applications and the Subcommittee on Science, Research, and Technology of the Committee on Science and Technology*, House of Representatives, 10 June 1985, p. 590.
46. See ibid. pp. 580–86; US Department of Commerce, *U.S. Industrial Outlook 1987*, p. 28–4; and US Department of Commerce, *U.S. Industrial Outlook 1989*, p. 26–5.

47. David Weston and Philip Gummett, 'The Impact of Military R&D: Hypotheses, Evidence and Verification', *Defense Analysis*, Vol. 3, no. 1 (March 1987), pp. 72–4.
48. NSF, *International Science and Technology Data Update: 1988*, p. 94.
49. For an example of Japanese leadership in the application of lasers in optical technology (optoelectronics) see Robert Haavind, 'Lighting the Way in Lasers', *High Technology*, August 1985, pp. 39–41.
50. Information on the DoD's Very High Speed Integrated Circuit Program and Japan's civilian work on semiconductor technology can be found in Thomas Howell, William Noellert, Janet MacLaughlin and Allan Wolff, *The Microelectronics Race* (Boulder, CO: Westview Press, 1988, pp. 118–25.
51. NSF, *International Science and Technology Data Update: 1988*, pp. 18–19.
52. OECD, *Science and Technology Indicators* (1986), p. 32.
53. NSF, *International Science and Technology Data Update: 1988*, p. 94.
54. NSF, *National Patterns of Science and Technology Resources: 1987*, p. 58.
55. US Department of Commerce, *U.S. Industrial Outlook 1989*, p. 26–1.
56. See Anthony DiFilippo, *Military Spending and Industrial Decline: A Study of the American Machine Tool Industry* (Westport, CT: Greenwood Press, 1986), pp. 53–7; and Anthony DiFilippo, 'Supply-Side Myopia, Subsequent Rationalizations and Machine Tool Industry Stagnancy', *The Social Science Review*, Vol. 7, no. 1, (1988) pp. 24–43.
57. US Department of Commerce, *U.S. Industrial Outlook 1989*, pp. 20–2 and 20–5.
58. Jeffrey Bairstow, 'Can the U.S. Semiconductor Industry Be Saved?', *High Technology* (May 1987), pp. 34–40.
59. US Department of Commerce, *U.S Industrial Outlook 1989*, p. 20–5.
60. See Seymour Melman, *The Demilitarized Society* (Montreal: Harvest House, 1988); David Alexander and Anthony DiFilippo, 'Beyond INF: Toward Progressive Arms Reduction', *Defense Analysis*, Vol. 4, no. 4 (1988), pp. 398–400; and see Marcus Raskin, *Draft Treaty for a Comprehensive Program for Common Security and General Disarmament* (Washington, DC: Institute for Policy Studies, July 1986) for a detailed disarmament plan.
61. This legislation is titled The Defense Economic Adjustment Act: H.R. 101, reintroduced on 3 January 1989 by Representative Ted Weiss (D-NY).
62. For an extended analysis of the industrialization issue and a detailed look at Japanese and West German industrial policies relative to the US see Anthony DiFilippo, 'Reindustrialization Politics: U.S. Industrial Policy at a Comparative Disadvantage', *Research in Politics and Society*, Vol. 3 *Deindustrialization and the Restructuring of American Industry* (Greenwich, CT: JAI Press, 1988), pp. 269–89.
63. See US Department of Commerce, *An Assessment of U.S. Competitiveness in High Technology Industries*, p. 27.
64. NSF, *The Science and Technology Resources of Japan: A Comparison with the United States*, p. 66.

65. NSF, *The Science and Technology Resources of West Germany: A Comparison with the United States*, p. 52.
66. See Jeffrey Hart, 'British Industrial Policy', *The Politics of Industrial Policy*, eds Claude Barfield and William Schambra (Washington, DC: American Enterprise Institute for Public Policy Research, 1986), pp. 128–60.
67. Kaldor et al., 'Industrial Competitiveness and Britain's Defence', pp. 36–9.
68. See Sir David Phillips, 'A Strategy for Science in the UK' *Science and Public Policy*, Vol. 15, no. 1 (February 1988), pp. 3–12.
69. Cf. Kaldor et al., 'Industrial Competitiveness and Britain's Defence', p. 48. Also see Jeffrey Hart, op. cit.
70. See *Contrasting Interests in National Security: Selecting Technology for Deterrence or Economic Growth*, by Anthony DiFilippo, presented at an international conference on 'Ethical Choices in the Age of Pervasive Technology', 27 October 1989, University of Guelph, Ontario, Canada.
71. OECD, *Science and Technology Indicators* (1986), p. 73.

2 Defense Spending as Industrial Policy: The Impact of Military R&D on the US Software Industry

Nance Goldstein

INTRODUCTION

Federal spending on research and development (R&D) has gained acceptance in the postwar US economy as a necessary means to promote basic research. The profit motive provides little incentive for companies to invest in long-term, expensive R&D which does not directly contribute to commercial success. In order to overcome this market failure, the US government has spent billions of dollars over the past decade on computer science (CS) and software R&D, primarily because it is viewed as technologically and economically central to the competitiveness of US industry. However, in recent years the Department of Defense (DoD) has come to dominate this public expenditure. This trend provokes a question as to how R&D spending for military purposes has influenced the direction of software technology development and the structure of the commercial software industry. Postwar industrial history provides examples of defense spending that propelled new technologies into widespread commercial use, but has this happened in the software industry during the 1980s?

This chapter attempts to address these questions about the economic role of military R&D spending in the software industry.[1] The computer software industry provides a useful case study of the relationship between, on the one hand, the research objectives of the DoD and the commercial sector, and on the other hand, the pattern of R&D funding and the changing industry structure. DoD spending on software seems to have affected the commercial industry's development in two distinct ways. First, it has shifted the industry's research and product development toward more applied and developmental work at the expense of basic research. Second, it has redistributed public resources toward large firms away from the industry's smaller firms. These trends have emerged precisely because the DoD relies heavily on the private sector to supply its software R&D. Yet high DoD spending on software R&D has favored large firms in the field, thereby aggravating the competitive problems for smaller firms, which have historically generated most software innovation. Thus, this pattern of defense spending may threaten the innovative and competitive potential of the commercial industry.

Examining recent military R&D spending on software also offers an opportunity to understand the emerging concern of defense planners for the deterioration in the competitiveness of US industry during the 1980s. In particular, the decline of domestic manufacturing capacity has been viewed by the Defense Department as endangering the weapons arsenal. Only vibrant industries operating in the US could create the technologies the DoD wanted for the future. Competitiveness problems have plagued industries which until recently were undisputed world leaders in critical high-tech fields such as semiconductors, computers and software. All of these fields have become important to the DoD's modern warfighting strategies. The DoD responded to the threatened loss of the nation's technological capabilities by promoting military R&D programs as a means to renewing the technology base and domestic industrial competitiveness.[2]

In spite of a national aversion to centralized planning, there has been surprising support for using Defense spending explicitly as an industrial policy to bolster US industries.[3] The postwar history of how defense spending helped to spawn the development of the computer and semiconductor technologies of the 1950s and 1960s has stirred support in Congress and within the business community for military sponsorship of industrial research. More recently, DoD officials have realized that public support for defense spending as an industrial aid might minimize the impact of anticipated budget-cuts.

This chapter will consider the extent to which Defense Department R&D spending has proven compatible with commercial objectives for advancing software technology. Experience in the software industry, an information technology industry strategically important to the competitive future of the US, may provide useful lessons for other sectors. This chapter has three sections. The first section highlights the trends of the Defense Department's spending on software R&D in the 1980s and the establishment of specific software-related research programs geared to the DoD's technological strategy. The second section reviews the economic relationship between defense CS R&D expenditures for military uses and technological progress and R&D investment in civilian industry. The chapter concludes by considering the implications of military R&D spending for national industrial policy.

DEFENSE SPENDING ON SOFTWARE

The DoD is the largest single consumer of software in the world. The Department has spent billions on large software systems since the early 1980s to develop new computing capabilities. The mammoth, complicated DoD bureaucracy requires big, complex information processing systems. Consequently, DoD's spending on data processing and general-purpose software and software services rose by 142 per cent from $1 688 580 000 in FY 1983 to $4 083 573 000 in FY 1987.[4] Another factor contributing to this rise in CS spending is the fact that current defense strategy relies heavily on a growing arsenal of 'intelligent' weapons systems, which are weapons with sufficient on-board information processing capability to make decisions and carry out a mission without human intervention. As a result, 80 per cent of US weapons systems depend significantly on software.[5] By producing weapons with embedded computer systems, the DoD intends to redress a major perceived US vulnerability, namely, the fact that it has far fewer troops relative to the Soviet Union. Thus, by acquiring technologies that give US weapons qualitative leverage over Soviet troops and systems, US forces can be enhanced by these technological advantages.[6] These so-called 'force multipliers' critically depend on large, extremely sophisticated software programs. The DoD is attempting to apply this approach across a wide range of dissimilar warfighting scenarios, from terrorist action to global conflict.[7]

As a result of this technological strategy, DoD spending on software embedded in weapons is projected to increase by more than sevenfold between 1983 and 1990, from $4 billion to more than $30 billion.[8] All of these factors have combined to cause software costs to claim a rapidly increasing share of the defense budget during the enormous Reagan Administration buildup. By 1989 software accounted for six to seven per cent of the entire DoD budget, with that share likely to grow.[9]

The skyrocketing cost of software development for complex systems partly accounts for this. The costs of software development and maintenance (that is, adapting it to changing uses) now far exceed hardware costs in the DoD.[10] The cost-escalation results partly from the process of developing software. The demand for software is growing faster than the ability to produce it because it is still largely an artisan-like process. It depends on individuals and their intellectual creativity to define the functional requirements, design systems, write the code and test it. This labor-intensity severely limits the speed, reliability and predictability of delivering a product.[11] For example, a complex weapons system like a guided missile requires a software program of hundreds of thousands of lines. Using contemporary technologies, a small sub-program of up to 125 000 lines of programming code (LOC) takes 18 months to produce.[12] The larger and more complex the program, the more unpredictable the development time and its cost. While the size of defense programs varies in length and complexity, the large ones are huge. For example, a defense software research group reported the largest as 3.2 million LOCs.[13]

These technological limits in producing software, coupled with the resulting delivery bottlenecks and the quality problems of complex systems, have threatened to curtail the DoD's strategic plans. As USAF Brigadier-General Charles F. Stebbins admitted, 'The senior Air Force leadership realizes that the software problem is really starting to eat our lunch.'[14] The cost and reliability problems constrain the number, type and effectiveness of the desired weapons and capabilities the DoD can purchase. The Air Force claimed that software problems were responsible for seven out of ten of the weapons systems that were in trouble in 1983.[15] The effort required for developing and testing software for the F-18 fighter-plane were so extensive that when changes were needed, they modified the plane to fit the existing software.[16]

Establishment of DoD's software-related research programs

In the past, software was simply a 'data' item, listed in the budget like office supplies. By the early 1980s, the growing importance of military software, coupled with the severity of emerging technological problems, made the software budget a crisis.[17] As a result, the Defense Department initiated a number of programs specifically to increase the effective use and quality of software and the productivity of developing it. The DoD acknowledged that technological advances in the civilian sector, particularly in smaller firms, were critical for achieving the DoD's goals.[18] The Software Technology for Adaptable Reliable Systems program (STARS) aimed to ensure that DoD personnel actually understood and used the newest, most effective technologies. A second goal focused on encouraging the industry to innovate by altering the way the DoD defined and contracted needed software R&D.[19] The STARS program founded the Software Engineering Institute to teach defense programmers the most modern methods of software development, and established the Software Productivity Consortium, a software R&D collaboration of defense prime contractors. To aid its effort, in 1982 the DoD adopted ADA, a high-order computer language, as the single programming language for all DoD mission-critical systems. ADA included many features to simplify and reduce the number of programming tasks and to encourage reuse. In 1984 the DoD initiated the Strategic Computing Program (SCP) – the biggest computer R&D program ever – to create 'a new generation of machine intelligence technology which will have unprecedented capabilities and which promises to greatly increase our national security and our economic strength'.[20] Administered by the Defense Advanced Research Projects Agency (DARPA), SCP is a ten-year $1 billion program initiated to bring six not-yet-accessible or existent technologies to the point of usefulness for new weapons systems.[21] The technologies include vision and speech recognition, planning and reasoning, gallium arsenide microchips and natural language and navigational programming.

The Strategic Defense Initiative (SDI) also funds CS research. The research for the proposed space defense system depends heavily on information processing and rapid communications. SDI's controversial computer battle-management system alone would require 10 to 30 million lines of code, which it is conservatively estimated would take more than 3000 programmers and analysts at least 10 years to complete.[22] These plans represent a major technological leap from contemporary systems. Research for SDI's battle management system received more than $275 million from 1984 through 1987, mostly for software R&D.[23] In 1989 the DoD identified 22 critical technologies that were deemed essential to develop in order to ensure long-term qualitative superiority of United States weapons systems, with seven of these being software or software-dependent technologies.[24]

In addition to general DoD programs, each Service contracts its own R&D. The Air Force spent 5 per cent of its total 1983 budget on software, which amounted to $3 billion.[25] The Army planned a $20 billion program over the period 1986–96 for communications, command and control software systems for its defense and warfighting capabilities.[26] This rising software demand fueled a 250 per cent real increase in DoD spending on CS and engineering research from FY 1976 to FY 1988. In FY 1988 the DoD spent $450 million on all forms of computer-related R&D.[27] Indeed, the DoD continues to dominate all federal funding of CS research, with military funding accounting for 63 per cent of all publicly-funded CS R&D in FY 1988.[28]

An implicit goal in most of these military software R&D programs was to develop the same economic and technological capacities that the civil sector needed. The emphasis was increasingly on process R&D geared to reducing software costs, increasing software development productivity, and improving product quality, as well as ending some of the contracting practices that had historically fostered inefficiencies in private-sector contractors.[29] For example, STARS has financed the development of so-called engineering tools to make new software understandable (transparent) and usable (portable) in a variety of situations. Moreover, STARS aimed to structure programs so that parts of it are reusable, thereby saving programmers from the trouble of always rewriting every function from scratch. DARPA, in particular, has viewed its CS research agenda as exactly the basic and applied research which the commercial industry has needed. Then DARPA Deputy Director Craig Fields claimed, 'I know of not one example anyone has ever come up with of how [the technology base] contents of the program would differ if it were a civilian program. We are serving a civilian purpose as well.'[30]

This apparent convergence of military and civilian sectors' interests on process innovation stands in marked contrast to the history of defense-targeted research. The DoD has most often demanded extraordinary performance requirements for its technology, which has resulted in an emphasis on product R&D, while ignoring production research and cost constraints.[31] In the past these research priorities have driven a wedge between the technologies appropriate to the two sectors. More recently, the DoD's recognition that software development problems were threatening the development of new weapons systems has created an unusual opportunity where military and commercial objectives might prove complementary.

The DoD's dependence on the commercial sector

As research and production problems mounted, the services' military labs could not supply the DoD's gargantuan demand for new software.[32] Consequently, the DoD has increasingly relied on the private sector to perform most of its software R&D.[33] For example, the DoD will spend approximately 60 per cent of SCP's funds in industry.[34] This dependence on civil industry derives from more than internal supply constraints. It was recognized early in the 1980s that design, testing and maintenance techniques in the commercial software sector were more advanced and better than internal DoD methods.[35] Also, the DoD's scientific advisers recognized that smaller independent software firms could provide the creativity and innovation so necessary for DoD's far-reaching technological plans. The similarity of military and civil technological needs and the DoD's dependence on a viable and innovative civilian industry suggests that defense software research priorities during the 1980s may have directly and positively enhanced productivity, technological development and growth in the commercial sector. Yet while defense R&D funding could conceivably produce real, direct technological benefits for the commercial industry, the other effects of DoD R&D policy may undermine efforts to stimulate innovation and protect the commercial base of the CS industry. In the next section we shall examine the distinctive ways in which military research policy has affected the industry's very competitive structure, and thereby the industry's potential for innovation.

DEFENSE SOFTWARE R&D FUNDING AND THE INDUSTRY'S COMPETITIVE STRUCTURE

An examination of the economic dynamics and structure of the US software industry in the late 1980s will provide a context for understanding the effects of DoD software R&D policy. R&D in the software industry has a distinctly different role from research in most other sectors. Because software is the set of instructions to make a computer perform particular operations, R&D dominates the work of a software producer. Thus, conceptual production precedes mass production of the software product. Mass-production manufacturing in the software industry merely refers to the reproduction of the information instruction set for the market, that is, copying the program on to floppy disks, printing the manual and packaging them for distribution. Because it supplies the product that makes computers and microelectronics equipment work, the industry must devote a higher-than-average share of resources to R&D to satisfy the phenomenal pace of technological change and increasing sophistication of customers in high-tech markets. New-product R&D is a necessity to maintain both short-run market share and long-run viability.[36] In addition, competitive pressures have increasingly demanded directing R&D resources to process improvements. As noted above, greater size and complexity of large software systems for an increasing array of uses has resulted in unpredictable time-and-cost escalation for production of new software. The failure to improve productivity has jeopardized future company growth.

At the same time the risks of R&D investments have risen because of considerable technological and market uncertainties. Rapid technological change prevents firms from reliably predicting near-term market demand. They hesitate to risk expensive long-term R&D commitments because it is notoriously difficult to predict the eventual payoff for a product that can so easily be copied or imitated.

Changes in the industry's structure have further hampered company spending on R&D, particularly longer-run investment. The industry is a fragmented one of mostly small entrepreneurial firms. For instance, in the mid-1980s about 85 per cent of the ever-increasing number of software firms employed fewer than 20 people.[37] During the 1980s the rising costs and risks of R&D coincided with increasing industry concentration. The increasing market concentration results in part from the necessity of gaining access to an effective national, even global, distribution network. The high resource costs of building proprietary access to markets effectively excludes smaller firms, and thus makes takeovers attractive to both the smaller firms and the acquiring firms.

These trends give competitive advantage to the computer and telecommunications giants which have claimed a growing share of software markets. Computer hardware and telecommunications giants have devoted ever-increasing shares of their vast resources to developing software. Software now overshadows the production costs of hardware, and now almost dictates product design and sales.[38] Computer firms spend most of their R&D dollars on software, and software systems development may involve a third or more of a large computer firm's employment. As a result, these firms moved first to develop software internally, and then began producing software products for the outside market. By 1987 leading computer corporations earned more than a third of their sales from software and expected that to increase in the near-term to 50 per cent of their sales.[39]

Large firms' needs for new products and greater resource requirements have fueled an increasing flurry of mergers and acquisitions by large software firms and computer corporations.[40] Large firms have voraciously acquired smaller firms to feed products to their starved distribution networks. Smaller firms agree to takeover in order to gain access to financial resources and to enhance job security. The numbers of acquisitions more than quadrupled during the 1980s, from 138 in 1982 to 434 in 1988 representing $8.4 billion in value.[41] The software industry has a much higher propensity for acquisition than most industries, and the economic squeeze sharply quickened the pace in the late 1980s.[42] The increased market power of large firms threatens the short-run and long-run viability of smaller firms. While economic studies on the relationship between market power, firm size, and R&D intensity have been mixed, many argue that in general, and particularly in this industry, a vibrant small-firm sector is essential to sustaining innovative activity.[43] In the case of oligopolistic high-tech firms, Rebecca Henderson has shown that these firms avoid introducing new generational and radical innovations.[44] If this holds true for the software industry, the industry's restructuring may have reduced the industry's R&D and innovative potential by squeezing out the small firm sector. Economic pressures would then further jeopardize the future competitiveness of a sector recognized as vulnerable in the early 1980s.

Development support at the expense of basic research

The DoD, in spite of public declarations to the contrary, has increasingly diverted its computer science funds away from long-term basic research to short-term weapons systems development. Despite the mushrooming of DoD CS-related spending, basic research funding fell sharply as a share of that funding, from 31 per cent in FY 1976 to 15 per cent in FY 1987. And while the level of expenditures for basic CS research did increase from $20 million to $57 million over the same period, the DoD's more specific applied research and development CS spending increased by more than 630 per cent. Basic research simply has not kept pace with the phenomenal growth, diversification and potential of the computer field.[45]

The Strategic Defense Initiative (SDI), the space anti-ballistic missile defense system, is an example of this shift towards more developmental work at the expense of basic R&D. SDI caused controversy within the scientific community partly because of its objective to push software technologies far beyond contemporary capabilities.[46] The largest military venture ever undertaken in the US, SDI spent most of its $276 million battle-management program R&D on software.[47] This program provides the communications, computing and control systems for the entire space defense system. In spite of the alleged objective of stimulating leading-edge R&D, independent analysts found that much of the funding targeted simulations and efforts not likely to produce basic advances in computer science.[48] Moreover, there is very little investment in the challenging and critical areas of software products and work processes. Persistent doubts about SDI's technical feasibility and increasing pressure to reduce defense spending have already squeezed SDI's more far-reaching, experimental efforts.[49] By 1988 SDI Office had scaled back the battle-management research program to gain demonstrable weapons, for example, prototyping kinetic energy weapons.

Changes in the activity of DARPA also partly explain this shift in CS research toward more applied and developmental work. DARPA, the DoD's leading R&D authority, and sponsor of high-risk, high-payoff technology research, supplies the R&D that the individual Services avoid because it falls outside their traditional warfighting roles. The R&D efforts by the Army, Navy and Air Force are also limited by the fact that military men make the decisions and they are traditionally oriented to very short time-horizons and operation-specific ventures.[50] Consequently, to compensate for this tendency, DARPA supports the farsighted R&D that will determine future military capabilities. It explores general technologies such as communications and data processing, which individual Services are unlikely to tackle. As a result, DARPA has been the major public source of artificial intelligence and advanced computing research since the mid-1960s. DARPA funding created time-sharing and networking for large computer systems and packet-switching for telecommunications systems: all major breakthroughs that transformed a wide range of commercial and scientific activities.

DARPA may prove unable to produce such economic bonanzas in

the 1990s. The traditional resistance of the Services to new technologies led to pressures in the mid-1970s and again in the mid-1980s for DARPA to prototype new discoveries. DARPA's role shifted to persuading each Service to accept new technologies by giving them specific, readily-usable applications.[51] In addition, late in the Reagan Administration there was a growing desire in Congress to see concrete results from years of extravagant spending. By producing workable weapons systems, the DoD might garner support for continued spending in a world of budget constraints and continued scepticism about high-tech programs like Star Wars.[52] The shift of DARPA and DoD spending to development, as opposed to basic research, represents a priority to produce mission-critical technologies which in turn ensures the completion of desired weapons before they are lost to budget cuts. The Strategic Computing Program (SCP), originally funded to achieve far-reaching capabilities in software, illustrates another case of a program which was shifted to near-term mission-critical applications.

Mission priorities

The DoD launched SCP to respond to the perceived competitive threat of the Japanese government's support for its Fifth Generation computing project. SCP focused its research on developing easily-usable systems built from standardized inputs, which would enjoy the economic incentives of commercial spinoff. To do this, DARPA placed about 60 per cent of SCP funding in industry, with universities receiving about one-third of the funding and the remainder going to national labs.[53] The reality of the program has not matched the adventurous intent. While SCP purports to undertake applied and even basic research, according to Mitch Marcus of Bell Laboratories, [m]ost of [the technology goals] require major breakthroughs in research. Expecting particular breakthroughs within a particular time frame is really going out on a limb.'[54] SCP's program structure demands that researchers create innovations, or 'scheduled breakthroughs', within short time-periods to meet weapons production schedules.[55] Using tight schedules to manage research prohibits the pursuit of multiple possible avenues of inquiry, and this may restrict the rate of new discoveries. Also, SCP has embedded general technologies in classified weapons systems, which tends to slow the diffusion of new technologies. Classifying basic technologies denies industry and academia access to information and innovation and consequently contradicts the prime economic rationale for state support of research. The actual structure of the program, then, hinders progress in true research and severely limits the possibility that it can supply the planned social benefits.

Furthermore, SCP seems to have cut or terminated funding for some of the long-term research that the DoD promoted as worthy of industrial support. In 1988 SCP stopped funding industry research on one of its advanced technologies, natural language programming. The DoD, it seems, considered the potential performance benefits too far in the future given the constrained budget. According to computer science analysts William Schatz and John Verity, '[where] DARPA had previously been supportive of much more pure computer science research, . . . never has [DARPA] so aggressively funded computing research with such specific weapons applications.'[56]

Many argue that the DoD's considerable spending on computer science through programs such as SDI and SCP has distorted the direction of economically important R&D away from civilian needs.[57] This distortion may result from the DoD's targeting technologies which commercial industry will not use or from R&D contracting practices that effectively limit competition.

Like the history of postwar military investment, defense software technology development continues to be performance-driven with almost no cost constraints. The DoD adopted ADA as a standardized computer programming language specifically to improve software engineering productivity and to reduce the costs over the whole life of the software running defense systems. ADA addressed many of the problems computer professionals consider critical for speeding up the design and writing of complex programs, improving the reliability of the software, and reducing costs. It is a standard for all DoD equipment and agencies and is written so that parts of it can be reused in order to save time in later programming.[58]

Yet ADA has so far been largely ignored by the commercial market. The language does not deliver its promise of higher productivity because it is too complex for widespread use in cost-conscious situations.[59] It was designed for a large bureaucracy and is considered too slow and too complicated for most business uses. Its complexity demands programmers be trained six months or more to use it skillfully. Some consider it beyond the capabilities of many programmers. In the words of CS expert C. A. R. Hoare,

At first I was extremely hopeful. The original objectives of the [ADA] language included reliability, readability of programs, formality of language definition, and even simplicity. Gradually these objectives have been sacrificed in favor of power, supposedly achieved by a plethora of features and notational conventions, many of them unnecessary and some of them . . . even dangerous.[60]

Overdesigning not only limits the technology's spinoff to commercial industry. Since 1987, the DoD has required all contractors to use ADA. This means firms must have ADA-specialized engineers. This effectively restricts the number of firms able to win R&D contracts. This is one among many defense R&D contracting policies that have limited software companies' access to DoD R&D support during the 1980s.

This contrasts with the DoD's sponsorship of the development of the COBOL language in 1959. Rather than choosing a product to meet the DoD's elaborate internal requirements, it recruited computer manufacturers' professionals and corporate computer users to create a language that the DoD could use for its many activities and which met the needs of the commercial world. Because industry representatives created a language they could use, COBOL became the standard business computer language.[61]

Defense R&D contracting

The Defense Department has acknowledged that small firms would make particularly valuable contributions to its major software R&D initiatives.[62] The SDI Office, for example, publicized a set-aside program to tap the creativity of entrepreneurial software firms and to break with the postwar practice of contracting primarily to large corporations.[63] This, like the Small Business Innovative Research Program for all DoD procurement, has not succeeded.[64] In fact, most of the industrial R&D contracts for software have gone to prime contractors that are large, long-established firms which are completely or significantly dependent on the DoD. Very few commercial software firms of any size have competed for defense R&D money.

A major example of this tendency was the early competition to submit concepts for SDI's software system and R&D proposals, which was won by major defense contractors like TRW, Boeing, Rockwell International and Martin Marietta.[65] Interestingly, all but

Boeing won large SCP contracts. In addition, established multi-national computer hardware corporations have also won large defense R&D contracts. Honeywell, IBM, Sperry, Unisys, and AT&T are among 49 large contractors for SCP industrial R&D.[66] While contractors subcontract much of the work, smaller independent software firms have largely refused to participate. According to a Defense Science Board Task Force report of 1987, there's evidence that the DoD actually lost many of its commercial software suppliers during the 1980s.[67]

The main reasons for this concentration of CS research in large firms result from traditional DoD practices, recent changes in DoD policy, and specific competitive factors in the US software industry. First, contractors need to have experts experienced in dealing with DoD bureaucracy and preparing the volumes of documentation for a proposal. Second, the DoD's extraordinary technology specifications are often long and time-consuming; therefore it is very expensive to compete for contracts and to carry out R&D. Many smaller firms cannot afford to tie up their workers because of the increasing uncertainty over the delay and the magnitude of DoD's payback. Relatively few firms have the resources to be able to bid for R&D projects. Moreover, the anti-bureaucratic structures and financial weaknesses of many independent software firms make them unlikely contenders.

Third, because the Department has channeled larger shares of its R&D funding into major weapons systems, the contracting process favors large firms.[68] Winning an R&D contract is the key to winning follow-on production contracts. The DoD frequently awards large production contracts to one source, so they are extremely lucrative. Prime contractors often duel for R&D contracts to get a piece of a new system because so few new weapons systems are started per decade. Moreover, tightening budget constraints make ongoing projects very uncertain. This oligopolistic competition can lead to below-cost bids in the expectation that the winner will make up the loss in a later contract. This may effectively exclude smaller firms. Further, the DoD selects contractors on the basis of their capability to handle the follow-on contract. This eliminates many smaller firms.

Finally, the DoD uses the same profit allowance for software R&D as for hardware procurement contracts in its cost-plus incentive contracts. However, R&D contracts for hardware producers are often followed by production contracts which have historically provided acceptable total profits levels. In contrast, software firms have no comparable follow-on production contracts. The ten per cent profit on hardware procurement contracts is insufficient for a return on custom-designing software.[69] Financially vulnerable software firms may not be able to afford to win an R&D contract.

The perverse effects of new competitive procurement laws

The 1984 law to structure real competition for all DoD awards dramatically altered R&D contracting. The Competition in Contracting Act lengthened DARPA's period for processing an R&D proposal from 90 days to 285 days and added paperwork and bureaucratic demands which tend to further deter innovative firms from bidding. Rather than promptly funding unsolicited research ideas from firms, DARPA and the DoD were required to respond by publicly requesting competitive bids for the same research effort. That process would likely disclose the innovator's proprietary information to its competitors, particularly the large firms.[70] These conditions discouraged smaller commercial firms from requesting DoD support.

In large measure, the DoD and Congress were responding to the public's outcry over waste and fraud and to pressures to reduce defense spending in the mid-1980s by shifting the risk of defense R&D on to contractors. Through legislation and regulation, the DoD further discouraged civilian firms from participating in defense-related research through the use of fixed-price contracts and cost-sharing on high-risk ventures, reduced profit allowances, reduced and delayed progress payments for completed work, and preference for low-priced awards.[71] These practices effectively excluded cash-constrained, smaller commercial firms. At the same time, the changes stymied efforts to gain innovations that result from longer-term R&D commitment and attention to methodology and quality.

Civilian software firms as subcontractors

While all these factors directed CS prime contracts to defense firms, 40 per cent to 60 per cent of all DoD funding usually gets to subcontractors.[72] Smaller commercial software firms could gain R&D support through subcontracts with the primes, but this did not happen, because of the problematic relationship between primes and sub-tier firms in general, and their particular competitive relationship in the software market. The problems stem from the fact that the

DoD has historically assumed that the primes will maintain the viability of supplier firms within the subcontracting chain, so the DoD does not have to deal with them directly.[73] There are, however, major conflicts of interest between the two. The primes off-load R&D risks on to their subcontractors. Where primes might have flexible, or even cushioned contracts with the DoD, subcontractors receive more restrictive terms from the primes. Subcontractors often get fixed-price contracts even though their role involves higher technical risks. Perhaps most important is that the primes do not protect subcontractors from competition. During a project's life, the product is often opened to competition, which is frequently with another large prime. Primes can decide at any point to supply the product internally, and that is easier to do once the prime has learned the technology from the subcontractor. Consequently the supplier base for defense contracts has dwindled. By 1980 50 per cent of small high-tech contractors were either bankrupt or refusing to subcontract.[74]

The nature of software technology sharpens the conflict between the primes and civilian software firms. Software firms have difficulty controlling the rights over their product because it is information.[75] Primes benefit from this relationship because they gain access to the software firm's technology through a subcontract and close contact with the firm's software personnel.

Primes gain up-to-date information that enables them to perform future R&D internally, thereby capturing the subcontractor's expertise without having to pay for the years of investment to learn the technology. This opportunity is most obvious when the prime is a leading computer corporation, many of which are major suppliers of software. Many of the commercial software suppliers for the DoD have dropped out in recent years.[76]

The downturn in defense spending has exacerbated this conflict. Prime weapons contractors began competing in the fast-growing commercial software market years ago as a protective strategy against the actual or potential loss of weapons contracts. Boeing, Lockheed, McDonnell–Douglas and others have attempted to sell software in civilian markets to amortize their huge software investments. These ventures also helped the firms keep their skilled personnel busy during periods of uncertainty in DoD contracting. The primes' entry into commercial markets serves the DoD's interests. These are the same firms that are the sole source of complex weapons hardware. Diversification can ensure that the DoD will not lose its weapons production capability by cushioning the primes financially during a lean period of defense funding.

DEFENSE SPENDING AS INDUSTRIAL POLICY

Despite DoD claims to champion the needs of US industry to regain global competitiveness, the DoD has presided over a dramatic increase in defense R&D spending during the Reagan years which has resulted in a shrinkage of the national technology base.[77] The recent history of military funding of software R&D has shown how that contradiction could develop.

Political pressure on the military establishment during the 1980s increasingly diverted spending away from general technological inquiry into the development work to make the desired weapons systems operational. Because developing applications of software focuses expertise and learning on the specific usage, this shift results in the increasing specialization of R&D inputs, particularly labor. Moreover, many of the specialized technologies which are created are unlikely to offer any usefulness to commercial industry. Further, much of the technology has been embedded in classified weapons systems, which tends to restrict commercial access. No matter how generalizable the defense-sponsored technologies, their potential economic value as commercial products or as the basis for further development into civilian uses is limited by embedding them in specific weapons systems.

Over the same period, the Defense Department has redistributed its software R&D funds toward short-term development at the expense of basic and applied research.[78] Underlying these trends is the fact that the DoD has skewed its research programs partly in response to increasing Congressional and budgetary pressures. Even the future-oriented mission and far-reaching technological hopes of DARPA surrendered to these demands. Clearly, the DoD's short-term institutional and political interests have won out over longer-term and broader goals.

These developments stem from the Defense Department's funding to meet military needs. However, these practices present economic problems for civilian industry as well. The current process of CS innovation and production technologies have reached the limits of their capabilities at a time when market demands for more complex, larger and more reliable software are increasing exponentially. These supply constraints are reflected by the skyrocketing costs, unpredictable delays, unreliable products and missed market opportunities, which will only continue unless technological breakthroughs change the way software is created. Simultaneously, extreme financial pressure on the independent software sector 'to get the product out' has depressed industry spending on longer-term research. Independent software firms, particularly small and medium-sized firms, have neither the resources nor the protection from fast-changing market competition to invest in longer-term risky R&D. Computer Associates, now the largest US independent software firm, has for years been buying up smaller firms to seize products and compensate for their own lack of internal R&D activity and expertise. Computer Associates' 1989 takeover of Cullinet Inc. – a former market leader – provides an example. Cullinet's financial weakness stemmed from their inadequate longer-term research into non-IBM, non-mainframe computer systems and their competitive failure in those growing market segments. This case illustrates the inability of private sector software firms to perform necessary longer-term R&D and foreshadows significant competitive problems not only in the software industry but in all sectors dependent on software and microelectronics.[79]

The most pressing need for industrial support, then, would be to allow the industry's most innovative firms the chance to invest in R&D. Review of the appropriate form of government assistance, including incentives or rewards, loan subsidies, improved protection of data rights, and other factors, is beyond the scope of this discussion. Clearly this is the direction policy should take to improve competitiveness. However, the Defense Department is by far the nation's largest public supporter of CS R&D. With budget pressures likely to continue to constrain public spending, DoD spending effectively diverts public money away from the civilian software industry.

The unusual coincidence of defense and civilian sectors' needs for productivity-enhancing technological advances has not rectified the situation. The ways the Defense Department has contracted its software R&D seem to have had a perverse effect. The DoD has directed most of its expenditure to sectors least reliable in creating innovations. For example, the DoD funded the Software Productivity Consortium, a group of defense-dependent contractors, to develop new production methods. This trend reflects the bigger problem, namely that the DoD has directed most of its industrial R&D funding to large computer corporations and defense firms.

Contracting and subcontracting practices have largely excluded smaller civilian firms. The elaborate bureaucracies and remoteness of these large militarily-dependent firms from potential customers tends to deny them the close communications with the market which are most critical to finding technological solutions that will be useful in industry. To the extent that the DoD's R&D has commercial potential, the prime contractors seem the least likely to be able to transfer these innovations to the commercial sector in a timely fashion. Further, most of these contractors want a larger share of the fast-growing civilian software market, so they are unlikely to restrict the dissemination of their findings from military work. Given the importance of both largeness and cash resources in today's software market, defense R&D spending has given potential competitive advantage to these big firms. This may be a particularly important advantage in the supply-constrained labor market. Concern over a shortage of computer professionals has contributed to rising salaries which large firms can more easily afford. Thus, Defense Department software R&D spending seems to have fortified the position of large firms in the software market and the CS labor market. The dynamics of concentration tend to favor larger firms.

Even without grand public interest aims, defense spending, because it is so large, does affect industry structure and competition, particularly in a relatively small industry like the software sector. Defense spending is an industrial policy, regardless of intentions. By devoting extensive public resources to large and less innovative firms, and to short-term military interests, public policy has effectively ignored the vulnerability of smaller civilian firms and may even have depressed the production of socially useful R&D.

The DoD's distortion of software R&D and the structure of the industry have resulted at least in part from the absence of any economic analysis of the industry and the possible impacts of DoD policies. Moreover, this has happened without public debate over the accountability for the economic repercussions on this industry and others. Relying on the DoD as the agent for national industrial and technology policy seems a costly and inappropriate response to problems of the US industry.

Notes

1. This chapter is based on preliminary research for a larger project on the US computer software industry. It considers the part of the independent software industry that supplies large- and medium-sized operating and applications systems for mini- and mainframe computers and telecoms and computer networks. Further, the categories of R&D used throughout the text (basic research, applied research and development) are similar to those used by the National Science Foundation. See for instance, *Research and Development in Industry, 1981*, National Science Foundation, Washington, DC, 1983, p. 2.
2. See *Holding the Edge* by the Office of Technology Assessment, US Congress, Washington, DC, 1989, for a thorough explanation of the technology base.
3. See 'Toward a Pentagon Inc.' in *The New York Times*, 23 October 1988.
4. See *Prime Contract Awards by Service Category and Federal Supply Classification, FY 1987* by the Department of Defense, Directorate of Information, Operations and Reports, Washington, DC, 1988, Table C p. 21 and 46.
5. See A. Bell, 'Defense Software Steady Despite Cuts', *Mass High Tech*, 5 June 1989, pp. 1, 24.
6. See William Perry and Lawrence Sumney, 'The Very High Speed Circuit Program' in *Review of Military Research and Development*, edited by Koska Tsipis and Penny Janeway (London: Pergamon, 1987).
7. See *Critical Technologies Plan*, by the Department of Defense, Washington, DC, 15 March 1989, p. 3.
8. See 'ADA Steps Out' by Edward Bernard, *Datamation*, Vol. 31, no. 17, 1 September, p. 117.
9. See *Critical Technologies Plan*, op. cit., p. A-13.
10. Maintenance refers to the long period in the lifecycle of a software system after it is installed. Costs during this period derive from changes in the software due to new functional needs and modernization. As software does not deteriorate, this may be a very·long period of time. It is now assumed that maintenance accounts for 80 per cent and more of the system's total costs.
11. For more technical explanations of the processes, technologies and their limitations, see *The Mythical Man–Month* by Frederick Brooks (New York: Addison-Wesley, 1975).
12. See 'Star Wars Won't Compute' by Jonathan Jacky, *Atlantic Monthly*, June 1985. Also see, *SDI – Technology, Survivability and Software* by the Office of Technology Assessment, US Congress, Washington, DC, 1988, p. 237.
13. Reported in A. Bell, 'Defense Software', op. cit., p. 24.
14. Quoted in John Morrocco, 'Coming Up Short in Software', *Air Force*, February 1987, p. 66.
15. See *Report of the USAF Scientific Advisory Board Ad Hoc Committee on the High Cost and Risk of Mission-Critical Software*, US Air Force, Washington, DC, December 1983, p. 2–2.
16. See Jacky, 'Star Wars', op. cit., p. 26.

17. For an assessment of this crisis, see *SDI – Technology Survivability and Software*, op. cit.
18. See *Defense Small Business Advanced Technology Program, 1981–1982*, US Department of Defense, Washington, DC, 1982. Also see Edward Lieblein, 'The Department of Defense Software Initiative – A Status Report', *Communications of the ACM*, Vol. 29, no. 8, August 1986, pp. 734–743.
19. Lieblein, ibid.
20. See William Schatz and John Verity, 'Weighing DARPA's AI Plans', *Datamation*, Vol. 30, no. 12, 1 August, pp. 34–43.
21. See Joel Yudken and Barbara Simons, *Computer Science Research Funding: Issues and Trends, Interim Report to the Special Interest Group on Automata and Computability Theory*, SIGACT, of the Association for Computing Machinery, 1988, p. 11.
22. For a discussion of this see Nance Goldstein, 'Software for SDI Goes Back to the Drawing Board' *Computing*, 1 May 1986, p. 20.
23. See OTA, 1988, op. cit., p. 248. There has been a long, vociferous debate among software experts about whether or not software technologies can be designed to perform the extremely complex functions for SDI, especially the capability to create a reliable management system for battle in space. The question of the technological feasibility of military requirements is beyond the scope of this paper; however, the fact that the debate triggered the commissioning of two presidential panels of inquiry (The Fletcher Panel of 1983, *Report of the Study on Eliminating the Threat Posed by Nuclear Ballistic Missiles: Battle Management, Communications and Data Processing*, Washington, DC, Department of Defense, October 1983, and the Eastport Group Report of 1985, *Report to the Director, Strategic Defense Initiative Organization*, Washington, DC, Department of Defense, 1985) indicates the centrality of software for current and future DoD strategy and expenditures.
24. These technologies include software producibility, parallel computing, machine intelligence/robotics, simulation and modeling, automatic data relay, and data fusion. All together these programs require funding of more than $600 million in FY 1990, according to the DoD. See *Critical Technologies Plan*, Washington, DC, Department of Defense, 15 March 1989.
25. USAF, 1983, op. cit. p. 2–2.
26. See *Battlefield Automation – Status of the Army Command and Control System Program*, Washington, DC, US General Accounting Office, August 1986 (NSIAD-86-184FS), p. 1.
27. This represents an increase from $60 million to $294 million. These spending levels in current dollars represent only spending in the DoD's 6.1 research category and 6.2 exploratory development category. Much of the R&D spending is in the 6.3A category known as advanced technology development, and some other lower categories of research classification. Also, these data do not include millions spent on R&D performed in industry through the DoD's independent research and development program which is off-budget. These matters are elaborated by Yudken and Simons, *Computer Science Research Funding*, op. cit., p. 8.

28. Ibid.
29. See *Embedded Computer Resources Acquisition and Management* by the Defense Science Board Task Force, Washington, DC 1982. Also see Richard Hanlon, *Software Modernization*, Maxwell Air Force Base, Air War College, 1986, and see Lieblein, 1986. op. cit.
30. Quoted by Jonathan Jacky in 'The Strategic Computing Program' in *Computers in Battle: Will They Work*, edited by David Bellin and Gary Chapman (New York: Harcourt Brace, 1987), p. 199.
31. For a more extensive treatment of this tendency see Seymour Melman, *Profits Without Production* (New York: A. A. Knopf), especially pp. 161–81. Also see Jacques Gansler, *The Defense Industry* (Cambridge, Massachusetts: 1985), especialy pp. 92, 106, 220–24.
32. For an examination of this see *Military Software*, Defense Science Board Task Force, US Department of Defense, Washington, DC, 1987. Also see *International Competition in Service*, Office of Technology Assessment, US Congress, Washington, DC, 1987.
33. Approximately 90 per cent of the DoD's entire research, development, testing and evaluation budget goes to private firms, as opposed to universities and national laboratories. This is documented by Lynne Brown in 'Defense Spending and High Technology Development', *New England Economic Review*, September/October 1988.
34. See Yudken and Simons, *Computer-Science Research Funding*, op. cit., p. 12.
35. See *DoD Should Change Its Approach to Reducing Computer Software Proliferation*, Report of the Comptroller-General of the United States, to the Chairman of the US House of Representatives Committee on Government Operations, 26 May 1983, US General Accounting Office, Washington, DC, (MASAD-83-26). Also see 'Conversation with Robert Kahn, Computer Science and Technology', *CPSR Newletter*, Vol. 5, no. 3, 1987. These same trends have been found in other sectors.
36. For example, the 1989 takeover of Cullinet, a leading independent software firm, resulted from financial problems that grew out of the firm's failure to recognize the commercial potential of new products such as minicomputers and workstations, and the resulting failure to devote R&D resources to creating products for these emerging markets. For a treatment of this see Alison Bell, 'Software Pioneer Reaches End of the Trail', *Mass High Tech*, 17 July 1989, pp. 1, 7.
37. *County Business Patterns*, 1983 through 1986 editions, Bureau of the Census, US Department of Commerce, Washington, DC, Table 1b, SIC groups 7372, 7374, 7379, p. 57.
38. See OTA, 1987, op. cit.
39. See Anne Field, 'Why the Hardware Giants are Hustling into Software', *Business Week*, 27 July 1987, pp. 53–4. Also, IBM, DEC Control Data and Sperry were four of the top suppliers of software services in 1981 and 1982, as noted in Peter Hall, Ann Markusen, Richard Osborn and Barbara Wachsman, *The California Software Industry: Problems and Prospects* (Berkeley: University of California Press, 1983), p. 65. And Hewlett-Packard spent nearly two-thirds of its R&D budget on software, as noted in the Office of Technology Assessment study, *Information*

Technology R&D, OTA, US Congress, Washington, DC, 1985.

40. See Hall et al., *California Software Industry*, op. cit. p. 69.
41. See *Mergerstat Review, 1989* (Chicago, Illinois: Merill Lynch and W. T. Grimm and Company, 1989) SIC groups 7372, 7374–79, Tables 872 and 873.
42. See OTA, 1987, op. cit. p. 168. Also see *The Massachusetts Software Industry, 1980–1984*, Cognetics, Boston, Massachusetts, 1985.
43. For a treatment of the general argument see Albert Link, Gregory Tassey and Robert Smud, 'The Induce versus Purchase Decision' *Decision Sciences*, Vol. 14, pp. 46–61. For a treatment of the particular case of the computer software industry see Hall et al., *California Software Industry*, op. cit, Cognetics, op. cit. and OTA, 1985, op. cit.
44. See Rebecca Henderson, *The Failure of Established Firms in the Face of Technical Change*, National Bureau of Economic Research, Summer Institute, July 1988.
45. See Yudken and Simons, *Computer Science Research Funding*, op. cit. p. 2.
46. See Eastport Group Report, 1985, op. cit. Also see David Parnas 'Software Aspects of Strategic Defense Systems', *Scientific American*, Vol. 73, September 1985, pp. 432–40.
47. This represented total spending from the program's beginning in 1984 through contracted research in 1987, but excludes spending through any of the SDIO's joint projects with other agencies. See OTA, 1988, op. cit. Furthermore, the official funding figures do not include privately funded R&D by companies. Company R&D spending on all SDI-related projects was estimated to be 36 cents for every federal R&D dollar. See Rosy Nimroody, et al., *Star Wars Spinoffs: Blueprint for a High Tech America?* (New York: Council on Economic Priorities, 1988).
48. These include the OTA report 1988, op. cit., the SDI-commissioned Eastport Group Study, op. cit., David Parnas, 'Software Aspects', op. cit. Parnas is a well-known SDI critic and has commented on this extensively. The Council on Economic Priorities (see Nimroody, *Star Wars Spinoffs*, op. cit.) quoted the opinion of Gordon Bell, the former Director of Computing at the National Science Foundation, 'Based on my interaction with SDI while at the National Science Foundation, I have no faith that their computer work is being carried out in a coherent or competent fashion. This techno-welfare program will result in absolutely no fallout [commercial spinoff] . . .' (p. 88).
49. To register the severity of these concerns, the House of Representatives cut almost $2 billion in SDI research money off the Administration's proposed FY 1990 defense budget in its own version, yet it remains to be seen what the House and Senate conference bill will appropriate. See Andrew Rosenthal, 'Uprising in the House', *The New York Times*, 29 July 1989, p. 1.
50. See Jacques Gansler, *Affording Defense*, (Cambridge, Mass.: MIT Press, 1989), pp. 217–18.
51. See for example, Packard Commission, *A Quest for Excellence: Final Report*, Washington, DC, June 1986. Also see 'Technology and the Military: DoD's DARPA at 25' in *IEEE Spectrum*, Vol. 20, August 1983, pp. 70–73.

52. It has also been suggested that funding constraints might reduce longer-term, more experimental CS research for a different reason. To reduce expenses DARPA adopted more bureaucratic measures for funding and managing research. Research is much more difficult to manage tightly than development, and consequently may lose funding. See Yudken and Simons, *Computer Science Research Funding*, op. cit.

53. See Yudken and Simons, *Computer Science Research Funding*, op. cit. p. 12.

54. As quoted in Schatz and Verity, 'Weighing DARPA's AI Plans', op. cit., p. 42.

55. See Mark Stefik, 'Strategic Computing at DARPA', *Communications of the ACM*, Vol. 28, no. 7, July 1985. Also see Jacky, 'Strategic Computing Program', op. cit. and Tom Athanasiou, 'Artificial Intelligence as Military Technology' in *Computers in Battle – Will They Work*, edited by David Bellin and Gary Chapman (New York: Harcourt Brace, 1987).

56. Schatz and Verity, 'Weighing DARPA', op. cit., p. 39.

57. For an elaboration of this argument see Clark Thomborson, 'Military Direction of Academic CS Research', *Communications of the ACM*, Vol. 29, no. 7, July 1985, pp. 583–5. Also see the various contributions in Bellin and Chapman, *Computers in Battle*, op. cit. Furthermore, these points are examined in Nimroody, *Star Wars Spinoffs*, op. cit., Bell, 'Software Pioneer', op. cit. and by Paul Selvin in 'Campus Hackers for the Pentagon', *Nation*, 28 November 1988, pp. 563–6.

58. For an explanation of the goals of adopting one language for all military uses and the specific advantages of ADA see the Defense Science Board Task Force report, 1987, op. cit., Edward Berard, 'ADA Steps Out' *Datamation*, Vol. 31, no. 17, 1 September 1983, pp. 114–26. Also see Benjamin Elson, 'Software Update Aids Defense' *Aviation Week and Space Technology*, 14 March pp. 209–21.

59. See Bell, 'Defense Software Steady Despite Cuts,' op. cit., p. 24.

60. C. A. R. Hoare, as quoted in Berard, 'ADA Steps Out', op. cit., p. 122.

61. See Jean Sammet, 'Software History' in *The Encyclopedia of Computer Science and Engineering* (New York: Van Nostrand Reinhold and Company, 1983).

62. See Defense Science Board Task Force, 1987, op. cit. and US Air Force, 1983, op. cit.

63. See Leslie Brueckner, 'Assessing the Commercial Impact of the VHSIC Program' Working Paper #5, Berkeley Roundtable on the International Economy, Berkeley, California, December 1984.

64. The Small Business Innovative Research Program was designed to correct the maldistribution of federal R&D money. This is discussed in Gansler, *Affording Defense*, op. cit., p. 221.

65. See Goldstein, 'Software for SDI', op. cit.

66. See Elizabeth Corcoran, 'Strategic Computing: A Status Report' *IEEE Newsletter*, Vol. 24, no. 4, 1987, pp. 50–54.

67. See Defense Science Board Task Force, 1987, op. cit., p. 30.

68. See Gansler, *Affording Defense*, op. cit, Chapter 7.

69. Defense Science Board Task Force, 1987, op. cit., p. 29.

70. This is suggested by defense industry expert Jacques Gansler in a personal communication with the author.
71. For a complete review of this process see Gansler, *Affording Defense*, op. cit., pp. 179–214.
72. Ibid., p. 258.
73. In fact there is little publicly available information on the extent of subcontracting for DoD prime contracts. The Department deals principally with the primes, and has compiled very few studies of subcontracting patterns and practices. See, for instance, *Geographical Distribution of Subcontract Awards Fiscal Year 1979*, US Department of Defense, Directorate for Information Operations and Reports, Washington, DC, 6 August 1980. Also see the last in a series of annual reports which was terminated after 1983, *Shipments to Federal Government Agencies, 1983*, Current Industrial Reports, US Department of Commerce, Bureau of the Census, MA-175(83)-1.
74. Gansler, *Affording Defense*, 1989, op. cit., p. 258.
75. For an explanation of the legal problems over data rights in the software industry see the OTA study, *Information Technology R&D*, Office of Technology Assessment, US Congress, Washington, DC, 1985.
76. Defense Science Board Task Force, 1987, op. cit., p. 30.
77. See Gansler, *Affording Defense*, op. cit., Chapters 7 and 8.
78. See Yudken and Simons, op. cit.
79. Interviews conducted by the author with venture capitalists, academics and industry representatives who are experts in software indicate that this was a general industry problem in 1988 and 1989.

Part II
Theoretical and Empirical
Issues of Military Economy

Part II

3 National Security, Noncontributive Activity and Macroeconomic Analysis: Theoretical, Empirical and Methodological Issues

Lloyd J. Dumas

INTRODUCTION

There is no denying that national security is a serious business. The desire of people to form nations with their own indigenous governments, and to shield them from the dictates of those living beyond their borders, has been a powerful force in modern human history. Within the confines of their own nation-state, people believed they could create a better life for themselves and their children, a life attuned to the particular culture and values with which they felt most comfortable. To achieve these goals, the nation-state did not need to be isolated from the rest of the world – trade, travel and exchange among the nations could in many ways be enriching – but it did need to be able to protect itself against unwelcome external interference and coercion.

In the last half of the twentieth century, much of the world has become obsessed with military means of protecting the nation-state, and so has lost the breadth of view that is critical to finding real security. In a troubled world of nations that have not yet learned to manage their conflicts without resort to violence, there is little doubt that military forces have a role to play in providing national security. But the security of a nation depends at least as much on the strength of its economy as on the power of its armed forces. No nation whose economy continues to deteriorate can long remain either powerful or secure.

In his book, *The Rise and Fall of the Great Powers*, Yale historian Paul Kennedy argues that for five hundred years, nations have become 'great powers' because of a strong and buoyant economy, then built large militaries to protect their interests, so burdening their economies with military spending that they receded from the center of the world stage, economically *and* politically. America is today following the same pattern. Four decades of vigorously pursuing the post-Second World War arms race has taken a heavy toll on the US economy. What was once the world's most powerful, vibrant, productive economy is increasingly finding itself unable to compete, unable to effectively do the most basic thing any economy must do – produce products people want at a price they can afford to pay. Yet the empirical and theoretical focus of conventional macroeconomics tends to obscure, rather than highlight, both the magnitude of this decline and its connection to nearly a half century now of unprecedentedly high military expenditures.

THE STATE OF THE AMERICAN ECONOMY

In 1982, unemployment soared in the US, reaching halfway to the horrendous rates of the 1930s, as the economy plunged into the worst economic downturn since the Great Depression. Since then, the unemployment rate has dropped to much more tolerable (though still historically high) levels, while inflation has remained well below the double digit rates of the late 1970s. Constant dollar GNP has been showing solid growth, rising over 20 per cent from 1982 to 1987, and reaching over \$4 trillion by the third quarter of 1988.[1] On the basis of these kinds of indicators, the period since 1982 has been labeled the strongest prolonged economic recovery of the post-Second World War period. We have been told that the economy has been revitalized, that America is 'back on the track'. But this is self-delusion.

There has been no real economic recovery, no thoroughgoing revitalization. What has happened to make things look so much better? An orgy of public (and private) borrowing has pumped up the surface of the economy. We have not returned to the sound base of efficient production that drove the impressive, widely-shared growth of the American economy throughout much of its history, the kind of solid foundation that can support real economic growth and make it sustainable. The erosion of America's economic base continues. And now, on top of that we have created a 'bubble'. The weakening economic base portends continued long-term deterioration in US economic performance. The bubble of debt raises the possibility of sudden collapse. Beneath the facade of rising GNP, the signs of America's serious economic trouble are clear and unmistakable.

Between 1948 and 1968, labor productivity (measured by output per hour of all persons in the nonfarm business sector) rose 67.7 per cent; however, from 1968 to 1988, it rose by only 23.7 per cent, a little more than one-third of the pre-1968 gain.[2] Paralleling this, purchasing power earned per hour worked (in the nonfarm business sector) rose by more than 38 per cent from 1948 to 1958, and had gained another 31 per cent by 1968. Then this twenty-year pattern of surging growth in real income dramatically shifted over the next twenty years. The gain from 1968 to 1978 was a mere 13.4 per cent. But even that looked good compared to the past decade. During the entire period from 1978 to 1988, purchasing power earned per hour worked gained only 0.6 per cent.[3]

There have been hundreds of bank failures since 1981. A post-Depression record of 120 bank failures was set in 1985. The record was shortlived: 1986 saw 138 bank failures; 1987 saw 184, more than 50 per cent above the record set only two years earlier.[4] In August 1989, federal legislation set in motion a bailout plan for the nation's troubled savings and loan industry, estimated to cost taxpayers $166 billion over ten years. Only two weeks later, the chief economist at the Federal Office of Thrift Supervision (newly created by the legislation) warned that savings and loans were still in deep trouble and that the cost of the bailout could go even higher.[5] At the same time, Peter Passell, economic columnist for the *New York Times*, reported on a study published by the Brookings Institution which argued that 'thinly capitalized commercial banks may be in no better shape than savings and loans were five years ago'. In this category were 226 banks with combined assets of nearly $1 trillion, including 13 of the largest 15 banks in the United States.[6]

While all this was happening, the national debt of the United States was undergoing an explosive increase. At the end of 1980, the interest-bearing public debt of the US reached $906.4 billion, an enormous amount of money. But only five years later, at the end of 1985, it had more than doubled to $1821.0 billion. By the end of September 1988, the national debt had reached $2.6 trillion. In less than *three years* after 1985, the federal government had *added* nearly $780 billion to the national debt, an amount equal to 86 per cent of the *total* national debt as of 1980.[7]

But it wasn't just the national debt of the United States that was rapidly increasing. The private debt of households and nonfinancial institutions, combined with the debt of state and local governments also underwent enormous increases during the 1980s, rising from nearly $3 trillion in 1980 to more than $6 trillion by September 1988.[8] Internationally, the pattern looked even worse. In 1980, the US was still a net creditor nation internationally, as it had been since 1914, with the rest of the world owing the US more than $106 billion. By 1985, the situation had completely reversed, with the US owing the rest of the world nearly $111 billion. By 1987, the net international debt of the US was almost $370 billion. In only seven years, we had added almost a half-trillion dollars of net international debt.[9] In sum, an enormous amount of borrowing, public and private, went on in America in the 1980s. And this much borrowing can temporarily paper over a lot of deepseated economic problems.

For all the rhetoric about revitalization, it is difficult to interpret stagnating real income, a rising tide of bank failures, an enormous increase in public and private domestic debt and a deep plunge from being the world's largest international creditor to being the world's largest debtor as signs of a healthy and strong economy. Yet as serious as these problems are, it may be that the most serious structural problem is that reflected by the nation's huge trade deficits. Here too we see a dramatic reversal of a longstanding pattern. Every year from 1894 to 1970, the United States exported more goods than it imported. After three-quarters of a century of annual trade surpluses, the US began to run consistent run trade deficits in the early 1970s. In 1983, the nation's merchandise trade deficit hit an all-time record of $64.2 billion. Within a year that record was shattered, as the trade deficit nearly doubled, reaching $122.4 billion. It continued to climb, to $133.6 billion in 1985, $155.1 billion in 1986, and finally peaking at $170.3 billion in 1987. In 1988, the trade deficit abated, running at an annual rate of $136.2 through October, but still more than double the record deficit that had been set only five years earlier.[10]

The nation's trade deficits reflect a fundamental failure of American competitiveness, an inability to produce efficiently enough to make domestic products attractive in price and quality to customers here and abroad. Once 'made in USA' meant made well, high in quality and reasonable in price. If that were still as true as it once was, exports would be higher, imports lower and trade surpluses rather than deficits would still be the order of the day. Americans have become accustomed to a high and rising standard of living. But an economy that cannot produce efficiently cannot continue to provide that kind of solid long-term economic growth.

Why has American industry become so inefficient? Why has it been so difficult to see this deterioration or to recognize just how basic and structural its sources have been? And what has this to do with the obsessive pursuit of national security through military means? The answers to these questions require a different perspective from that of conventional macroeconomic theory, and would be greatly assisted by a somewhat different way of organizing economic data, guided by that perspective.

Because it is common, among economists as well as the general public, to treat money value as synonymous with economic value, it is easy enough to overlook the fact that different money-valued activities have very different impact on the functioning of the economy. On the empirical side, a measure like GNP – the total money value of goods and services produced in a nation in a year – is taken as a measure of total economic value generated, of the population's level of material wellbeing. But a high or rising GNP actually tells us little about the public's real standard of living, about the presence or absence of real economic prosperity. A billion dollars spent on housing, or on the building of the nation's transportation system will add exactly the same amount to GNP as a billion dollars spent on public monuments. On the theoretical side, both of the dominant schools of macroeconomic thought focus attention on the size of an aggregate of money value: in Keynesian theory, it is the dollar volume of total spending; in monetarist theory, it is the money supply. From this point of view as well, a dollar spent is a dollar spent. For example, Keynesians would argue that if the government wants to stimulate a sluggish economy, it can do so by spending more money. It makes no macroeconomic difference whether the money is spent on housing, roads or public monuments. Yet particularly over the long run, the impact of these different forms of spending on economic wellbeing are in fact very different.

The theoretical basis for a more useful perspective has more to do with the works of Adam Smith, Karl Marx and Thorstein Veblen, than with the works of modern mainstream macroeconomists. For Smith argued that not all forms of economic activity were productive,

Marx that the activities of at least some persons engaged in economic activity were more expropriative than productive, and Veblen that 'conspicuous waste' was an institutional fact of life with significant economic consequences.

As an attempt to modify conventional macroeconomic theory so as to highlight rather than obscure the answers to the questions raised above, I offer the theory of resource diversion. This approach, elaborated in *The Overburdened Economy* (University of California Press, 1986), creates two taxonomies. The first and most important is a categorization of activities using productive economic resources, by the nature of their output; the second, a categorization of productive resources themselves by function. Some of these categories, or the potentially measurable concepts they imply, are congruent with or can be constructed from existing data; some are completely different, and difficult if not impossible to directly reconstruct from existing data categories.

The empirical testing of the theory raises some interesting methodological issues, having little or nothing to do with data categories as such, that may well have broad relevance. The theoretical relationships postulated involve cumulative processes, asymmetries, structural rigidities, and at least potential discontinuities or threshold effects that substantially complicate testing. Indicative empirical evidence is provided in *The Overburdened Economy* to demonstrate the plausibility of the theory. But rigorous, unbiased testing requires attention to these issues of data and technique.

THE THEORY OF RESOURCE DIVERSION

The core of the theory of resource diversion can be stated quite succinctly. It begins by defining the economy as that part of society that provides the material standard of living. The economic value of a good or service is accordingly defined by the extent to which it contributes to that material standard of living. And in turn, the economic value of an activity depends on the contribution of that activity to the provision of a good or service that adds to material wellbeing.

Ordinary consumer goods add to the material standard of living directly. Producer goods increase the standard of living indirectly, by adding to the economy's capacity to produce those goods that add to material wellbeing. Thus, both consumer and producer goods are classified as economically 'contributive'. However, unnecessary activities carried out in the course of producing either of these, such as the useless 'paperpushing' that has become commonplace in the overstuffed bureaucracies of American business and government, are clearly 'noncontributive'.

There are goods and services that are economically 'noncontributive' as well. By their nature, design and intention, they are oriented to purposes other than enhancing material wellbeing. Churches, for example, are intended to provide spiritual value, not economic value. Public monuments may be constructed to instill pride in the nation, and encourage a spirit of coherence. However, they do nothing to enhance material wellbeing. Similarly, military goods and services have no economic value – they neither contribute to the material standard of living directly, as do consumer goods, nor are they tools with which to produce. This is not to say that military goods have no value – they may, for example, have political value. But it is clear that they were not intended to and do not fulfill either consumer- or producer-oriented functions. They do not add to material wellbeing. Therefore, they are *economically* 'noncontributive'.

It is important to emphasize that the terms 'contributive' and 'noncontributive' are not to be viewed as the functional equivalent of 'good' and 'bad', or 'useful' and 'useless'. Organized societies have many goals. The production of the material standard of living is only one of them. There is no intention here to elevate that particular goal above the rest. We are focusing here on the question of material wellbeing because that is the central function of the economy.

To the extent that noncontributive activities absorb labor, machinery and other productive resources, those economically valuable resources can be said to be 'diverted' from the central purposes of the economy. The opportunity cost of such diversion can be viewed in terms of consumer goods forgone, as in the 'guns vs. butter' tradeoff, or in terms of investment forgone – a kind of 'guns vs. machine tools' tradeoff. If the society trades 'butter' for 'guns', the standard of living will be depressed year-by-year relative to what it could be in the absence of resource diversion. It may, however, be possible to maintain a respectable rate of investment. If the society trades 'machine tools' for 'guns', year-by-year the standard of living may be kept higher for a time, but the economy's productive competence will deteriorate. In the long run as this process continues, it will undermine competitiveness and force the standard of living down as well.

Whether consumer goods or investment are being sacrificed as a result of resource diversion depends not only on what kinds of production continue to be emphasized, but also on the nature of the diverted resources. Some kinds of labor and capital, such as engineers and scientists and the R&D equipment and facilities with which they work, are inherently investment-oriented. Diverting them to noncontributive activity has little or no effect on productive capacity and so on the standard of living in the short run. But as such diversion is sustained year after year, it can have devastating effects on productive competence, competitiveness and hence the standard of living in the long run.

Productive competence – the capability for efficient production – is primarily the result of three things: an appropriately skilled and motivated workforce; a sufficient quantity and quality of capital (primarily direct production capital and infrastructure capital); and an up-to-date process and product technology. Without conscious and ongoing efforts to maintain it, productive competence will erode. The maintenance or improvement of productive competence requires a flow of resources adequate to preserve and strengthen these three pillars on which it stands. Consequently, diverting significant amounts of the key resources required for this investment to noncontributive activity will tend to cause productive competence to deteriorate. From the point of view of the real business of the economy, it is as though some resources had been destroyed, leaving the economy poorer.

The continued decay of productive competence will sooner or later cripple the efficiency of production, and thus interfere with the critical process on which real, widespread economic growth depends. Because the vast majority of the population of any nation earn the largest part of their income in the form of wages (and salaries), broad-based economic growth requires a continuing rise in the real wage. This in turn implies that money wages must grow relative to the level of prices. But since wages (and salaries) are the largest part of cost for most producers, rising money wages (along with any increases in the price of other inputs) mean rising costs, which tend to force product prices upward. Thus, avoiding the erosion of real wages by cost-push inflation in such an environment requires continuing improvement in the efficiency of production. Decaying productive competence undermines this critical ability of producers to offset higher input costs with improved efficiency. At first, this may merely limit the increase in real wages, but it will eventually cause real wages to stagnate, then decline.

The deterioration of real wages (and ultimately other forms of real income as well) may occur by a number of different routes. Money wages may continue to rise, perhaps even rapidly, while cost-push inflation escalates, destroying the purchasing power of those wages. In an open economy, such a cost-generated rise in the level of prices will put domestic producers at an increasing disadvantage relative to foreign producers whose input costs are lower and/or whose productive competence is not being undercut by a heavy burden of noncontributive activity. As domestic producers price themselves out of the market, they will lose export markets to foreign competition and see their domestic market share eroded by an increasing flow of imports. This will eventually result in rising balance of trade deficits, along with serious employment problems at home. The loss of markets by domestic producers will force cutbacks in local production, causing the unemployment rate to rise. Stagflation, rather than being a bizarre aberration, is one natural route by which persistent resource diversion leads to a deterioration in real incomes through the intervening process of decaying productive competence.

Declining productive competence may also lead to a deterioration of real wages in the presence of little or no inflation. The pressure of foreign competition, for example, may ultimately compel domestic producers to limit or eliminate increases in the price of their products. In the absence of cost-offsetting capability, this can only be accomplished by either holding wages and other input costs to anemic increases at best, or actually forcing them down. If local labor will not accept lower wages, domestic firms may move production to cheap labor havens abroad, and real incomes will be pushed down by rising unemployment. If the costs of inputs other than labor (e.g. oil) are falling, it may actually be possible to increase real wages for a time while continuing to produce locally – even in the absence of cost-offsetting capability – providing foreign producers are not also experiencing the same falling input costs. This would be an extremely fortuitous circumstance, and one that is unlikely to persist. If, on the other hand, costs of other inputs are rising, the downward pressure on wages will be correspondingly stronger.

There is no way to win in such a circumstance. If employees refuse to accept sufficient wage restraint or reduction, inflation will destroy the purchasing power of their incomes, and domestic production will be unable to hold markets against foreign competition. Production will be cut back locally, and the deterioration in living standards will be transmitted via rising unemployment, and perhaps by inflation as well. If employees do accept wage concessions, the pressures toward both inflation and unemployment will be mitigated, but the decline in living standards will not. It will simply be transmitted in the form of falling money wages.

Closing the economy by erecting protectionist barriers will not help. Employment may be maintained but the rate of inflation will tend to increase, as pressures for wage restraint are reduced and the flow of low-priced foreign goods is restricted or eliminated. If wages are forced down even in the presence of protection, inflation will not erode real wages; falling money wages will. It is possible to prefer one or another of these different mechanisms by which the drop in material wellbeing is transmitted – they do, for example, have different implications for the distribution of income – but none of them is a very pleasant prospect. Declining productive competence will result in a falling standard of living. Conventional macroeconomic policies can only alter the transmitting mechanism.

Resource diversion is thus a powerful and fundamental process. If noncontributive activities divert significant amounts of the resources most crucial to the maintenance and improvement of productive competence over a sufficiently long period of time, the cost-offsetting ability of domestic producers will deteriorate, and living standards will eventually decline. The contributive economy will have been undermined. Though the symptoms may vary, this process is so basic that it will produce the same essential effect – falling material wellbeing – whether it occurs in the context of a market-oriented or socialist economy, in a more developed or less developed nation.

It is not difficult to see the relevance of the theory of resource diversion to the US. Since the end of the Second World War and especially since the 1950s, the US has maintained a large military along with a substantial system of bases, military-oriented industrial firms, research laboratories and 'think-tanks' to service it. This noncontributive sector has been lavishly provided with resources that otherwise could have been available to the contributive economy. A vast expansion in the bureaucratic structures of government, business and nonprofit institutions has created a great deal of unnecessary administrative activity that supplemented the military diversion.

Not only has a substantial quantity and quality of resources been diverted, but the military diversion in particular has emphasized scientific and engineering talent and capital – resources that are especially important to productive competence. The R&D carried out by engineers and scientists is the primary source of the improvements in product and process technology that keeps industry efficient. And capital is the means by which many of the improvements developed by engineers and scientists are actually applied in industry.

At least 30 per cent of the nation's engineers and scientists have been and continue to be drawn into military-related R&D.[11] The negative effect of this large and prolonged internal 'brain drain' on the progress of contributive technology has clearly overwhelmed any positive effect produced by the spinoff of military R&D results to civilian application.[12] The US has been losing the critical technological edge to its economic rivals, particularly those, such as West Germany and Japan, whose economies are much less heavily burdened by noncontributive military activity.[13]

The extensive capital diversion has compounded the problems of maintaining productive competence. It is possible to convey a rough impression of the magnitude of this diversion by considering gross comparisons of both physical and financial capital. In 1983, the reported book-value of the stock of physical capital directly owned by the Department of Defense was 46 per cent, as large as the reported book-value of the stock of physical capital owned by all US manufacturing establishments combined.[14] The military's drain of financial capital is equally impressive.

In terms of current dollars, narrowly-defined defense outlays over the five years 1983–87 alone amounted to more than $1245 billion. Even adjusted for inflation in constant 1982 dollars, these outlays were well over a trillion dollars. This is enough financial capital to purchase, at book-value, all the machinery, equipment, structures *and* inventories owned by all US manufacturers combined in 1987. Adjusting these figures for inflation does not materially change the result.[15] All these comparisons actually understate the diversion because capital owned by military firms and used to manufacture military products is included with 'all manufacturers', rather than with diverted capital. It should be subtracted from the former and added to the latter.

The US experienced serious stagflation from the late 1960s through the 1970s. During the 1980s, the respite from high rates of inflation has been accompanied by chronically high unemployment. Yet even these high unemployment rates may understate the employment problem, because underemployment appears to have been growing in recent years. Large numbers of relatively high-paying jobs (mainly in manufacturing) have involuntarily been traded for much lower-paying jobs (mainly in the much-touted service sector). Wage concessions, freezes or at best minimal increases have become common. The failed competitiveness of American production is made painfully obvious by the enormous and still-rising balance of trade deficit – this despite generally falling oil prices, a weakening dollar and lower relative US wages in the past few years.[16] And, of course, the longstanding productivity problem that underlies this loss of competitiveness is also consistent with the theory of resource diversion.

THE NEED FOR REVISED DATA COLLECTION

In the world of social science, as in the world of natural science, the empirical testing of theory is vital to the progress of understanding. Yet constructing empirical tests is often more difficult than it would at first appear. Any such test must begin with the collection of a sufficient quantity and quality of data, a process which tends to be considerably more problematic in the social sciences. In part, this is because of the inability of social scientists to construct controlled laboratory experiments. While this is also a problem in natural sciences such as astronomy, it is compounded in social science by the fact that the units from which data are collected may not be neutral to the collection process. Planets and stars neither alter their behaviour in response to data collection nor have vested interests that are potentially affected by the uses to which the data may be put. Human beings and their organizations do.

For these reasons among others (not the least of which is cost), economists are often forced to rely on existing data sources. This is perhaps especially true in macroeconomic analysis. The definitions used for data categories of conventional economic analysis are critical because they control how data are collected and aggregated. These critical category definitions are influenced by well-accepted mainstream theories, as well as a complex of sociopolitical factors.

Theories influence data collection because they are essentially ideologies, ways of thinking about the world that organize a confusing mass of facts into patterns that are simpler to understand and manipulate than the complex reality they purport to model. They achieve this simplification in part by directing attention toward certain phenomena and away from others, i.e. by telling us which aspects of the real world to pay attention to and which to ignore. The well-accepted theories that are part of the mainstream thus clearly condition which data are collected and how they are categorized, by in effect telling us what is and what is not important.

Because of the critical role of accepted theory in shaping data collection, existing data categories may obscure rather than illuminate the source of the problem when prevailing theory no longer yields accurate conditional prediction and thus effective policy guidance. By directing attention to the wrong phenomena, these data may inadvertently conceal aspects of reality that have become important. With such a misdirection of attention, it may be exceedingly difficult to determine whether a minor modification of that theory or a more dramatic paradigm shift is in order.

Furthermore, as new theories (or substantial modifications of existing theories) are offered, they tend to be evaluated at least initially by empirical tests using existing data categories to operationalize the new theoretical variables. While this is completely understandable, it may introduce an unrecognized degree of bias. To the extent that present data categories have been shaped by prevailing theory, they are likely to be less than accurate representations of the concepts introduced by the new theory. As a result, the empirical tests may be misleading. None of this is to say that appropriate tests of even revolutionary new theory can never be constructed with existing data, but rather that full and proper tests *may* sometimes require new data categories, new data collection, ingenious methodological innovation or some combination of these.

The manner in which data are presently collected and categorized does not make clear the crucial distinction between contributive and noncontributive activities. At the highest level of aggregation, the GNP is structured by the underlying assumption of prevailing theory that equivalent money value represents equivalent economic value. As a result, the GNP combines contributive and noncontributive activities in an indistinguishable blend, rendering its meaning as a measure of economic activity ambiguous. A high and rising GNP does not necessarily indicate that an economy's system of production is well-developed and functioning effectively. Nor does it necessarily indicate that the material wellbeing of the population is high or rising.

GNP has been rightly criticized in the past for being overly exclusive, for ignoring productive activities such as those performed without pay in the household. But GNP is also overly inclusive, adding in activities that do nothing to enhance material wellbeing, the economy's *raison d'être*. Both of these problems are the result of treating money value and economic value as synonymous: that for which we don't pay money cannot be relevant to our economic wellbeing, that for which we do must be.

This approach to measuring aggregate economic activity has made GNP an increasingly misleading indicator of economic status or growth. For example, it used to be a joke in basic economics courses to point out that if neighbors were paid to clean each other's houses that would add to the GNP, while if they each cleaned their own house without pay the GNP would not be increased. But increasing economic pressures, combined with changes in social attitudes, have pushed more and more families to become multiple wage-earner households. More and more of the housework that was excluded from GNP, because it was unpaid, is now counted because others are being hired to do it for us.

Suppose, for example, a family of four finds that it needs a second income to support its standard of living. With both adults working, yearly family income rises by, say, $12 000. But now they must pay for daycare, eat out more often and perhaps hire someone to help occasionally with housecleaning, etc. Suppose that costs the family $3000 a year. As a result of all of this, GNP would rise by $15 000. But the amount of productive activity in the economy would rise by only $12 000, and the family's net income by only $9000. If half of the 'family (more than one person) households' in the US in 1987 did spend an average of $3300 per year ($275 per month) on all such activities, that would have amounted to more than $106 billion that year, or nearly 2.5 per cent of GNP.[17] That is particularly impressive, since constant dollar GNP grew a total of less than 10 per cent in the preceding four years (1984–87).[18]

There is something very misleading about an economic indicator that treats what is really an economic 'treadmill effect' as if it represented progress. Yet this is a straightforward consequence of ignoring the nature of activities as a determinant of economic value – a concept central to the theory of resource diversion – and focusing on the presence of money exchange instead. The same approach results in the misleading inclusion of noncontributive activities as part of total economic product. That this constitutes a significant distortion is, for example, indicated by the fact that narrowly-defined defense outlays amounted to about 6.4 per cent of GNP in 1987, and growth in these constant-dollar defense outlays directly accounted for just over 13 per cent of the growth in constant-dollar GNP between 1981 and 1987.[19]

In Keynesian terms, assuming a marginal propensity to consume in the reasonable range of 0.75–0.85 for the US, implies that somewhere between 52 per cent and 87 per cent of the growth in GNP in those seven years was the multiplied result of this expansion in noncontributive military activity. There is apparently something to be said for the view that the GNP growth during the 1980s was due more to the effects of old-fashioned military Keynesianism than to the effects of 'supply-side' economics.

The point, of course, is not that military Keynesianism is a more effective tool for short-term economic stimulation than supply-side policies, but that the measurement of economic product by GNP greatly distorts the picture of what is really happening in terms of economically useful activity. Equivalent expenditure on the repair of the decaying American infrastructure, or even more important, on investment in state-of-the art production capital for civilian-oriented industry would have produced the same short-term stimulation. But it would also have improved productivity – something the military buildup has clearly not done. A measure which cannot distinguish between the economic meaning of these alternative uses of the nation's economic resources must be considered deeply flawed.

What is needed on the aggregate level is a measure that includes all those activities that contribute to material wellbeing and excludes all those activities that do not. I have elsewhere discussed in greater detail some of the conceptual dimensions of such a measure, which I refer to as the 'social material product', or 'SMP'.[20] A reasonable first approximation might start with GNP and subtract the value of those final products that clearly do not add to material wellbeing, such as military goods and services. It would then be necessary to subtract the value of that part of the investment component of GNP that supports the production of those noncontributive goods and services, particularly those that are specialized to such use. That is a bit more tricky. Trickier still is attempting to subtract the value of all those activities imbedded in the production of contributive output which are useless, such as unnecessary management. If we can agree to move beyond the money economy, it would also be a good idea to add an appropriate estimate of the value of those unpaid goods and services that contribute to material wellbeing. Accurately estimating the full contributive output of a nation is likely to be a fairly complex process. But even a rough attempt to correct by eliminating such obviously noncontributive activities as the production of military goods and services, should lead to a better, more meaningful measure of economic output than GNP.[21]

The same basic data problem continues at lower levels of aggregation. The theory of resource diversion highlights the importance of both contributive R&D and capital investment to the maintenance and improvement of productive competence. Yet neither the present form of R&D data, nor the present form of capital investment (and capital stock) data permits a clear picture of the extent to which these resources have been diverted to noncontributive activity.

It would be helpful to simply have R&D expenditure data divided into contributive and noncontributive categories. But it would be even more useful to have contributive and noncontributive R&D data further disaggregated into labor and capital components. In a sense, the extent to which R&D labor, i.e. engineers and scientists themselves, have been diverted is perhaps the most basic issue, since they are the most fundamental technology-generating resource. But though it is possible to roughly estimate, for example, the fraction of the nation's scientists and engineers engaged in military-related R&D from currently published data, it is quite difficult to develop an accurate estimate. Plausible estimates run from 25 per cent to 50 per cent, an unacceptably large range for such an important datum.[22] This is compounded by the inability to distinguish investment in R&D facilities and equipment from other forms of capital investment in currently published data.

Data on capital investment (and capital stock) generally suffer from overaggregation. Apart from the need to disaggregate into contributive and noncontributive components, the theory of resource diversion calls for a division of durable capital into four subcategories: R&D capital, production capital, infrastructure capital, and control capital (the equipment and structures used in conjunction with management and administration). Investment in each of these forms of long-lived capital has very different economic meaning. Combining them, as we currently do, is both confusing and misleading. For example, equivalent dollar investments in control capital and production capital – say, building office buildings as opposed to state-of-the-art production facilities – are likely to have dramatically different effects on productivity. Yet presently, the data are virtually indistinguishable.[23]

METHODOLOGICAL ISSUES

It is a clear implication of the theory that the effects of resource diversion on productive competence are both cumulative and long-term. The ongoing processes of labor-force attrition, physical depreciation and technological obsolescence can only be overcome by continuing investment of sufficient resources in human and physical capital. If the noncontributive sector claims a sufficiently large fraction of *any* of the key resources required, it will impede this critical investment process, and the economy will become less and less competent as time goes by. Each year of insufficient investment increases the investment required to regain the previous level of productive competence. And to the extent that foreign competitors, perhaps less burdened by noncontributive activity, are investing enough to improve their productive competence, the competitive position of domestic producers will deteriorate.

Methodologically, this means that year-by-year multivariate time series analysis, for example, pairing levels of military spending with a measure of productivity or economic growth, will not capture the full impact of resource diversion. Some means of cumulating the effect of this diversion must be incorporated. This is further complicated by a structural rigidity implied by the theory: the environment of the contributive and noncontributive sectors is likely to be sufficiently different that both labor and capital may become specialized to their sector of employment. They may consequently be unable to cross the sectoral boundary without undergoing a transition process which itself requires time and resources. Not only are the resource markets likely to be segmented, but the transition between them may also be asymmetrical; it may be easier to move from contributive to noncontributive activity than to move in the opposite direction.[24] This is certainly true for the military/civilian industry dichotomy.

This 'one-way valving' is a very considerable complication. But even in its absence, the wall between the sectors creates real problems. It means that a reduction in noncontributive activity may lead to unemployment, rather than the fluid movement of displaced workers and facilities into contributive activity. In the absence of a purposeful transition process, this inability to move into contributive activity may persist for an extended period. Therefore, a reduction in noncontributive activity does *not* by itself imply *any* necessary mitigation of resource diversion, let alone one that is equivalent to that reduction.

In practical terms this means, for example, that actual employment or expenditure in the military sector at any point in time may not be an accurate indicator of the existing level of military resource diversion. This is yet another reason why there may not be a period-by-period correlation between military spending and productivity in at least the short-to-medium run. Methodologically, it is necessary to measure military resource diversion in terms such as highest previously-sustained level of military expenditure (within a reasonable time horizon), rather than as present military spending. And since all the postulated relationships are long-run, even the productivity or growth variables must be smoothed in some way to reflect their trends.

Specifying a distributed lag structure will cope with some of the cumulative effect issues raised earlier, but is not a sufficient response to the problems of rigidity or asymmetry. Nor will it cope with yet another complication – the possibility of threshold effects. It may be that until the amount of resource diversion reaches a certain threshold, its effects on relative productive competence are minimal. Beyond that threshold, growing diversion may produce an increasingly severe effect. Furthermore, if domestic producers begin with a competitive edge, the decline in productive competence will appear to have little effect until it proceeds to the point at which relative competitiveness has significantly shifted. Only when that threshold is crossed will real impacts on the sales of domestic producers be felt.

More ominous, it is possible that there is a critical threshold of diversion beyond which negative effects on productive competence may be extremely difficult to reverse. Such a threshold might, for example, occur if the diversion has produced a severe distortion or deterioration of key components of the nation's education system. If any of these thresholds exist, they are more likely to depend on both the size and duration of diversion than on size alone. Neither a large, short-lived diversion, nor a small long-lived one is likely to have any lasting effect on productive competence.

SUMMARY AND CONCLUSIONS

The decline in the competitiveness of American industry is real and unmistakable. But the underlying causes of this decline are still a matter of considerable controversy. Conventional macroeconomic theory has been able to shed relatively little light on this crucial matter, in part because its fundamental assumption that money value and economic value are equivalent obscures certain critical distinctions.

The theory of resource diversion takes a different view. It argues that only those activities which contribute to material standard of living have economic value. It further contends that too large a diversion of productive resources to activities that do not contribute to material wellbeing will result in a long-term deterioration in the economy's ability to produce efficiently. And as the economy's capacity for efficient production declines relative to foreign producers, so does its competitiveness. Accordingly, the theory points an accusing finger at the long-term effects of more than four decades of high military expenditures in the US, supplemented by an explosion of unnecessary bureaucracy, as primary sources of America's severe competitiveness problems.

The powerful effects of resource diversion are masked in part by the overaggregation of key economic variables, under the guidance of prevailing theory. In some ways, they have come to be more confusing than illuminating. Our measures of total economic product, capital investment and capital stock, R&D and various categories of labor need to be disaggregated and otherwise revised. The theory of resource diversion provides some useful guidelines for such revision.

Studies of the economic effects of military spending done in the past have tended to concentrate on short-run opportunity costs, rather than on the longer-term, more structural impacts highlighted by the theory of resource diversion.[25] But it is no simple matter to correct this deficiency. Trying to estimate the kind of long-run relationships on which the theory focuses requires coping with problems of cumulative effect, structural rigidities, asymmetries and the possibility of a number of thresholds that introduce discontinuities into the model.

The combination of data problems and methodological complications certainly makes it difficult to estimate the precise nature and strength of the effects of resource diversion on the nation's economic performance and prospects. Yet the conceptual case for a powerful connection between diversion and competitiveness is sufficiently strong to hold out the promise that such work will have a considerable payoff.

There is an old story about a man who sees his friend searching the road underneath a street lamp, and asks what he is looking for. 'My car keys', his friend replies. 'Where did you drop them?', he asks. 'In the middle of that field.' 'Then why are you looking in the road?', he asks. 'Because the light's better over here.'

We cannot afford to keep letting the lamp post of existing data and theory determine where we look for the causes of our failed competitiveness. It may be more difficult to look elsewhere, but the search is far too important to allow habit or convenience to keep us looking in the wrong places.

Notes

1. In 1982 dollars. See *Economic Report of the President (January 1989)*, (Washington, DC: Government Printing Office, 1989), app. B, Table B-2, p. 310.
2. Ibid., Table B-46, p. 360. Note that the data for 1988 is only through the third quarter of that year.
3. Ibid.
4. Dumas, L. J., 'The Economic Cost of Ineffective Weapons', in A. Ehrlich and J. Birks (eds), *Hidden Dangers* (Sierra Club Books, 1990), fn. 5.
5. Nash N. C., 'Losses Still High at Savings Units, U.S. Agency Warns', *New York Times*, 23 August 1989.
6. Passel, P., 'Are Banks Broke Too?', *New York Times*, 23 August 1989.
7. *Economic Report of the President (January 1989)*, Table B-84, p. 406.
8. Ibid. These data were calculated by subtracting data for federal debt in Table B-84, p. 106, from data for total public and private debt of the nonfinancial sector in Table B-67, p. 385.
9. Ibid., Table B-106, p. 429.
10. Ibid., Table B-105, p. 428.
11. Dumas, L. J., *The Overburdened Economy* (Berkeley: University of California Press, 1986), pp. 208–11.
12. Ibid., pp. 213–17.
13. Ibid., pp. 215–17.
14. Dumas, L. J., 'Commanding Resources: the Military Sector and Capital Formation', in D. R. Lee (ed.), *Taxation and the Deficit Economy* (San Francisco: Pacific Institute for Public Policy Research, 1986), pp. 330–34. \
15. Department of Commerce, Bureau of the Census, *Statistical Abstract of the United States, 1989*, (Washington, DC: US Government Printing Office, 1989), Table 526, p. 326, for 'defense outlays' and Table 1270, p. 728, for manufacturing capital, including inventories.
16. The wage data are particularly striking. The Bureau of Labor Statistics has published a comparison of hourly compensation costs for production workers in 30 countries. These include both developed countries and

those classified as 'newly industrialized countries' (e.g. Mexico, Brazil, Taiwan and Hong Kong). As of 1987, the US ranked ninth, with three countries paying over 20 per cent more per labor-hour than the US. Even what used to be called 'cheap Japanese labor' cost about 83 per cent as much as labor in the US. See Department of Labor, Bureau of Labor Statistics, *International Comparisons of Hourly Compensation Costs for Production Workers in Manufacturing, 1975–87* (Report 754, August 1988), p. 5.

17. *Statistical Abstract of the United States, 1989*, Table 58, p. 45 provides data on households, and Table 685, p. 421 provides data on GNP.
18. Ibid., Table 685, p. 421.
19. Ibid., Table 526, p. 326 and Table 685, p. 421.
20. Dumas, L. J., *The Overburdened Economy*, p. 150–52.
21. A variety of economists have argued the deficiencies in GNP. See, for example, Tsuru, S., 'In Place of GNP', in H. Nijkamp (ed.), *The Political Economy of the Environment* (The Hague, 1971). Some have suggested alternative national measures. See, for example, Measure of Economic Welfare (modified later to Net Economic Welfare) in Nordhaus, W. and Tobin, J., 'Is Growth Obsolete?', *Fiftieth Anniversary Colloquium V* (National Bureau of Economic Research, Columbia Press, 1972); and Net Social Welfare in Barkley, P. W. and Seckler, D. W., *Economic Growth and Environmental Decay* (New York: Harcourt, Brace Jovanovich, 1972), pp. 43–7.
22. An example of the lower limit estimate can be found in Dumas, L. J., *The Overburdened Economy*, pp. 208– 11; the upper-range estimate was given in testimony by Murray Weidenbaum, in US Senate, Committee on Labor and Public Welfare, Sub-committee on Employment and Manpower, *Hearings: Nation's Manpower Revolution, Part 9* (Washington, DC: US Government Printing Office, 1964), p. 3146.
23. A further argument, on similar grounds, is made for a four-way subdivision of labor: managers (decision-makers), administrators (decision-implementers and monitors), technologists, and production workers. However, with the exception of the manager/administrator division, it is generally possible to distinguish these classes of labor from existing data.
24. Dumas, L. J., *The Overburdened Economy*, pp. 164–7.
25. See for example, Bezdek, R. H., 'The 1980 Economic Impact – Regional and Occupational – of Compensated Shifts in Defense Spending', *Journal of Regional Science*, Vol. 15, no. 2, 1975; Chase Econometric Associates, *Economic Impact of the B1 Program on the U.S. Economy and Comparative Case Studies* (Cynwyd, Pennsylvania: Chase Econometric Associates, 1975); Employment Research Associates, *The Empty Pork Barrel: The Employment Impact of the Military Build Up, 1981–1985* (Lansing, Michigan: Employment Research Associates, 1986).

4 Manufacturing Productivity and Military Depletion in the Postwar Industrial Economy

J. Davidson Alexander

INTRODUCTION

The growing debate over the economic effects of defense spending underscores the need for wider economic studies. Here we examine how military spending affects manufacturing productivity in the United States, with special attention to the slowing of productivity growth since 1970, using a simultaneous equation econometric model. Unfortunately, there are about as many economic approaches to the effects of military spending on economic performance as there are kinds of economic theory. Before continuing, then, it is necessary to bring several prominent approaches under some manageable classification.

In neoclassical economic theory, it makes little sense to isolate military spending from other kinds of government spending. Any increase in government spending, in this view, requires households to pay higher taxes either now or later, and thus to adjust their consumption (and labor supply) downward to a new full employment equilibrium level. If government finances military expenditure by borrowing, this may crowd private investment out of the market for funds. As with any government spending, then, the major neoclassical prediction for defense spending is that it decreases consumption and investment.

Keynesian theory covers more diverse approaches to military spending. In Keynesian models the economy is more vulnerable than it is in neoclassical models to demand-shocks reducing economic

The author would like to thank Greg Bischak, Anthony DiFilippo, Richard DuBoff, Seymour Melman and Iris Young for helpful comments on earlier drafts.

)yment level. Under such conditions, ny new government spending revives in the Keynesian tradition deny that between military spending and other ture when it comes to stabilizing the ry goods employs about as many people r education, and it stimulates about as in the new plant and equipment that nes's own approach to public expenditure between military and other government economic textbooks such as Paul Samuel- ote it, though usually by omitting any dis- ding.[1]

rsion of this neutralist perspective focuses on following the work of P. J. Verdoorn and loorn's Law states that the rate of productivity grow... ial economy depends upon the growth rate of manufacturing ... t. While sometimes this effect is interpreted as one of growing output inducing new manufacturing investment in more productive capital (or a rising amount of capital per worker), Kaldor himself attributed the induced boost in productivity to dynamic economies of scale rather than to a rising capital–labor ratio.[3] High military demand for manufactured goods, then, should stimulate productivity growth through the Verdoorn effect.

Others within the Keynesian tradition hold that military spending has a certain distinction, if only because it is easier to justify large federal spending on defense than on other public projects. At the very beginning of the Cold War, military Keynesians succeeded in tying economic policy to Cold War politics. Paul Nitze of the National Security Council, economist Summner Slichter and columnist David Lawrence were among those associated with this military Keynesianism in the early postwar period.[4] More recently, others add the argument that military R&D is an important source of technological change, and thus productivity growth, in a modern economy.

In a parallel analysis neo-Marxian critics note the reliance of the US economy on high levels of military spending. In this view, high military demand supports high profits and employment without expanding manufacturer's capacity for producing consumer or capital goods in an economy which already suffers from excess capacity. Some also add the proposition that elite policymakers reject alternative forms of government outlays which might maintain aggregate demand as well as military expenditure. For example, social spending similar to that of the North European social democracies would commit government in both principle and deed to improving social welfare and increasing economic equality, and thus threaten the interests of corporate and other elite groups. Some critics also observe that the military sector is an essential source of technological dynamism in an otherwise anemic national R&D effort.[5]

A third trend within the Keynesian tradition, and also within the radical tradition, holds that military expenditures damage the economy by crowding out public investment. The harm comes not because military spending is necessarily harmful in itself, but because it reduces government expenditure on productivity-increasing civilian investments in public infrastructure such as transportation, communications, education and civilian research and development.[6]

Finally, economists in the depletion tradition, such as Lloyd J. Dumas and Seymour Melman, with roots in both classical and institutionalist economic theory, hold that military spending is in itself harmful to long-run growth and effective corporate organization. Military spending not only crowds out public investment in infrastructure, but also diverts important productive resources to economic uses that increase neither our material wellbeing nor our productive capacity. While, in the short run, defense spending may create jobs and raise incomes, in the long run it depletes the economy of capital and R&D resources necessary for raising productivity, substituting non-contributing activity for contributing activity. Moreover, it turns corporations into inefficient seekers of Pentagon subsidies.[7]

Among these several approaches six propositions emerge about the general ways that military spending can boost or lower manufacturing productivity. Military spending may have no effect on macroeconomic performance other than lowering consumption. Military purchases of manufactured goods boost productivity by stimulating manufacturing growth (the Verdoorn effect). Military spending on R&D helps (or hurts) civilian technological progress and thus productivity. Military capital spending raises (or depletes) the economy's capacity to supply civilian equipment and structures. Defense spending diverts government funds from infrastructure projects. Finally, the subsidy dimensions of military spending alters corporate decision-making structure.

The sections that follow develop a model of productivity growth which incorporates some of these propositions about military spending and productivity growth, and tests them using econometric estimates of two model specifications. The first section contrasts alternative views of productivity growth and establishes some conditions that a model must meet to be useful in exploring the propositions about military spending and productivity growth. Sections two and three define a classical production model that satisfies these conditions as well as general requirements of a production model. Section four briefly distinguishes between two specifications of the production model: an aggregate or macroeconomic model; and a resourse use model that has more of a microeconomic orientation. Sections five and six specify these models and report estimates of the specifications using postwar US data. Section seven discusses these results with respect to the slowdown in productivity growth after 1970.

PRODUCTIVITY IN DECLINE: EFFICIENT ALLOCATION OR RESOURCE DIVERSION?

The slowdown in manufacturing productivity growth is now almost two decades old. From 1951 to 1972 manufacturing labor productivity, defined as manufacturing output per hour of production labor, rose at an annual average rate of about 2.58 per cent. During the next decade, it rose at about a 1.94 per cent annual average rate, a dramatic 25 per cent decline in the growth rate.[8]

Few analysts doubt the seriousness of the productivity slowdown in the US and elsewhere. Increased output per hour is a necessary condition for a rising average standard of living (as measured by a rising level of consumption and/or leisure). Those who view the US economy as caught in intense competition, moreover, regard continuously and rapidly rising productivity as a necessary condition for competitively lowering production costs. Even small changes, such as the 0.64 percentage point decline just noted, translate into serious changes in the long-term trends of our standard of living and production costs. Designing policies capable of reversing this decline requires careful assessment of alternative hypotheses about the sources of the decline.

Conventional neoclassical production approaches implicitly preclude testing an important set of hypotheses about the sources of this slowdown in manufacturing productivity growth in the United States.

Apparently relying on the tenet that any institution subject to market forces will evolve and operate efficiently, explanations using these models assume that institutions affecting productivity have all functioned efficiently. This chapter develops a different kind of productivity model to examine the postwar productivity, a model built upon basic ideas of classical economic theory to explore resource diversion.

According to the general resource diversion perspective, during the post-Second World War era crucial institutions, including military institutions, have evolved in such a way that they misallocate productivity enhancing resources. This has deprived manufacturers of the capital, research and development and organizational resources they need to increase the product of available labor. Before turning to a classical model to frame particular hypotheses about resource use and diversion, let us look at the conventional view.

Conventional neoclassical studies of the productivity slowdown in the US generally assume, in two important respects, that there are no fundamental structural aberrations in the economy responsible for the slowdown. First, many economists have replaced the concept of labor productivity (Q/L, output per hour of labor) with the measure of total factor productivity (Q/F, output per a composite total factor that represents capital and labor inputs). In constructing a measure of total factor, they use the shares of income that labor and capital each receive to represent the contribution that the quantities of labor and capital employed respectively make. This choice of income shares to reflect the respective contributions of capital and labor to production, however, assumes that capital and labor markets are operating efficiently in the sense that these factors each earn the value of their marginal product.

Second, the assumption of efficient institutional allocation is also often built into the investment model which conventional studies use. To explain the productivity slowdown, these studies typically opt to explore the effects of exogenous forces that can retard capital formation. Notable among such exogenous shocks are energy price shocks, policy shocks, labor force composition shocks, and declining technological progress. In this view the energy shocks of the 1970s made much new productive equipment and techniques too expensive to use. Moreover, policy shocks in the form of government regulations upgrading pollution and safety standards have made some production techniques obsolete. Another explanation holds that a younger, more female labor force allegedly possessed of less experience and skill has lowered average productivity. Yet another accounts suggests that a decline in technological advances, perhaps stemming from a slowdown in R&D expenditure, diminished the ability of manufacturers to raise productivity.[9] From this perspective, markets and enterprises continue to allocate efficiently. However, facing unfavorable exogenous shocks, optimal managerial decisions are necessarily short-run and result in slower productivity growth. Despite considerable work with this model, few find its results very encouraging.[10]

This study explores postwar productivity and the recent productivity growth slowdown under alternative theoretical perspectives. Within these alternative perspectives, it explores the contribution of military spending to the slowdown. First, in the Keynesian and post-Keynesian perspectives, high demand for manufacturing goods induces productivity growth as firms expand to achieve dynamic economies of scale (the Verdoorn effect). To test this hypothesis we require a model which captures rising military and other demand for manufacturing output.

Second, lower productivity growth, including the slowdown of the 1970s, results from an institutional diversion of resources away from what classical economists called 'productive' activity or what Dumas has called 'contributive' economic uses, that is, from the production of consumption or investment goods and services.[11] For example, institutional rigidity has prevented manufacturing firms from adjusting properly to new shocks; furthermore, institutional changes themselves have both biased choices of new techniques and have restructured markets. Each bias diverts important resources to less productivity-enhancing employments. Thus the institutional diversion hypothesis holds that the way economic institutions have evolved (or failed to evolve) over the past two or three decades accounts for much of the productivity slowdown in the United States.

Several unconventional diversion hypotheses come under this theoretical perspective. One hypothesis holds that the productivity slowdown has been caused by the substitution of a short-run money-making orientation for long-run production perspectives in management (the managerialism hypothesis). Another hypothesis posits that the Pentagon has lowered productivity growth by preempting a significant share of R&D resources, skilled labor and capital resources (the depletion hypothesis); and has replaced cost-minimizing management with cost-escalating decision-making in military industries (the subsidy search hypothesis). A final diversion thesis holds that changes in industrial relations and labor markets have reduced actual labor effort (the social relations hypothesis).[12]

To test these specific diversion hypotheses we require a model which can capture a variety of structural changes that affect the productivity growth: changes in the use of research and development personnel and laboratories; other changes in the direction of the growth-path of knowledge; changes in the flow of capital funds both within firms and among industries; changes in desicion-making processes away from cost-minimization; changes in the organization of production processes and labor markets; and changes in educational processes.

In the following, a production model is elaborated which explores the effects of a subset of such institutional changes on manufacturing productivity in the United States. It focuses primarily, but not exclusively, on the military's role in diverting resources by preempting R&D resources, preempting capital funds from manufacturing, and influencing changes in the organization of industrial firms.

A CLASSICAL MODEL OF PRODUCTIVE COMPETENCE

Let us define production as deliberate transformative action of two kinds: (1) the transformation of natural and intermediate resources into goods and services, and (2) the background transformation of the knowledge of nature, of tools, of skills and of work organization. The transformation of nature and intermediate goods is 'direct labor', while the other transformations – the production of knowledge, skills, intermediate goods, capital goods and work organization – are 'background labor'.

At any time direct labor has a level of productive competence determined by background labor. Let total manufacturing output be the product of the interaction of manufacturing labor with the level of productive competence. More formally, the level of manufacturing output is the product of an index of manufacturing labor input, L, with an index of productive competence in manufacturing, C. Thus, in standard production function form,

$$Q_t = L_t^a \, C_t^b \qquad \text{equation (1)}$$

where Q is manufacturing output at time t and a and b are constants.

Dividing both sides of equation (1) by L gives us an index of manufacturing output per worker

$$(Q/L)_t = L_t^{a-1} C_t^b \qquad \text{equation (2)}$$

where Q/L is labor productivity at time t, and a and b are constants.

Finally, expressing this productivity function in terms of rates of change, we obtain

$$q_t = (a - 1) \, l_t + bc_t \qquad \text{equation (3)}$$

where the rates of change q, l, c are the differences between natural logarithms of current and last period values of Q/L, L and C respectively, and a and b remain parameters. The rate of growth of labor productivity is the sum of the rates of growth of actual direct manufacturing labor utilized and of productive competence.

Changes in the labor utilized may reflect changes not only in the quantity of labor employed but also in the quality, the intensity or the composition of labor. For simplicity, this study abstracts from the changing skill, sexual and racial composition of the labor force, and from changing intensity of work effort, although in principle the index L could be expressed as a function of these variables.

Before turning to the determinants of the rates of change of C, we should note the absence of an index of physical capital in this production function. It is well known that measuring the quantity, quality and services of capital goods presents serious problems to economic accounting theory and to production theory.[13] This model follows the tradition of classical political economy in treating capital goods as intermediate goods whose design characteristics, like characteristics of any physical resource, enhance labor.[14] The significance of capital goods for productivity stems from their increasing availability, from improvements in this design (embodied technical change) and from improvements in their organization (disembodied technical change). Thus if we can sufficiently capture those sources of embodied and disembodied technical change which make labor more productive, we can omit a measure of the intermediate good, capital, from the model's production function.[15]

As in much production theory in economics, we could treat the index of productive competence, C, as a level of *knowledge* or technology, and in turn, assume that this knowledge increases at a constant rate. While we shall treat productive competence as a growth function, we shall depart from convention in two ways. First, in the resource diversion models of this study, production competence involves institutional practices as well as knowledge. Changing institutional practices include managing manufacturing assets principally as financial assets rather than production assets, as well as passing high costs on to the Pentagon through cost-plus contracting and other subsidies, rather than minimizing costs. Treating production assets as financial assets may render otherwise quite promising production decisions impractical, especially long-run research, development or production projects. Passing on cost increases to the Pentagon may render certain production techniques profitable to firms which are otherwise quite expensive from a social point of view. To take another example of institutional changes affecting productivity, new worker-participation practices make the introduction of greater skill-utilization and on-the-spot troubleshooting practical, whereas traditional Taylorist hierarchical practices, in which managers make most decisions, make these worker-participation practices impractical.[16]

One way that economists approximate unmeasurable technical change is with measured changes in the ratio of capital to labor used in manufacturing; presumably a rising stock of capital embodies much new know-how.[17] For reasons given above, however, this study seeks to avoid problems of measuring both the amount of capital used and the intensity of its use.

Second, this model also departs from convention by treating the growth rate of production competence as a variable. Production competence grows at a rate which is a composite of other rates of growth and decay. Some of these other rates reflect the resource diversion we are examining. Thus, assume that the rate of competence growth is a weighted sum of other growth rates, or

$$c_t = B_1 + B_2 r_{2t} + B_3 r_{3t} + \ldots + B_n r_{nt} \quad \text{equation (4)}$$

where c is the growth rate of the index of productive competence in manufacturing at time t, each r is the growth rate of one of the $(n-1)$ determinants of the level of productive competence, and each B is a constant.

The determinants of the changes in the productive competence of direct manufacturing labor fall under three broad classifications: changes in the deliberate generation of useful technical knowledge; changes in the level and quality of mechanization in manufacturing (embodied technical change), reflected in the changes in capital services per worker; and changes in the goals and organization of manufacturing firms (disembodied technical change), as reflected in changing manufacturing practices. In three sections below we shall break down these forces in an attempt to state how their rates of change affect the growth rate of production competence.

DETERMINANTS OF PRODUCTIVE COMPETENCE

Technical knowledge

Research and development activities, and the dissemination of their results, constitute intentional efforts to upgrade productive competence and have widely been regarded as major determinants of technical change. Changes in R&D efforts, however, have not generally been found to be major influences on the recent productivity slowdown in the US, perhaps in part because of measurement and definitional problems.[18] We do have some indications that federally-financed R&D has been less effective than civilian-financed R&D, and has been a drain on productivity growth.[19]

A further cause of concern is the proportion of R&D expenditures devoted to military projects, which comprises the largest part of federal R&D expenditure (amounting at times to over half of all US R&D spending). Indeed while R&D spending in the US as a proportion of GNP matches that of our main commercial rivals, Japan and West Germany, when we count only civilian R&D, the US civilian R&D effort as a proportion of GNP is only about 75 per cent of the Japanese and West German effort. Studies suggest, moreover, that military R&D may be the specific federal drain on measured productivity growth.[20] Although these studies are hampered by lack of data and by measurement problems, they lend some support to one major diversion thesis, the military depletion hypothesis.

The depletion hypothesis asserts generally that military spending has harmed US manufacturing by depriving it of important resources. With respect to R&D, the depletion hypothesis holds that significant R&D resources have been deleteriously preempted by military and space research and development. The main support for the depletion hypothesis has come from industrial and institutional studies.[21] Since high-paying and challenging defense industry work bids technical and scientific laboratories and workers away from ordinary industrial employment, the rate of civilian invention falls with high or increasing levels of investment in military R&D. The rate of return to civilian manufacturing from the spinoffs of military R&D, the depletion hypothesis maintains, has never been as high as the rate of civilian return from direct civilian R&D, and it has been decreasing in significance as military R&D has become increasingly specialized and secret. The inventions actually produced by military R&D, moreover, may also bias the shape that further R&D takes in favor of less cost-conscious, less productivity-enhancing innovation by placing the R&D process on different development paths and learning curves than civilian-dominated R&D would generate. This bias includes skewing education incentives for science and engineering students.[22]

To test this hypothesis we shall distinguish between total technology effort in the United States and military R&D expenditures. The latter, according to the depletion hypothesis, has a negative effect on progress in productive competence and thus productivity growth.

Mechanization

The generation of new knowledge by R&D efforts will not enhance productive competence unless it actually affects production processes, by becoming embodied in new physical capital or by shaping the organization of production (see below). Mechanization is literally the replacement of human and animal-powered production by machine-powered production, but here we define it more generally as a change in the level of capital services available, reflecting embodied technical knowledge. In order to avoid problems of measuring a growing and improving stock of capital, we go behind that change in capital stock to model several determinants of the relevant investment decision.

A cost-minimizing firm (and, to a different extent, one that is merely cost-conscious) will introduce new labor-saving capital when the ratio of wages and other labor compensation relative to physical capital costs rise, a ratio which we call 'the alternative cost of capital'. At least in the longer run, rising labor costs and relatively smaller increases in capital costs explain much of productivity gains in the United States and elsewhere. A number of classical studies established this connection between the alternative cost of capital and either mechanization or innovation.[23] We shall explore the effect of changes in the current levels of alternative costs on productivity.

Demand conditions may also directly affect this adjustment of the capital–labor ratio. In general, measured productivity rises before the upturn in the business cycle and falls before the downturn.[24] More important, 'Verdoorn's Law' holds that growth in manufacturing output stimulates productivity increases. As we saw earlier, sometimes such productivity gains are interpreted as an achievement of dynamic returns to scale and sometimes as a matter of 'anticipated demand' stimulating investment. For our purposes this Verdoorn relationship between rising manufacturing output and productivity gains is a mechanism of efficient macroeconomic allocation rather than resource diversion. The primary significance of the Verdoorn effect here is that it is a major avenue through which military spending can exert a positive influence on manufacturing productivity. Increasing military demand can induce investment and help manufacturers attain economies of scale.

While there has been some controversy about the role of the cost of funds on investment during the postwar period, changes in interest rates are often thought to govern the rate of capital investment. There is some evidence that cheap investment funds contributed to growth during some periods of US history.[25]

The discussion of capital investment above has assumed a sufficient level of capital resources flowing into manufacturing through retained profits and borrowing. Money capital flowing persistently out of even a growing manufacturing sector, however, can affect productivity adversely in two ways. Investment outflows can increase the average age of capital equipment, and they can deprive background labor of resources necessary for improving production competence.

We can distinguish two kinds of relative disinvestment in manufacturing. The first is the broad structural shift which renders manufacturing less and less important in the economy (usually attributed to shifts in consumption). When capital flows away from manufacturing, say to the expanding service sector, we expect measured manufacturing productivity to fall (perhaps after a lag, during which the least productive parts of capacity are retired). Conversely, an increasing manufacturing share of GNP will precede rising productivity.[26]

Second, the narrower stagnationist hypothesis about disinvestment holds that falling investment opportunities in the maturing manufacturing sector induce outflows of surplus earnings to nonproductive or speculative sectors of the economy, such as financial services, real estate and marketing.[27] While this will not of necessity slow productivity growth, it will cause productivity growth to tail off to the extent that profit-seeking outside manufacturing becomes the dominant strategy in manufacturing firms. For example, to the extent that finance, financial services, and marketing departments grow in importance, or that investments outside manufacturing become major portions of manufacturing firms' assets, firms will devote fewer resources to enhancing their manufacturing productive competence. The big steelmakers have been the most widely-cited example of this diversion of internal funds. From this perspective, a rising ratio of investment in 'speculative' (financial, real estate and marketing) sectors, relative to investment in manufacturing, signals declining manufacturing competence growth.

Organization of production

At least some of the potential returns to R&D require that a firm be organizationally able to translate technology gains to production. It is also likely, as much of the new literature on Japanese manufacturing observes, that productivity gains rely on continuous small improvements in laboratories and on the shop floor.[28] In each case organizational flexibility guided by cost-minimization (or cost-consciousness) are two key aspects of productivity decision-making.[29]

The cost escalation hypothesis – a cousin of the depletion hypothesis already encountered in the discussion of R&D – holds that the militarization of the US economy has constrained and actually transformed decision-making processes in manufacturing firms. There are several avenues through which this occurs. First, Pentagon contracting practices are often competitive only in name, and once obtained, contracts guarantee profits as markups over costs. This contracting procedure gives defense firms the incentive and ability to drive up actual costs. In particular, one criterion for awarding defense contracts is that the bidder possess demonstrable, available capacity to take on new projects. Thus, firms will often have unused capacity. The Department of Defense itself often provides capital to military suppliers through outright grants to hold excess capacity in plant and personnel. Thus defense firms have considerable license and motive to inflate not only reported costs, but more importantly, their actual costs by choosing expensive R&D and manufacturing production techniques. Cost accounting, moreover, follows historical estimation procedures based upon previous costs (which don't acknowledge subsequent cost-improvements) rather than engineering costing procedures (which do acknowledge recent cost-reduction).[30]

To the extent that similar decision practices spread to other manufacturing sectors where firms hold some market power, firms will practice cost escalation (or 'cost maximization'), and they will lose some cost-minimizing ability and incentive. This slows productivity growth. The recent tendency to outsource much production formerly undertaken within the firm is an indication that central administrations have lost the ability to control costs of their manufacturing divisions.[31]

A second avenue for military-generated change in corporate decision-making is the R&D investment bias discussed earlier. Such bias implies that the technological frontiers being explored are often irrelevant to lowering manufacturing cost because they are biased toward costly, precise and extremely high-performance military products. This kind of expensive know-how raises the cost of labor-saving mechanization and discourages productivity-enhancing investment.

Third, to the extent that the Pentagon bids scarce labor and material resources away from civilian production, civilian manufacturing may have less ability to improve productivity.[32]

In this chapter we test this complex depletion hypothesis only in the aggregate: the stronger the influence of military production criteria in the manufacturing sector, the slower the growth of production competence will be. To make this operational in this study, we shall narrow the range of this influence sharply. The larger the military share of manufacturing sales, the lower productivity growth will be. The ratio of military investment (military purchases of major equipment and structures) to the output of the manufacturing sector will serve as an aggregate index for changes in the strength of this influence.

It is important to note that the phenomenon of military Keynesianism complicates any test of the depletion hypothesis. One can hold both the depletion hypothesis, expecting military spending to have a long-run negative effect on productivity growth, and still believe that military spending increases manufacturing output in the short run. The latter, by the Verdoorn connection, stimulates productivity through a succession of short-run stimuli. We use a simultaneous equation model in this study, in part, to separate and compare the depletion and the Verdoorn effects on productivity.

The managerialism hypothesis proposes a second way in which organizational change has affected manufacturing performance. There are actually various forms of the managerial hypothesis, often corresponding to different theoretical perspectives. In one form, for example, the managerialism thesis holds that new managers in manufacturing have been technically trained to emphasize moneymaking over production. Notably, their business-school education emphasizes short-run returns on assets at the expense of long-run planning of production.

It is difficult, however, to distinguish empirically this sociological business-school version of managerialism from a conventional explanation of the recent short-run orientation of managers. In the conventional view, the international economic shocks of the 1970s created an environment of uncertainty in which the short-term planning horizon, rather than a long-term capital formation horizon, is precisely the rational one for any manager, regardless of whether she or he is a new financial technician or not.

Consequently, this chapter tests a second, stronger managerial hypothesis which can be distinguished from the conventional view. Unlike the well-known example of Japanese institutions, American corporations allow and even encourage a high degree of mobility of managerial labor. The stronger managerial thesis holds that in order to enhance their mobility, US managers seek general knowledge of financial planning techniques above particular knowledge of specific firms or production processes. New managers make a splash by revamping a firm's financial and organizational profile, rather than by formulating wise production plans. In other words, bureaucratic management practices raise short-run careerism above longer-run production planning. Consequently, under this stronger managerialism hypothesis, both business-school techniques and short-term orientation are consequences of the shape of managers' mobile career paths within and across corporate bureaucracies.

The weaker managerialism hypothesis does not necessarily imply that managers will aggrandize themselves by multiplying and expanding their corporate departments, but the stronger managerialism hypothesis does imply this: a prime way to demonstrate one's talent and to build up a strong track record is to expand the responsibilities and the staff of one's own department. Productivity growth thus declines not only because of short-termism but also because of the incompetence of a burgeoning bureaucracy. We know that administrative offices have grown during the post war period. We will test the hypothesis that a growing ratio of nonproduction personnel to production workers slows productivity growth. In the conventional theory of the firm, rising nonproduction to production worker ratios should be rational, that is contribute to productivity growth, *ceteris paribus*, while the strong managerialism thesis holds that the net effect of a rising ratio is negative.[33]

It should be noted that military contracting practices can also promote managerialism and rising proportions of nonproduction workers. Military bidding and contracting require a great deal of accounting and engineering paperwork, a practice now under attack by those who would reform Pentagon inefficiency piecemeal. The nature of much military production, moreover, requires considerable science and engineering staffs. Since costs can be passed on to taxpayers, moreover, cost considerations do not always affect the growth of nonproduction staffs.

TWO ECONOMETRIC PERSPECTIVES ON PRODUCTIVITY

Now we can fit the several parts of the diversion perspective together. Since to date we have not developed very satisfactory econometric models of either productivity changes or the economic effects of military spending, it would be a mistake to close off diverse approaches prematurely. It is in that spirit that this study develops the classical model. It is also in that spirit that this study now develops and tests two different specifications of the classical model of resource use.

We will examine two different kinds of models of productivity growth reflecting two different ways of thinking about productivity growth. On the one hand, we can think about productivity growth as an aggregate or macroeconomic phenomenon. In this case, Verdoorn's Law, attributing productivity growth to the growth of manufacturing output (via dynamic economies of scale and/or induced investment) is one prominent aggregate approach. On the other hand, we can think about productivity growth as the outcome of many decisions about resource use. In this case we associate productivity changes with changes in influences on decisions about resource use: changing relative costs of production; changing organizational goals of firms; changing organization of industries; changing technology effort; and so on.

From the perspective of conventional macroeconomic aggregates, military economic variables can sometimes appear relatively small. For example, Department of Defense outlays as officially measured only rarely have run above 10 per cent of GNP in the postwar period and typically have not exceeded 7 per cent. Even more accurate measurements add only a few percentage points to these figures.[34] From a real resource use perspective, on the other hand, military use of resources has a much larger magnitude. For example, estimates place the proportion of scientists and engineers employed on military projects as high as 50 per cent during some postwar years.[35]

We shall, moreover, explore simultaneous equations specifications of the two productivity models. This choice is based upon the apparent interdependence between the rate of productivity growth and several other variables in each model. For example, the aggregate model makes the rate of manufacturing productivity growth not only a function of the growth rates of manufacturing production labor and of manufacturing output (Verdoorn's Law), but also a determinant of the level of these growth rates. Similarly, the resource use model makes productivity growth both an influence on and an outcome of capital outflow from manufacturing and a proxy for the rise of managerialism. Since this interdependence violates ordinary least-squares assumptions, each model of productivity growth has been expanded to a three-equation econometric model.

In the aggregate model explored here we will examine the effects on productivity of changes in three military explanatory variables: military spending; the ratio of military capital investment in equipment and structures to total manufacturing output; and the ratio of net military capital stock to net manufacturers' capital stock. In the resource use model, we shall examine the effects in two variables: the rates of change of the ratio of military capital investment to total manufacturing output (as above) and military R&D expenditures. (All rates of change are per cent changes.)[36]

AN AGGREGATE MODEL OF PRODUCTIVE COMPETENCE

The following three equations express the aggregate model of manufacturing productivity growth.

$$q_t = B^1 + (a - 1) l_t + B_2 CMQ_t + B_3 CALT_t + B_4 CMIMQ_t \quad \text{eq. (5)}$$

$$l_t = b_1 + b_2 q_t + b_3 CMQ_t + b_4 CMIMQ_t \quad \text{eq. (6)}$$

$$CMQ_t = A_1 + A_2 DCU_t + A_3 q_t + A_4 CIM_t + A_5 CM_t + A_6 CMK_t \quad \text{eq. (7)}$$

In these equations, q is the growth rate of manufacturing productivity; CMQ is the growth rate of manufacturing output; $CALT$ is the growth rate of the alternative costs of capital (the ratio of labor compensation to machine prices); $CMIMQ$ is the ratio of military capital investment in equipment and structures to manufacturing output, a proxy for the influence of military demand; CMQ is the growth rate of manufacturing output; DCU is the annual difference in capacity utilization; CIM is the growth rate of manufacturing investment; CM is the growth rate of military expenditure; and CMK is the rate of change of the ratio of net military capital stock (military structures and equipment) to net manufacturing capital stock. A, B, b and the single a are all constants.

Simultaneity occurs in this system for several reasons. The growth rate of manufacturing labor productivity both is determined by those of manufacturing output and manufacturing labor and determines their growth rate. Faster manufacturing productivity growth decreases the growth rate of hours worked but increases the growth rate of manufacturing output. Additionally, manufacturing output is allowed to influence manufacturing labor directly.

Equation 5 attributes rising production competence, *ceteris paribus*, to falling quantities of manufacturing labor input, to rising manufacturing output (CMQ – the Verdoorn effect), and to a rising alternative cost of capital ($CALT$), as postulated earlier. Further, according to the diversion hypotheses, rising military influence on manufacturing practices decreases the manufacturing productivity growth rate by preempting capital-producing resources, changing manufacturing decision-making processes, and biasing technological progress. In this aggregate model we do not separate these sources of resource diversion: instead they are together proxied by the ratio of major military investment expenditure to manufacturing output ($CMIMQ$). In estimating equation 5, then, we are interested in testing the hypotheses that the parameters a, B_2 and B_3 are positive, and B_4 is negative.

To allow for a positive military expenditure impact on productivity through the Verdoorn effect, we add a manufacturing output function, equation 7, to the model. In order to focus on resource flows, equation 7 diverges somewhat from the Keynesian income–expenditure model of manufacturing output growth. The growth rate of manufacturing output rises as a consequence of increases in short-run demand, reflected in a higher rate of capacity utilization (DCU), increases in the growth rate of productivity itself (q), and increases in the growth rate of manufacturer's investment (CIM), holding capacity utilization changes constant.

Manufacturing output, moreover, will change as a consequence of changes in two military variables included in equation 7. First, faster growth in military expenditures should lift the growth rate of manufacturing output through the ordinary spending multiplier. This growth in manufacturing output in turn should boost the productivity growth rate. Second, as we saw earlier, the depletion thesis holds that the military absorption of capital diverts capital-producing resources from civilian use. Thus a rising rate of change of the ratio of net military capital stock to manufacturers' net capital stock (CMK), reflecting a drain on the growth of the civilian capital stock, reduces the growth rate of manufacturing output. This would decrease the productivity growth rate through the Verdoorn effect. In sum, all of the coefficients in equation 6 are expected to be positive except A_6.

Finally equation 6 allows the military economy to work on productivity by changing the growth rate of production labor hours (l). We assume that the rate of growth of production labor hours slows as productivity growth (q) rises, and increases with a rising manufacturing output growth rate (CMQ). We allow, moreover, for the quantity of labor input to be affected by military spending – here measured by the relative importance of the military investment demand to the manufacturing sectors ($CMIMQ$), holding constant the level of manufacturing output.

Whether military spending has a positive or a negative impact on manufacturing production hours worked is problematic and controversial, since there is considerable debate over whether military economic activity generates more or less employment than alternative forms of expenditure. To the extent that manufacturers produce a larger share of their output as military investment goods and construction materials, we might expect production labor to decline, holding GNP growth constant, since producing military investment goods employs relatively more nonproduction scientists and engineers than much manufacturing. In equation 6 we would thus expect b_4 along with b_2 to be negative, and b_3 to be positive.

We can now turn to the results of simultaneous ordinary least-squares estimation of the three equations. The estimates and econometric tests cover the period 1951 to 1982. Relevant R&D and technology data are difficult to interpret and in some cases unavailable before 1951. I decided *a priori* to end with the recession year of 1982 to avoid two kinds of abrupt regime changes about that time.

First, in response to a decade of declining economic performance and relatively ineffective government policy, economic policy veered sharply enough that a structural shift in the macroeconomy might affect the productivity model parameters: far-reaching federal tax reductions; rapidly-expanding military procurement and military R&D expenditures; an enlarged budget deficit, sharply higher real interest rates, and the surging dollar shutting down much manufacturing (temporarily raising measured productivity and ushering in a new era of capital goods imports); and a new explosion of private debt and financial activity relative to manufacturing activity, all changed the environment in which the productivity-enhancing effort takes place.

Second, sharp and controversial changes in the Labor Department's measurement of production and productivity began in the early 1980s to reflect the rising importance of computers and related products in the US manufacturing output mix. This appears to have biased the estimates of output and productivity upward.[37]

The Data Appendix presents definitions of variables and sources of data used. Table 4.1 presents an ordinary least-squares estimate of the aggregate model in three simultaneous equations. The coefficients, mostly elasticities, have the anticipated signs and are significant at the 1 per cent or 5 per cent levels.

In equation 5 the relatively large coefficient on the growth rate of manufacturing output indicates that the Verdoorn relationship is strong; manufacturing expansion increases productivity growth. The negative coefficient of the depletion thesis variable, growth of military investment share of manufacturing output supports the depletion thesis: we cannot reject the hypothesis of a negative direct influence of Pentagon purchases of physical capital on manufacturing productivity growth. This direct depletion effect is considerably smaller than the Verdoorn effect, however (-0.02 to 0.70); it is also much smaller than the impact of changes in the growth rates of alternative costs and production labor hours on productivity growth.

In this aggregate model, ironically, the strongest depletion impact works indirectly on productivity through the Verdoorn effect, by negatively affecting manufacturing output. In equation 7, the depletion variable, the annual rate of change in the ratio of net military capital stock to the net manufacturing capital stock, expresses military preemption of capital resources. Here a one per cent increase in this measure of military preemption of capital resources brings about a 0.17 per cent decrease in manufacturing output. (At this point,

Table 4.1   Estimate of Aggregate Simultaneous Equations Model, (1951–82)

Equation Dependent variable: (Growth rates)	5 Mfr. labor productivity	6 Production labor	7 Manufacturing output
Constant	0.503 (1.98)	−0.660 (−1.78)	1.34** (3.43)
Variable (growth rate)			
Manufacturing production labor	−0.561** (−8.48)		
Alternative cost of capital	0.155** (3.45)		
Manufacturing output	0.669** (10.73)	1.096** (21.43)	
Military investment share of mfr's output	−0.020** (−3.35)	−0.031** (−3.23)	
Manufacturing labor productivity		−1.14** (−7.61)	−0.522** (5.58)
Capacity utilization (difference, not growth rate)			0.796** (7.39)
Manufacturing share of GNP			0.302* (2.30)
Manufacturing investment			0.089* (2.26)
Ratio of military capital to mfr's capital stock			−0.174** (−3.43)
Military expenditures			0.041** (5.01)
ADJUSTED r^2	.86	.94	.98
F statistic	47.8	178.4	239.8
Durbin–Watson	1.97	1.97	1.80
Standard error	0.81	1.33	0.89

*   significant at the 5% level
** significant at the 1% level
t–statistics in parentheses.

several other military depletion variables were experimented with, including the rate of change of the ratio of military capital investment to manufacturing output, and several had outcomes stronger than this.)

We can compare the relative impacts of the two military variables reflecting military depletion and military stimulus as they affect productivity via the Verdoorn effect in equation 7. A 1 per cent increase in the depletion variable has a negative effect on manufacturing output, and thus on productivity growth, about four times larger than the positive effect of a 1 per cent increase in military expenditure stimulus (-0.17 to 0.04). To establish the scale of these effects on manufacturing output growth, note that this depletion coefficient is about one-quarter as large as the impact of a change in manufacturing demand, proxied by the annual change in capacity utilization, and about one-third as large as the impact of a change in the productivity growth rate.

We should also note that the non-military resource diversion variable, the growth rate of the manufacturing share of GNP, reflecting relative stagnation and divestment in manufacturing, has a significant positive coefficient. If manufacturing were a growing portion of GNP, that would have given a large boost to manufacturing productivity, with an elasticity almost twice the size of the military depletion variable. However, the actual historical decline of the share of manufacturing in the US economy has contributed to falling productivity through the Verdoorn relationship.

Finally the coefficients of equation 6 have the anticipated signs. We cannot reject hypotheses that make the growth rate of manufacturing production hours rise with a growing output rate and fall with a rising productivity growth rate. Nor, more importantly, can we reject the hypothesis that the faster the military share of manufacturing sales grows, the more slowly manufacturing production labor grows.

In summary, to the extent that any econometric test can confirm a hypothesis, these tests support the military diversion hypothesis. Rising military demand decreases the growth rate of manufacturing employment. Rising military capital stock of equipment and structures relative to manufacturers' capital stock decreases the growth rate of manufacturing output, with a negative impact larger than the stimulative impact of military spending on manufacturing output. The indirect impact of military economic activity on productivity growth through the Verdoorn effect, then, is negative. Lastly, the direct effect of military resource diversion on productivity growth is negative but small.

To obtain an estimate of the total net effect of the military variables on manufacturing productivity, we need comparable estimates of their elasticities with respect to productivity growth. We can obtain such an estimate from a single reduced-form equation.[38] This estimate, however, raises some problems. For one thing, in the aggregate model the military share of manufacturing output variable has both a negative impact (equation 5) and a positive impact (via equation 6) on productivity growth. A reduced form estimate of the elasticity for this military influence variable, then, must be interpreted problematically as a net effect. More important, we suspect serious multicollinearity in the data, particularly among the growth rate of military spending and both the growth rate of manufacturing labor and the change in capacity utilization; and further, between the growth rates of the military investment share of manufacturing output and the ratio of military capital stock to manufacturing capital stock.

To guard against the problems associated with estimates based on multicollinear data, Table 4.2 presents estimates of four reduced-form equations derived from the aggregate model. The first estimate includes all of the predetermined variables. The next equation drops capacity-utilization changes. The third equation drops one of the three military variables, the growth rate of the ratio of military capital to manufacturers' capital. The fourth equation drops each of the variables dropped in the second and third equations.

There does seem to be significant multicollinearity among the military variables, particularly affecting the t-statistics for the ratio of military capital to manufacturers' capital. Nevertheless, whether that variable is dropped or not, the coefficients on the growth rates of military spending and the military investment share of manufacturing output maintain their expected signs. In each equation, moreover, the negative net elasticity of the military depletion variable is slightly larger than the positive elasticity of the military spending variable. (The values of their coefficients vary as much as 25 per cent across these estimates.)

The actual relative values of these two military variables, however, overpowers much of the differences in their coefficients. From 1951 through 1982 the annual average growth rate of real military spending is roughly twice as large as the rate of increase of the military investment share of manufacturing output (5.17 per cent to 2.65 per cent). Substituting these values into the four reduced-form estimates in Table 4.2 and adding the positive and negative impacts, gives us the average annual net effect of these two military variables (ignoring the presumably negative effect of the third military variable). This substitution yields a slight net positive annual military impact on manufacturing productivity growth, ranging from 0.10 to 0.15 percentage points annually (or an average of 0.12 of a percentage point

Table 4.2 Reduced-form estimate for the aggregate model (1951–82)

Equation	I	II	III#	IV#
Constant	3.671**	3.653**	3.493**	3.496**
	(8.22)	(8.36)	(7.65)	(7.72)
Variable (growth rate)				
Alternative cost of	0.293**	0.292**	0.345**	0.349**
capital	(3.29)	(8.36)	(3.57)	(7.72)
Manufacturing share	0.220	0.295**	0.265	0.335**
of GNP	(1.04)	(2.83)	(1.16)	(3.13)
Manufacturing investment	−0.100	−0.821	−0.119	−0.106*
	(−1.50)	(−1.68)	(−1.70)	(−2.02)
Military expenditures	0.058*	0.610**	0.444	0.046*
	(2.45)	(2.73)	(1.86)	(2.10)
Manufacturing investment	−0.064**	−0.660**	−0.048*	−0.049*
share of mfr's output	(−3.29)	(−3.27)	(−2.48)	(−2.56)
Capacity utilization	0.072		0.064	
(difference, not	(0.41)		(0.33)	
growth rate)				
Ratio of military capital	0.156	0.160		
to mfr's capital stock	(1.55)	(1.62)		
ADJUSTED r²	.55	.56	.51	.53
F statistic	6.32	7.60	5.56	6.71
Durbin–Watson	1.92	1.88	1.94	1.94
Standard error	1.44	1.42	1.50	1.48

* significant at the 5% level
** significant at the 1% level
t–statistics in parentheses
\# estimated with Cochrane–Orcutt correction for autocorrelation

for the four estimates). However, the relatively smaller military depletion largely offsets the positive military Verdoorn effect.

We can now turn to the particular question of whether the military economy factors identified above share responsibility for the slowdown in manufacturing labor productivity growth, in the models developed here. Over the period of productivity slowdown 1970–1982, military spending *fell* at an annual average rate of 3.33 per cent annually, while the ratio of military investment to manufacturing output fell at a rate of 3.80 per cent. Thus we get inverted results. Because our model is based on rates of growth or decline, falling levels of military spending will boost productivity growth and falling levels of military investment relative to manufacturing output will boost productivity growth.

Substituting these negative annual rates of growth from 1970 to 1982 into the four reduced-form estimates of Table 4.2, and averaging the four, we get the following results. The declining military share of manufacturing output (declining military influence on manufacturing) boosted the productivity growth rate by almost 0.22 of a percentage point while declining military spending, through the Verdoorn effect, cut the productivity growth rate by over 0.17 of a percentage point. The net result of these declining military expenditures over 1970–82 was to boost the productivity growth rate by a slight 0.04 of a percentage point. This boost is even smaller than the 0.12 annual percentage point boost for the entire period. For reasons stated above, the subsequent period of rearmament in the 1980s has not been examined.

A RESOURCE USE MODEL OF PRODUCTION COMPETENCE

In the resource-use perspective, productivity growth varies with the extent to which a variety of resources are mobilized for productivity enhancement or are diverted to alternative use. The following is a simultaneous equation model of productivity growth from this resource-use perspective.

$$q_t = A_1 + A_2 l_t + A_3 T_t + A_4 CMRD_{t-1} + A_5 CALT_t + A_6 CR_t$$
$$+ A_7 CMSHARE_t + A_8 CSMI_t + A_9 CNPW_t \qquad \text{eq. (8)}$$

$$CMSHARE_t = b_1 + b_2 q_t + b_3 T_t + b_4 CNPW_t + b_5 CSMI_t$$
$$+ b_6 CMIMQ_t \qquad \text{eq. (9)}$$

$$CNPW_t = a_1 + a_2 CCRD\ (-\ 1)_t + a_3 CMSHARE_t$$
$$+ a_4 CMIMQ_t \qquad \text{eq. (10)}$$

where all variables are rates of change: q is manufacturing labor productivity, l is manufacturing production labor hours, T is an index of technology effort explained below, $CMRD(-1)$ is military R&D expenditure lagged one period, $CALT$ is the alternative cost of capital as before, CR is the real rate of interest, $CMSHARE$ is the manufacturing share of GNP, $CSMI$ is the ratio of investment in financial, real estate and marketing industries to manufacturing investment, $CNPW$ is the share of nonproduction employment in manufacturing employment, $CMIMQ$, as before, is the ratio of military investment in substantial equipment and structures to manufacturing output, and $CCRD(-1)$ is lagged nonfederal R&D expenditure, all at time t. A, b and a are constants.

Simultaneity occurs in this model for two reasons. A rising rate of growth of manufacturing labor productivity raises the growth rate of the manufacturing share of GNP (by lowering costs), and in turn it is increased by a higher growth rate of the manufacturing share, through induced investment, a version of the Verdoorn effect. Also, a falling manufacturing share of GNP both stimulates additional growth of nonproduction employment, as manufacturing firms diversify (and perhaps put more resources into sales), and in turn is induced by such a rise in nonproduction efforts. These relationships are discussed below.

The resource-use perspective allows us to consider the more complex set of determinants of productivity growth set out in the third section under three categories: technical knowledge; mechanization; and organization of work. These appear in equation 8.

To reflect technical knowledge growth, we include in the first equation an index of technology effort (T) suggested by David Gordon.[39] This is a composite variable created by principle component factors based on corporate patents granted for inventions, the annual rate of change of total R&D expenditures, and the growth rate of newly-published technology books. To reflect R&D depletion caused by military preemption of R&D resources, we include the annual rate of change of military R&D expenditures lagged one period, $CMRD(-1)$.

To reflect mechanization that embodies labor-saving technical change, we include the growth rate of alternative costs $(CALT)$ and of the real rate of interest (CR). To reflect a relative outflow of profits from the manufacturing sector we also include an industrial maturity variable, the change in manufacturing share of GNP $(CMSHARE)$, and the stagnation variable, the rate of change of the ratio of speculative (financial, real estate and marketing) investment to manufacturing investment $(CSMI)$. As we have seen, the diversion perspective predicts that slowing or falling manufacturing share of GNP and accelerating speculative investment will dampen productivity growth.

The growth rate of the manufacturing share of GNP also reflects resource-use dimensions of the Verdoorn relationship. A rising manufacturing share of GNP generally indicates rising manufacturing output, and this (holding production labor constant) indicates rising economies of scale or much new investment. A falling manufacturing share, on the other hand, while consistent with rising manufacturing output, also probably means that output expansion is being constrained on the supply side as capital resources flow to other sectors of the economy.

To reflect resource diversion stemming from the organization of production, equation 8 includes the rate of change of the ratio of nonproduction employment in manufacturing to total manufacturing employment (*CNPW*). This reflects the strong managerialist version of the diversion hypothesis, which predicts that a rising nonproduction share of manufacturing employment lowers productivity growth. Thus in equation 8, we expect A_3, A_5 and A_7 to be positive and the other coefficients to be negative.

Equation 9 expresses the rate of change of the manufacturing share of GNP (*CMSHARE*) as a function of technology changes, various costs conditions, and military demand. Rising productivity (q) and greater technology effort (T) should increase the rate of growth of the manufacturing share by lowering costs. Faster growth of nonproduction workers relative to total manufacturing workers (*CNPW*) should lower manufacturing share under the diversion assumption that the net effect of increasing nonproduction workers reflects declining emphasis on manufacturing *per se* and declining managerial competence in manufacturing.

Rising growth of investment in speculative and commercial sectors relative to manufacturing investment (*CSMI*), reflecting higher capital costs and relatively lower demand for manufacturing output, should be negatively related to the manufacturing share. Finally, a faster growth in the ratio of military capital investment to manufacturing (*CMIMQ*), holding other things constant, reflects the portion of the defense budget which has a positive demand stimulus on the manufacturing share (and thus indirectly on productivity growth, i.e. the military Verdoorn relation). Thus in equation 9 we expect b_4 and b_5 to be negative and the other coefficients to be positive.

Equation 10 expresses the growth rate of nonproduction workers relative to total manufacturing workers as a function of civilian and military factors. First, some growth of nonproduction labor relative to manufacturing labor is a consequence of rising inhouse technology effort. Accelerating a firm's R&D effort increases nonproduction workers employed in manufacturing, especially scientists and engineers. By increasing productivity, moreover, rising private R&D effort lowers the number of production workers for a given level of nonproduction labor. To proxy for firms' R&D effort, we use nonfederal R&D expenditures, lagged one year to reflect some of the indeterminate period of time it takes for R&D to affect production techniques.

Second, changes in the manufacturing share of GNP (*CMSHARE*), reflecting an outflow of profits from manufacturing sector to other sectors, in equation 10, may increase the relative size of nonproduction departments in manufacturing firms, notably financial departments. Third, a rising growth-rate of military capital investment relative to manufacturing output (*CMIMQ*) reflects greater military influence on manufacturing firms' technology, R&D direction and contracting practices. This, according to the depletion perspective, will also raise the portion of nonproduction workers in manufacturing.[40] Thus in equation 10, only a_3 is expected to be negative.

Table 4.3 presents results of the ordinary least squares estimate of the three simultaneous equations in the resource use model. While the measures of overall fit do not match those of the estimate of the aggregate model, the first equation of this model still explains over two-thirds of the variation in the productivity growth rate. Most of the coefficient estimates are significantly different from zero at least at the 5 per cent level. The military and other resource diversion variables have the expected signs.

In equation 8 of Table 4.3, productivity growth is negatively related to lagged military R&D growth rate. The net effect of rising military R&D expenditures is that a 1 per cent increase in these expenditures reduces productivity growth by a small 0.035 of a percentage point. Accelerating growth of both the index of technology effort and the real interest rate do positively affect productivity growth, as expected, although the coefficients are not significant at customary levels (and generally are not in estimates of alternative specifications). On the other hand, we cannot reject the hypotheses that increasing growth rates of both the alternative cost of capital and the manufacturing share of GNP do stimulate productivity growth.

Turning to the non-military depletion variables, we can reject the hypothesis that they have no negative influence. Faster growth of the stagnation proxy, investment in financial, real estate and marketing industries relative to manufacturing investment, lowers the manufacturing productivity growth rate. And faster growth of the strong

Table 4.3   Estimate of resource-use model (1951–82)

Equation Dependent variables: (rates of change)	8 Mfr labor productivity	9 Mfr share of GNP	10 Nonprod. labor share of mfr employment
Constant	4.614** (11.38)	−0.568 (−0.81)	0.353 (0.97)
Variables			
Mfr production labor hours	−0.407** (−4.19)		
Index of technology effort	0.544 (1.84)	0.945** (2.80)	
Alternative cost of capital	0.426** (3.53)		
Real interest rate	0.082 (1.052)		
Military R&D expenditures (−1)	−0.035* (−2.50)		
Nonprod. share of mfr employment	−0.613** (−3.51)	−0.871** (−5.33)	
Manufacturing share of GNP	0.453** (3.18)		−0.530** (−6.15)
Speculative investment mfr investment ratio	−0.121** (−2.81)	−0.077* (−2.24)	
Mfr labor productivity		0.386* (2.15)	
Military investment manufacturing output		0.039* (2.47)	0.049** (4.75)
Nonfederal R&D expenditure (−1)			0.107** (2.88)
ADJUSTED r^2	.68	.68	.73
F statistic	9.27	14.00	28.79
Durbin–Watson	1.93	1.20	1.25
Standard error	1.21	1.74	1.45

*   significant at the 5% level
** significant at the 1% level
t-statistics in parentheses

managerialism proxy, the nonproduction labor share of manufacturing employment, is associated with a lower productivity growth rate.

In equation 9, these same two nonmilitary depletion variables negatively affect the growth rate of the manufacturing share of GNP. The growth rate of strong managerialism, proxied by the nonproduction labor share of manufacturing employment, has a particularly large effect. This suggests that managerialism is a significant part of the story of declining manufacturing share of GNP.

With respect to the military Verdoorn effect, in equation 9 the growth rate of the ratio of military investment to manufacturing output, the index of military influence on manufacturing, positively affects the growth of the manufacturing share of GNP, and thus indirectly influences productivity positively. Finally rising growth rates of both productivity and technology effort sharply boost the growth rate of the manufacturing share.

In the estimate of equation 10 the growth rate of the ratio of nonproduction employees to total manufacturing employment is indeed positively related to the rate of growth of lagged nonfederal R&D expenditures. Presumably, this is both because science and engineering employment rises with private R&D effort and because production labor falls with successful R&D effort for any level of demand. On the other hand, accelerating industrial maturation, proxied by faster decrease in the manufacturing share of GNP, increases the growth rate of the nonproduction labor share of manufacturing employment. This suggests that manufacturing maturity promotes managerialism. Lastly, faster growth in the proxy for military influence on manufacturing practices – the ratio of military investment expenditure to manufacturing output – positively affects the nonproduction proportion of manufacturing employment, which in turn negatively affects productivity.

To estimate the actual magnitude of the impacts of military R&D and investment expenditure on manufacturing productivity, we need comparable coefficients for the military variables. Since in the productivity equation, equation 8, only military R&D expenditures appear, we estimate a reduced-form equation, as we did for the aggregate model. Doing this raises similar problems, because the proxy for military influence on manufacturing sales, the ratio of military investment to manufacturing sales, enters the model in a complex way. It reflects both positive military stimulus in equation 9 and military depletion of capital resources in equation 10. Its coefficient in a reduced form estimate, then, will reflect both a positive and negative impact on productivity, which we shall interpret as a net effect. Similarly, there is high probability of multicollinearity in the reduced form estimate, at least between the two military variables and between the R&D variables.

Table 4.4 presents estimates of the reduced form equation for the

Table 4.4   Reduced form estimate for resource use model (1951–82)

Dependent variable	Growth rate of manufacturing labour productivity
Constant	4.441**
	(8.73)
Variables (growth rates)	
Real interest rate	0.013
	(0.15)
Mfr production labor hours	−0.278**
	(−3.16)
Alternative cost of capital	0.600**
	(4.01)
Manufacturing share of GNP	0.515**
	(3.37)
Index of technology effort	0.424
	(1.32)
Nonfederal R&D expenditures (−1)	−0.076
	(−1.73)
Speculative investment/ mfr investment ratio	−0.151**
	(−2.80)
Military R&D expenditures (−1)	−0.046**
	(−2.95)
Military investment manufacturing output	−0.026*
	(−2.32)
ADJUSTED^2	0.62
F statistic	6.73
Durbin–Watson	1.88
Standard Error	1.31

* significant at the 5% level
** significant at the 1% level
t-statistics in parentheses

resource use model with manufacturing labor productivity as the dependent variable. The relatively high standard errors of the estimates of coefficients for real interest rates and nonfederal R&D suggest that multicollinearity is present in the data. Dropping variables as we did for the aggregate model, however, does not change the magnitudes of the military variables. The elasticity for the overall impact of changes in the ratio of military investment to manufacturing output is negative, −0.026. Similarly, the elasticity for the growth rate of real military R&D is negative, −0.046. We conclude that the net effect of military expenditures was to lower manufacturing productivity growth.

Over the period 1951–82, the first military variable, the military influence proxy grew by an annual average rate of 2.65 per cent, while real military R&D expenditure grew by 5.62 per cent. Substituting these values into the reduced-form estimate of Table 4.4, we find that the net effect of military activity over 1951–82 was to lower the productivity growth rate by about 0.33 of a percentage point annually.

Over the period of the productivity slowdown, 1970–82, the military investment to manufacturing output ratio fell by an annual average rate of 3.80 per cent, while real military R&D expenditures fell by 3.19 per cent annually. Given the elasticities of Table 4.4, the net effect of this declining military expenditure from 1971 to 1982 was to raise the productivity growth rate approximately 0.25 of a percentage point annually.

CONCLUSION

Conventional analyses of productivity growth and slowdown in the US have relied on the neoclassical production model's institutional assumption of efficient resource allocation. On the other hand, theories of the economic consequences of military economic activity and of other forces of diversion, such as industrial maturation, stagnation, and managerialism, have tended to be less rigid than the productivity literature, but perhaps not always so thorough in their qualitative and quantitative argument.

This study attempts to relax the standard assumption of efficient resource allocation in productivity studies and to sharpen the various military and non-military diversion hypotheses about postwar economic performance. This approach can be extended to more recent years and to other economies. No matter how successful these attempts turn out, however, they rely on data which need qualitative improvements. We especially need better measures of productivity, R&D expenditure, other components of technology effort and effects, including civilian spinoffs, and nonproduction labor.

Given the aggregate model and the resource use model, we find that data for 1951–82 support three hypotheses identified at the outset. Aggregate military spending as such contributes to economic expansion, and thus to both employment growth and productivity growth. In the longer run, however, negative depletion effects at least counteract, if not overwhelm, these positive Verdoorn effects. Apparently if government policy had devoted expenditures to non-depleting civilian uses, there would be little or no counter to the Verdoorn effect of the expenditures.

Estimates of the aggregate model support the depletion thesis that military spending and military investment have deprived US manufacturing of capital resources. Estimates of the resource model also support the depletion thesis that military R&D has retarded the technology effort in the US. Estimates of neither model, however, support the claim that military activity is responsible for the recent productivity slowdown.

Surely this is not a result that lends unqualified support to any particular policy perspective. Military Keynesians and critical stagnationists predict that military activity will generally raise, not lower, production during the long run, and that the military cutbacks up to 1979 would retard productivity growth. The depletion hypothesis, of course, does imply that military economic activity will lower productivity growth. The depletion hypothesis, however, also implies that military cutbacks are necessary to restore high growth. The 1970s cutbacks were not sufficient to restore productivity.

These results of the resource model do not necessarily falsify the depletion hypothesis. Depletion theorists have generally associated the 1970s productivity slowdown with accumulated changes in corporate practices and institutional forms over the years.[41] The kinds of econometric models explored here, however, do not capture such cumulative effects of military economic activity. The models examine only annual rates of change in military and productivity factors, rather than absolute levels or other measures which reflect cumulative institutional changes. A productivity slowdown based on cumulative effects and rachet effects might be remedied by reducing military economic activity, but then the benefits would only become apparent slowly at some far point in time. Certainly an econometric exploration of cumulative institutional effects would be fruitful.

On the face of it the results of this study should prompt us to reconsider industrial and military policy in the United States. First with respect to the nonmilitary diversion variables, results suggest that, contrary to conventional wisdom, managerial domination of production decisions and market competition are not sufficient to induce the innovation the manufacturing sector requires. Internal organizational expansion and capital outflows have retarded productivity growth over the long run.

Second, since the Second World War, military policy has been based on the untested popular belief that military economic activity contributes to economic growth, just as it contributed to ending the Great Depression. During this period, military Keynesianism and Cold War politics fit conveniently together. Among the consequences of this belief has been a relatively unchallenged expansion in military production quite independently of our national security needs, a result which certainly contributed to the spiraling arms race.

If, as this study implies, military enterprise has not been the long-run economic stimulus previously assumed, policy formation must take account of the economic burdens of military expansion, many of which have been largely ignored in most policy discussions and academic debates. In this light military expansion appears relatively more costly for the nation; and alternative security strategies, including serious arms negotiations, become relatively less costly for the nation. Clearly this result supports an economic and political reassessment of our national security needs.

Data Appendix: Definitions and Sources

ABBREVIATIONS

ERP	US President, *Economic Report of the President* (Washington, DC: US Government Printing Office, 1984).
HS	US Department of Commerce, *Historical Statistics of the United States* (Washington, DC: US Government Printing Office, 1976), Vol. II.
HLS	Bureau of Labor Statistics, US Department of Labor, *Handbook of Labor Statistics* (Washington, DC: 1983).
HT	US President, *Historical Tables, Budget of the U.S. Government, FY 1990* (Washington, DC: US Government Printing Office, 1989).
SA	US Department of Commerce, *Statistical Abstract of the United States* (Washington, DC: US Government Printing Office, various years).

VARIABLES

q	Annual rate of change of real manufacturing output per employee hour. *HLS*, Table 92.

l	Annual rate of change of hours of manufacturing production labor. US Bureau of the Census, *1985 Annual Survey of Manufacturers* (Washington, DC: January 1987).
CALT	Annual rate of change in the alternative cost of capital: ratio of nonfarm labor compensation to machine tool price index. *ERP*, and Association of Machine Tool Makers, *Economic Handbook of the Machine Tool Industry* (Washington, DC, 1985).
CMQ	Annual rate of change of real manufacturing output. *ERP*.
CMIMQ	Annual rate of change of ratio of military capital expenditure (measured over the fiscal year) to manufacturing output. *HT*, Table 9.1; ERP.
DCU	Annual difference in manufacturing capacity utilization. US Department of Commerce, Bureau of Economic Analysis, *Business Conditions Digest* (December 1986).
CMSHARE	Annual rate of change of ratio of manufacturing output to GNP. *ERP*.
CIM	Annual rate of change of real manufacturing investment. *ERP*.
CMK	Annual rate of change of ratio of net military capital stock to net manufacturer's capital stock. US Department of Commerce, *Survey of Current Business* (January 1986).
CM	Annual rate of change of defense expenditures, deflated by the producer price index for capital goods. (The Bureau of Economic Analysis deflator for defense expenditures begins only with 1972.) *ERP*.
CR	Annual rate of change of rates of return on Moody's Aaa bonds, deflated by producer price index for capital goods. *ERP*.
CMRD	Annual rate of change of military R&D expenditures, fiscal years. *HT*, Table 10.1.
CNPW	Annual rate of change of the ratio of nonproduction labor to total manufacturing labor. *HLS*.
T	= .7 CRD + .72 CTB − .89 PAT, normalized.
CRD	Annual rate of change of real non-farm non-government investment in R&D. Leo Sveikauskas, 'The Contribution of R&D to Productivity Growth', *Monthly Labor Review*, March 1986, Table 1.
CTB	Annual rate of change in the moving average of new technology books. *HS* R-216; SA – various editions 1970–86. 1982 value extrapolated using figure for new technology books and editions, *SA*.
PAT	Corporate patents issued. *HS* and *SA* 1977 and 1986.
CSMI	Annual rate of change of ratio of investment in financial, real estate and marketing industries to manufacturing investment. *ERP*.
CCRD	Annual rate of change of nonfederal R&D expenditures. *SA* 1951, 1955, 1959, 1986. Figures for 1951 and 1952 are spliced.

Notes

1. Paul Samuelson, *Economics* (New York: McGraw-Hill, various editions); recent editions have been co-authored with William D. Nordhaus.
2. Nicholas Kaldor, *Strategic Factors in Economic Development* (Ithaca, NY: Cornell University Press, 1967); Robert E. Rowthorn, 'A Note on Verdoorn's Law', *Economic Journal* 89 (March 1979), 131–3; Thomas R. Michl, 'International Comparisons of Productivity Growth: Verdoorn's Law Revisited', *Journal of Post Keynesian Economics* 7, no. 2 (Summer 1985), 474–92.
3. This interpretation can be found in A. P. Thirwell, 'A Plain Man's Guide to Kaldor's Growth Laws', *Journal of Post Keynesian Economics* 5, no. 3 (Spring 1983), 345–58; and John S. L. McCombie, 'Kaldor's Laws in Retrospect', *Journal of Post Keynesian Economics* 5, no. 5 (Spring 1983), 414–29.
4. See, for example, Fred J. Cook, *The Warfare State* (New York: Macmillan, 1962), Ch. vi, esp. 169–72, and 65–7. See also Richard DuBoff, *Accumulation and Power: An Economic History of the United States* (Armonk, NY: M. E. Sharpe, 1989), 98–9.
5. Paul A. Baran and Paul M. Sweezy, *Monopoly Capital* (New York: Modern Reader, 1966), esp. Ch. 7; Michael Reich, 'Military Spending and Production for Profit', in Richard C. Edwards, Michael Reich and Thomas E. Weisskopf (eds), *The Capitalist System* (Englewood Cliffs, NJ: Prentice-Hall, 1978), 409–17; L. J. Griffin, M. Wallace and J. Devine, 'The Political Economy of Military Spending: Evidence from the United States', *Cambridge Journal of Economics*, Vol. 6 (1982), 1–14; James M. Cypher, 'Military Spending, Technical Change, and Economic Growth: A Disguised Form of Industrial Policy?', *Journal of Economic Issues*, Vol. 21, no. 1, March 1987, 33–59.
6. Two articles in a recent issue of *Challenge* state the thesis with varying degrees of urgency: Richard B. DuBoff, 'What Military Spending Really Costs', and Francis M. Bator, interview by Richard D. Bartell, 'GNP Budgeting: Old Theory, New Reality', *Challenge*, Vol. 32, no. 5, Sept.–Oct., 1989, 4–10 and 21–27.
7. Lloyd J. Dumas, *The Overburdened Economy* (Berkeley: University of California Press, 1986) and Seymour Melman, *The Permanent War Economy* (New York: Simon and Schuster, 1974).
8. As I explain in the discussion of data, I use a measure of manufacturing output per labor hour that is available only through 1982. Bureau of Labor Statistics, *Handbook of Labor Statistics* (Washington, DC: Government Printing Office, 1983). Subsequently the Labor Department revised its estimation method, probably overestimating the value of computer industry output and the domestic content of some manufacturing output.
9. For summaries of these hypotheses, se Zvi Griliches, 'Productivity Puzzles and R&D: Another Nonexplanation', *Journal of Economic Perspectives* 2, no. 4 (1988), 9–21; Martin Neal Baily and Alok K. Chakrabarti, *Innovation and the Productivity Crisis* (Washington, DC:

Brookings, 1988); Edward N. Wolff, 'The Magnitude and Causes of the Recent Productivity Slowdown in the United States: A Survey of Recent Studies', in *Productivity Growth and U.S. Competitiveness*, ed. William J. Baumol and K. McLennon (New York: Oxford University Press, 1985).

10. Ibid.
11. Dumas, ibid.
12. Now echoed frequently in the business press, the spark behind the many recent versions of a managerialist hypothesis was probably Robert H. Hayes and William J. Abernathy, 'Managing Our Way to Economic Decline', *Harvard Business Review* 58 (1980), 67–77; see also Seymour Melman, *Profits without Production* (New York: Knopf, 1983). An early statement of the social relations model of labor effort was developed by Samuel Bowles, David M. Gordon and Thomas E. Weisskopf, *Beyond the Wasteland: A Democratic Alternative to Economic Decline* (New York: Anchor Books of Doubleday, 1983). Classic statements of the depletion hypothesis and the subsidy search hypothesis appear in Seymour Melman, *The Permanent War Economy* (New York, Simon and Schuster, 1974) and Melman, *Profits without Production*. A theory of resource diversion in the classical tradition, with specific reference to military production, appears in Lloyd J. Dumas, *The Overburdened Economy* (Berkeley: University of California Press, 1986).
13. See, for example, Geoffrey C. Harcourt, *Some Cambridge Controversies in the Theory of Capital* (Cambridge: Cambridge University Press, 1972).
14. By 'classical tradition' I mean the general theoretical orientation on production of political economists from Adam Smith through Ricardo and even Marx. As I understand classical production theory, it treats land, labor and capital as irreducible factors of production only in the sense that the classes that own them and derive incomes from them are each socially inseparable from capitalist production. Productive labor alone, however, is technically irreducible as the primary factor in the origin and measurement of value. For example, we can reduce the measure and value of any capital good to a series of laboring activities. In the classical framework, these propositions about property and labor summarize the social and technical context in which improving productivity occurs.

    Two advantages of the classical model for this study stand out. This model avoids the problem of measuring capital, capital services and embodied technical change by treating capital as an intermediate rather than primary production factor. And in examining a situation of general institutional resource diversion, the model is not confronted with the paradoxical neoclassical problem of comparing second-best allocations.
15. For this general approach I am indebted to Earl Yang, whose engineering model treats productivity growth as a function of engineering variables. Yang thus omits both labor and capital from his production function; Earl Yang, Dissertation Seminar, Department of Industrial Engineering and Operations Research, Columbia University, 1987.
16. Some examples appear in Lee O. Smith, 'The Cuomo Commission's "New Realism"', *Challenge* 31, no. 5 (1988), 37–45; see also, Michael J.

Piore, 'A Critique of Reagan's Labor Policy', *Challenge* 29, no. 1 (1986), 48–54.

17. See, for example, Assar Lindbeck, 'The Recent Slowdown of Productivity Growth', *The Economic Journal* 93 (March 1983), 13–34.

18. See Griliches, 'Productivity Puzzles'; Wolff, 'Magnitude and Causes'; and Martin Neal Baily, 'What Has Happened to Productivity Growth?', *Science*, 24 October 1986, 443–51.

19. Frank R. Lichtenberg, 'The Effect of Government Funding on Private Industrial Research and Development: A Re-assessment', *The Journal of Industrial Economics* 36, no. 1 (1987), 97–104; Frank R. Lichtenberg, 'The Relationship Between Federal Contract R&D and Company R&D', *American Economic Review* 74, no. 2, May 1984, 73–8; and Nestor E. Terleckyj, *Effects of R&D on the Productivity Growth of Industries: An Exploratory Study* (Washington, DC: National Planning Association, 1974).

20. Frank R. Lichtenberg, 'The Impact of the Strategic Defense Initiative on U.S. Civilian R&D Investment and Industrial Competitiveness', TMs [photocopy], Columbia University, January, 1988; Nathan Rosenberg, 'Civilian "Spillovers" from Military R&D Spending: The U.S. Experience since World War II', in *Strategic Defense and the Western Alliance*, ed. Sanford Lakoff and Randy Willoughby (Lexington, Mass.: Lexington Books of D. C. Heath, 1987), 165–88; see also David Weston and Philip Gummett, 'The Economic Impact of Military R&D: Hypotheses, Evidence and Verification', *Defense Analysis* 3, no. 1 (1987), 63–79.

21. Dumas, *Overburdened Economy*; Melman, *Profits without Production*; Robert W. DeGrasse, Jr, *Military Expansion, Economic Decline* (Armonk, NY: M. E. Sharpe, 1983); Melman, *Permanent War Economy*; Anthony DiFilippo, *Military Spending and Industrial Decline: A Study of the Machine Tool Industry* (Westport, Ct: Greenwood, 1986); and Anthony DiFilippo, *From Industry to Arms: The Political Economy of High Technology*, TMs [photocopy], Lincoln University, Pa., 1989.

22. N. Rosenberg, 'Civilian "Spillovers"'; Carl Barus, 'Military Influence on Electrical Engineering Curriculum Since World War II', *IEEE Technology and Society Magazine* (June 1987), 3–9. See also Richard M. Cyert and David C. Mowery, 'Technology, Employment and U.S. Competitiveness', *Scientific American* 260, no. 5 (May 1989), 56 and 62.

23. E. Rothbard, 'Causes of the Superior Efficiency of U.S.A. Industry as Compared with British Industry', *Economic Journal* (1946), 383–90; Seymour Melman, *Dynamic Factors in Industrial Productivity* (Oxford: Basil Blackwell, 1956); H. J. Habbakkuk, *American and British Technology in the Nineteenth Century: The Search for Labor Saving Inventions* (Cambridge: Cambridge University Press, 1962).

24. Geoffrey H. Moore and John P. Cullity, 'Trends and Cycles in Productivity, Unit Costs and Prices: An International Perspective', in *Business Cycles, Inflation and Forecasting*, ed. Geoffrey H. Moore, National Bureau of Economic Research, Vol. 24 (Cambridge, Mass.: Ballinger, 1983).

25. See Richard DuBoff, *Accumulation and Power: An Economic History of the United States* (Armonk, NY: M. E. Sharpe, 1989), 29.

26. On productivity and changing output composition, see Wolff, 'Magnitude and Causes', and Martin Neal Baily, 'The Productivity Growth Slowdown by Industry', *Brookings Papers on Economic Activity* (1982).
27. Paul A. Baran and Paul M. Sweezy, *Monopoly Capital* (New York: Monthly Review Press, 1966); John Bellamy Foster and Henryk Szlajfer (ed.), *The Faltering Economy* (New York: Monthly Review Press, 1984).
28. For example, Ralph E. Gomory and Roland W. Schmitt, 'Science and Product', *Science* 240, 27 May 1988, 1131ff.
29. For example, Smith, 'New Realism'; Piore, 'Critique'; and Cyert and Mowery, 'Technology'.
30. Seymour Melman, *Permanent War Economy* (New York: Simon and Schuster, 1974).
31. Whether this loss of control over costs derives from military production practices and if so, how it is spread, are questions which have not been addressed in great detail for the entire economy. One possible channel from military contracting practices to cost escalation is that engineers are increasingly attracted to and trained within a military-influenced culture. Another possibility is that since the most dynamic firms and divisions of firms in the 1950s and 1960s have often been military production units, their managers have gained disproportionate prominence in corporate managements. Neither of these hypotheses has been tested.
32. For example, Rosenberg, 'Spillovers'. For views that military R&D has been neutral and that it has boosted civilian technology see, respectively, Lynn E. Browne, 'Defense Spending and High Technology Development: National and State Issues', *New England Economic Review* (Sept.–Oct. 1988), 3–22; and James M. Cypher, 'Military Spending, Technical Change and Economic Growth: A Disguised Form of Industrial Policy?', *Journal of Economic Issues* 21, no. 1 (March 1987), 33–59.
33. The implication that nonproduction workforces in manufacturing will grow faster than production workforces, we should note, is not sufficient to distinguish this strong version of the managerial thesis from still other versions of the managerial thesis. The stagnation thesis stated earlier, for example, also suggests that the growing speculative, nonmanufacturing activities of firms will expand nonproduction personnel relative to production workers. This growth may reflect either expanding financial offices or, as Baran and Sweezy, *Monopoly Capital*, argue, expanding marketing effort in the face of stagnant sales.
34. Hugh G. Mosley, *The Arms Race: Economic and Social Consequences* (Lexington, Mass.: Lexington Books, 1985), Ch. 3.
35. For reports of several estimates see Dumas, *Overburdened Economy*, 209–11; DeGrasse, *Military Expansion*, 79–80.
36. The method of calculating CX, the annual percent change in any variable X, is $CX = 100[\log(X_t/X_{t-1})]$, where log is the natural logarithm.
37. See Edward F. Denison, *Estimates of Productivity Change by Industry: An Evaluation and Alternative* (Washington: DC: Brookings Institution, 1989). As a consequence, later Labor Department tables of productivity data depart somewhat from earlier ones. Until we know better how to interpret and use the revised data, it appears less risky to use an earlier measure; hence the 1982 cutoff.

38. A reduced-form equation for a simultaneous equation system makes the dependent under study a function of all of the predetermined variables in the system. Here this means making the manufacturing productivity growth rate a function of all the other variables in the system except the two other dependent variables.

39. David M. Gordon, 'What Makes Epochs? A Comparative Analysis of Technological and Social Explanations of Long Swings', in *Technological and Social Factors in Long Term Fluctuations*, ed. M. Dimatteo, R. Goodwin and A. Vercelli (Springer-Verlag, 1989). Since Gordon's article does not include values of this technology effort index, it was reconstructed. The plot of this reconstructed variable differs a bit from the one Gordon presents. Apparently, I was able to obtain some values he estimated through extrapolation and splicing.

40. From a macroeconomic perspective it would make sense to include an index of demand conditions, instead of the ratio of military investment to manufacturing output, to reflect differences in layoff practices for production and nonproduction workers over the business cycle, and in fact such a variable improves the estimated equation's fit considerably. From the resource diversion perspective, however, focusing on the flow of resources in and out of manufacturing has some theoretical priority.

41. Melman, *Profits Without Production*; Dumas, *Overburdened Economy*.

Part III
Towards a Peace Economy

5 The Political Economy of an Alternative Security and Disarmament Policy for the United States

Gregory A. Bischak

INTRODUCTION

In the wake of the dramatic changes in Eastern Europe and the Soviet Union, some in the West have proclaimed the end of the Cold War. Yet the forty-five year legacy of the Cold War leaves in place a formidable array of military institutions which block the way to disarmament and an alternative framework for international security. These barriers to a new security policy are even higher as a result of the Reagan Administration's $2.25 trillion military buildup. Despite these realities, many on the right and left of the political spectrum have argued that the signing of the Intermediate Nuclear Weapons Treaty (INF), together with the growing fiscal and economic pressures on both the United States' and the Soviet Union's economies, create real prospects for further arms limitation agreements. Indeed, President George Bush, following the lead of President Reagan, has pledged to negotiate a strategic arms reduction treaty (START) which would reduce the number of strategic nuclear warheads in US and Soviet arsenals by at least 30 per cent and 35 per cent (not the widely advertised 50 per cent usually presented for public consumption).

Less sanguine peace activists, however, have noted that terms of the INF treaty and the proposed START agreement offer far less hope for real disarmament than would be suggested by the wave of public optimism. These critics point to the fact that US military planners are already replacing the intermediate-range missiles that have been removed under the INF Treaty with newly deployed air-launched and sea-launched cruise missiles not covered under the Treaty. Meanwhile, the START treaty currently being negotiated by the US and the Soviet Union will permit wide-ranging modernization of nuclear forces in both countries. For the US the treaty would allow the deployment of the Trident II missile, the B-2 Stealth bomber, the MX multiple warhead missile with a rail garrison basing system, the Midgetman land-based single warhead mobile missile, the advanced cruise missile, and the SRAM II attack missile.[1] Soviet strategic modernization would also proceed with deployment of improved versions of the SS-13, the SS-25 and the submarine ballistic missile forces.

The failure of arms control and arms limitation treaties to achieve a real reversal of the arms race is not surprising to many critics of US militarism, who have argued for decades that military spending and the arms race perform essential political economic functions in maintaining American hegemony in the world economy. Indeed, it is the thesis of this article that current arms control policy precludes a thorough reevaluation of the nation's security policy. Moreover, arms limitation policies currently under negotiation do not constitute disarmament and therefore eschew any consideration of economic conversion planning. Because both strategic and conventional forces modernization programs will remain intact under current proposals, there is little economic pressure for conversion planning.

In this chapter I will explore the nature of the political economic function of the arms race and the prospects for real disarmament, as opposed to another round of arms control. In the first section, I assess the current conjuncture and evaluate the political prospects for adopting an alternative framework for international security. In the second section I review the central concepts of alternative security proposals which have been advanced in Europe and the US. In the third section I review the estimates from several studies of the possible budgetary savings which might accrue from adopting a wide variety of arms limitation and disarmament proposals. However, none of these studies have attempted to evaluate the impact on the US economy from implementing a serious disarmament initiative. In the final section of this article, I attempt to examine and compare the relative economic effects of implementing two fundamentally different approaches to strategic arms reduction: one which permits the wide-ranging strategic modernization; and another which significantly curtails the strategic modernization currently underway. These estimates of the economic and employment impacts of the two different approaches illustrate graphically the political economy of arms control, as opposed to disarmament. Moreover, these comparisons show why there is so much institutional opposition to, and need for, economic conversion planning as an essential component of the disarmament process.

THE CURRENT CONJUNCTURE AND THE PROSPECTS FOR PROGRESSIVE INITIATIVES

Political economists in the US have long argued that military spending is used to prop up domestic aggregate demand in periods of stagnation. Presumably influential elites prefer military rather than civilian spending to stimulate the economy because it doesn't compete directly with private production. Nor does military spending redistribute income in favor of labor and the unemployed, so it doesn't undermine the disciplinary mechanisms of the labor market. Perhaps more importantly, the constant development of new weaponry has ensured the maintenance of US international hegemony through the projection of military force. This military capacity has allowed the US to enforce the international order of the world capitalist system, which rests on the promotion of free trade, international capital mobility and a secure environment for foreign investment. Accordingly, critics of this system argue that American foreign-policymakers and their corporate supporters will never support a permanent curtailment of military spending and overseas commitments in favor of disarmament. Moreover, America's allies in Western Europe and Japan also have a stake in continuing their support for US military spending, since it acts as a guarantor for the integrity of the system as a whole.

For these reasons left political economists have often argued that efforts by peace and disarmament groups to advance programs for disarmament and economic conversion of military industries are doomed to failure because they don't address the fundamental causes of militarism.[2] The inherent requirements of the postwar system and America's unique role in integrating and maintaining it have meant that there are substantial systemic political and economic pressures to defeat a program for disarmament, conversion and a realignment of federal budget priorities away from military spending and towards civilian spending.

This assessment has generated much critical analysis of the political economy of militarism, but not much in the way of a programmatic alternative to further military buildups. Unlike their Western European counterparts,[3] political economists in the US have not contributed to a positive programmatic analysis on how to overcome the economic inertia of the military–industrial system. Nor have they contributed to the development of a disarmament and alternative security policy which is so necessary to seize the initiative and build a popular movement for fundamental change in US foreign and military policy. Despite this pessimistic assessment there are compelling economic and political reasons to believe that the present conjuncture provides a real opportunity to press for a redefinition of defense policy, real arms reduction agreements and lower military spending.

On the international front, perhaps the most fundamental changes in East–West relations have come about largely as a result of the foreign and domestic initiatives advanced by Soviet President Mikhail Gorbachev since his accession to power in 1985. His political overtures to the West for reduced military tensions, the settlement of regional conflicts, and multilateral agreements for phased nuclear and conventional disarmament have been motivated both by a desire to end the Cold War and by a need to reduce the onerous burden of the arms race on the Soviet economy. Indeed, many analysts both within and outside the Soviet Union have recognized that the success of domestic economic reforms in the Soviet Union partly depend upon reductions in military spending in order to free crucial economic resources necessary for revitalizing the moribund civilian economy.[4] In addition, forging peaceful political relations with the West is an essential prerequisite for increased East–West trade, which is critical for the modernization of the Soviet Union's civilian economy. Nowhere is the substance and meaning of these policies clearer than in Eastern Europe, where the policies of *glasnost* and *perestroika* have fostered rapid democratization and economic change within the Warsaw Pact nations. Yet, in order for these changes to move forward unhampered, the confrontation of the two military blocs must be removed.

Within the Atlantic Alliance, there is growing pressure, especially in West Germany, to remove short-range nuclear weapons which could only be used in a conflict in central Europe. Further, there is questioning on both the right and left of the political spectrum that future modernization of tactical nuclear and conventional weapons might make war more thinkable in central Europe. So widespread are these reservations about nuclear and conventional modernization, that a popular slogan has been coined in the Federal Republic of Germany, 'The shorter the weapon's range, the deader the German.' These criticisms of NATO's modernization plans focus on the implications of using weapons whose destructive consequences would be confined to central Europe. Critics argue that such an approach to military doctrines actually increases the disparity between the security interests within the Alliance.

In Western Europe the acceleration of economic integration as planned for 1992 poses yet another challenge to US domination of the Atlantic Alliance, and this development will accentuate the shift towards a more polycentric distribution of political and economic power in the world. Further economic integration of Western Europe will undoubtedly create internal pressures leading to more economic concentration, and also create greater pressures for external trade, especially with Eastern Europe.

Already, a new era of economic detente seems to be developing between Western and Eastern Europe. Indeed, in 1988 Western European financiers agreed to provide the Soviet Union with over $9 billion in loans to underwrite the Soviet's economic modernization program.[5] This sum represents more than all Western loans to the Soviets over the entire three years from 1984 to 1987. In addition, the recent relaxation of Soviet restrictions on joint ventures with foreign firms now permits foreign ownership of more than 49 per cent of the operation. Another sign of the new economic detente was marked by the pronouncements by Vadim Medvedev, the Soviet chief of ideology, who has argued that there is no longer a historical necessity for an armed struggle between the East and West. Clearly, there exist new incentives in Western and Eastern Europe for disarmament and increasing economic integration.

At home, liberal Democrats and Republicans alike have moved slowly in addressing the changes in Eastern and Western European relations and warn that further economic detente could produce deep divisions within the Atlantic Alliance. Moreover, US initiatives for conventional arms control in Europe have been extremely modest, with most politicians being content to accept the current NATO proposals for the Conventional Forces in Europe disarmament talks in Vienna.[6] Indeed, there is little to indicate that the US and NATO will attempt to use these talks to curtail their expensive plans for conventional force modernization.

Yet the American economy faces limitations on further real spending increases for the military budget. The persistent fiscal budget deficits have constrained military spending so that real spending crested at a peak of $249.8 billion in FY 1987 (as measured in

Table 5.1   Selected current forces and plans for modernization

Forces	Equipment
	ARMY
18 Active Divisions	M1 Tank, Bradley Fighting Vehicle
10 Reserve	Apache Attack Helicopter
	New Light Attack/Reconnaissance Helicopter (LHX)
	NAVY
580 Deployable Ships	Nimitz-Class Aircraft Carrier
15 Carrier Battle Groups	Guided Missile Destroyer (DDG–51)
15 Carrier Air Wings	New Submarine (SSN–21)
(13 Active, 2 Reserve)	New Tilt-Rotor Aircraft (V–22)
	AIR FORCE
35 Tactical Fighter Wings	Stealth Strategic Bomber (B–2)
	New Tactical Fighter (ATF)
	STRATEGIC DEFENSE INITIATIVE
	Annual real growth of 3 per cent in research funding, with no deployment

Source: Congressional Budget Office, 'Costs of Supporting and Modernizing Current U.S. Military Forces', September 1988.

1982 dollars) with a flattening-out of outlays at an estimated $241.6 billion in FY 1989. Further increases are in doubt, and it is unlikely that future budgets will grow fast enough to allow for the full range of weapons procurements and modernization that were initiated by the Reagan Administration.

Indeed, budget planning by the Defense Department and Congress has begun to reflect these fiscal constraints on the pace of modernization and the degree of preparedness for strategic and conventional forces. Budget planning has focused on adjusting the pace of modernization and the growth of operational overhead to these new fiscal constraints. A faster pace of strategic and conventional force modernization – which means a more rapid process of research, development, testing, procurement and deployment – would imply a growth rate in the Defense budget of 3 to 4 per cent over the period from 1990 to 1994. This pace of modernization involves the deployment of the aforementioned strategic weapons systems, plus the other strategic and conventional weapons systems which are outlined in Table 5.1. In addition, Table 5.1 shows the force levels which were planned as part of the overall military buildup in the late 1980s and into the 1990s.

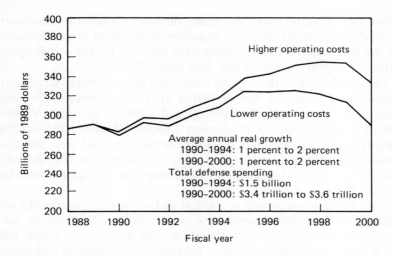

Figure 5.1 Projected Defense Budget; slower pace of modernization, 1988–2000
Source: Congressional Budget Office Staff Paper, 'Costs of Supporting and Modernizing Current U.S. Military Forces', September 1988.

However, this budget plan is really untenable because the outlays required for such a pace are greater than the outlays which will be available under the Gramm–Rudman budget restraints. Therefore, budget planners have considered lower operational overheads as one way to deal with the shortfall of appropriated funds. Another approach is illustrated in Figure 5.1, where a slower growth rate in modernization is considered, along with the deferment or cancellation of certain weapon systems. This approach yields a slower pace in average annual real growth of 1 to 2 per cent between 1990 and 1994, and beyond to the year 2000. Yet even these budget scenarios are being pared back, as the current Secretary of Defense Richard Cheney has instructed the services to cut back their spending plans, allegedly by $180 billion over 1992–1994.[7]

For its part Congress has principally focused its budget-trimming efforts on reducing operational outlays, thus sparing the procurement budget for major weapons systems.[8] In typical pork-barrel fashion, several weapons systems which the services had chosen to cut, such as the Osprey rotor tilt aircraft and the F-14D, were kept alive by Congressional efforts. Despite the alleged concern for improved preparedness, it may be compromised to provide funding for the big ticket items in the strategic and conventional modernization programs.

Moreover, Congress and the Pentagon have chosen to stretch-out several procurement programs and delay deployment of such systems as the B-2 bomber while pushing back the date for the initial operational capability of the Midgetman missile.

However, none of these budget scenarios have budgeted significant monies to provide for the estimated $175 billion required by the Department of Energy to clean up and improve the safety of the ageing nuclear weapons production complex. Another $35 to $50 billion would be required to complete the planned new nuclear production reactors and to renovate the balance of the military nuclear fuel cycle, if all the plans for strategic modernization were to be met.[9]

Clearly, there are very real political and economic pressures developing which are undermining the whole unilateralist strategy advanced by the Reagan Administration. The attempts to revive US leadership of the Alliance and to rehabilitate US political and economic hegemony have rested on a militarist posture. Star Wars represents a critical aspect of this strategy to reassert both US technological leadership and US dominance in the Alliance. Yet the Star Wars strategy has run up against technological and economic constraints which have necessitated a considerable scaling-back of the Reagan Administration's initially ambitious plans. As a result, it seems doubtful that Star Wars will prove to be the decisive political, technological and military strategy that was first envisioned by President Reagan. Indeed, the Star Wars budget was the one component of the DoD budget which suffered deep cuts in the FY 1990, falling by about $1 billion, from a requested $4.5 billion to $3.5 billion in budget authority.[10] Nonetheless, SDI poses a real danger to the future of bilateral restraints on space-based weapons as set forth under the Anti-Ballistic Missile Treaty of 1972.

Despite these blows to a unilateralist military posture, defense planners continue to emphasize the development of more unilateral military capabilities. Most notably, the report of the Commission on Integrated Long Term Strategy entitled *Discriminate Deterrence* calls for greater flexibility in US military capacities geared increasingly to intervention in the Third World 'to assure our adversaries that military aggression at any level of violence against our important interests will be opposed by military force'.[11] This approach aims to integrate strategies for a wide range of conflicts, from the 'lowest intensity and highest probability [conflicts] to the most widespread, apocalyptic, and least likely'.[12] While this doctrine purports to offer greater political and military stability through the use of a more 'discriminate' deterrent, this new dimension of US unilateral military projection will most likely create more instability in political and military rivalries, especially because it places such an emphasis on new military technologies which could foment a new phase of the arms race.

These developments demonstrate the need to think about a progressive initiative on US defense policy which can respond to both the new threats to and opportunities for an alternative security and disarmament policy for the United States.

CONCEPTS OF ALTERNATIVE SECURITY

In this context there are very real openings for advancing an alternative defense program based on principles of a non-provocative defense, which is non-interventionist and less nuclear-dependent. Alternative defense proposals represent an intermediate step between the current unabated dynamic of the arms race and complete and comprehensive disarmament. Alternative defense proposals call for the restructuring of military forces and the development of confidence-building measures with the aim of denuclearization and conventional arms reduction. An intermediate strategy of alternative defense could recast the terms of public discussion on national security and point the direction towards a real common security which isn't predicated on a hegemonic conception of foreign relations and military power. Further, it could lay the groundwork for a real disarmament process.

The European discussion of alternative security

Discussions of alternative defense concepts have developed both in Western Europe and, to a lesser degree, in the United States. These discussions have advanced a number of proposals which are not necessarily completely compatible. Nonetheless, there are several general concepts that have developed from the Western European debate which are relevant for the US discussion.

In Western Europe, especially Britain and West Germany, a debate has been initiated by peace activists, left political parties and Social Democratic parties on the dimensions of an alternative defense posture for Western Europe. The concept of 'defensive defense' or 'non-provocative defense' has been explored in the context of a unilateral reformulation of defense strategy for the UK, and a multilateral reformulation of defense in Western Europe, especially as it relates to West Germany.

The basic determining principle of 'defensive defense' rests on formulating a national defense posture which is non-threatening, or non-offensive in character. More precisely, the weaponry of the force structure is geared for defense by virtue of the limitations on the range, and destructive impact of its firepower. Moreover, the array of forces and troops are to be deployed so as to maximize the difficulty of a quick and short victory through the concentrated use of force by an adversary. A corollary of this posture is that forces and troops should be decentralized so that there aren't a set of distinct targets which invite preemptive first strikes by one's adversaries. Numerous variants of non-provocative defense have been developed, ranging from more radical proposals such as those for a civilian-based defense to more esoteric military concepts like defense-in-depth which have attracted the attention of NATO generals.[13] Despite important differences among these approaches to non-provocative defense – especially in regard to the extent of new types of military hardware required to implement some of them – the central principle of a truly defensively-oriented military posture has helped redirect discussion of security policy in both Western and Eastern Europe. Indeed, the Soviet Union has advanced the concept of 'reasonable sufficiency' to describe their new defense policy, and has begun to give substance to this policy by the changes in the structure of its Eastern European-based forces and troop deployments.[14]

On strategic nuclear defense, advocates of alternative defense have argued for either the elimination or reduction of the role of nuclear weapons for the defense of Europe as a whole. Research has explored a range of options, from a minimum nuclear deterrence posture to a non-nuclear defense. Proposals for the creation of denuclearized zones in central Europe and Scandinavia have been advanced as a means of removing the nuclear tripwires inherent in the current NATO doctrine of 'flexible response'; a doctrine which holds open for NATO commanders the option of escalating a conventional European land war into a tactical nuclear war.[15] These proposals are usually complemented by calls for zones of military disengagement, which require more general conventional demilitarization. Minimum nuclear deterrence proposals have come from other quarters and have emphasized the need to retain an independent Western European nuclear force that is decoupled from the US and NATO nuclear doctrine. Some advocates have proposed that the Western European nuclear force be deployed strictly as a retaliatory weapon, with a 'no first use' pledge accompanying this nuclear posture. Even some American Cold Warriors have joined in this call, as McGeorge Bundy has advanced a similar 'no first use' position for the American and NATO nuclear forces in Europe.[16] A related minimum deterrence concept has been proposed defining a threshold, or set of conditions, which when crossed would trigger a nuclear response against the aggressor. This implacable set of conditions would presumably deter an adversary from crossing the nuclear threshold.[17]

What is common to this alternative nuclear defense concepts is that they presuppose a fundamental change both in nuclear strategy and forces levels, and in the relationship between the US and the rest of the NATO countries. The salience of these issues was clear in the Western European debate and protest over the deployment of the Intermediate Nuclear Forces in the early 1980s, and in the renewed debate over the modernization of short-range nuclear weapons in NATO. The deployment of these weapons was seen as compromising the security of all Europeans in central Europe. Yet, the debate hasn't exclusively centered on nuclear weapons alone, as the modernization of conventional forces poses similar concerns.

NATO military planning for the so-called Follow-on Forces Attack concept has sought to integrate army and tactical airforces into a coordinated force through the use of new surveillance and targeting technologies which can strike distant targets with destructive new conventional weapons.[18] With the use of precision-guided munitions, this extended battlefield strategy aims to destroy Warsaw Pact targets through deep strikes using non-nuclear weapons. Thus, conventional war seems to become possible without the catastrophic consequences of nuclear weapons. Yet, the mere adoption of such a military doctrine increases the instability during a crisis situation, thereby inviting a nuclear first-strike by the Warsaw Pact forces against NATO command, control, communications and intelligence centers so as to preempt such a conventional military strike.

In the end, the adoption of such an integrated war-fighting strategy would seem to only increase instability, and compromises the common security of all of Europe. This outcome, together with similar considerations for nuclear weapons strategies, has given rise to increased discussion of the concept and dimensions of common security arrangements. The basic idea of common security is that security ultimately depends on the actions and reactions of one's opponent. Real security can only be achieved when one acknowledges the security needs of one's opponent in one's own calculations of security. This may sound like the present state of deterrence theory, yet it really represents a middle ground; one that looks beyond mere military and technological considerations to define the institutional parameters for a common security between opponents. Advocates of common security have argued that the political rivalry between East and West and the technological dynamic of the arms race have continually introduced instability into the deterrence relationship, and therefore undermined any sense of common security. For these reasons it is necessary to develop non-military means to curb the arms race and reduce tensions.[19] Yet the practical differences between common security and deterrence are perhaps clearer to those who live in central Europe, than to those on the other side of the Atlantic.

The concept of common security obviously points beyond military means for defense to various bilateral, and multilateral measures to reduce armaments, verify international agreements and develop manifold non-confrontational security arrangements. What animates this pursuit for common security is the recognition that neither side can gain a military advantage without elevating the risks to the other side, and hence to one's own side due to the threat of recourse to nuclear war.

In this sense, alternative security concepts involve the creation and development of new institutions to ensure common security through disarmament agreements, international monitoring agencies and enforcement processes. Thus, at the other end of the spectrum of alternative security concepts lie comprehensive disarmament proposals such as those that have been outlined by Grenville Clark and Louis Sohn in the 1950s and 1960s, and more recently, by Marcus Raskin of the Institute of Policy Studies in Washington, DC.[20] Clearly, the pursuit of such an approach would require a tremendous political mobilization and fundamental institutional change. It is for this reason that many proponents of alternative security have advocated that peace and progressive social movements press for numerous confidence-building measures through various unilateral, bilateral and multilateral efforts which prepare the way for more comprehensive disarmament agreements. US peace activists and alternative security advocates, however, have usually emphasized unilateral measures of military budget reductions, economic conversion and arms reduction and confidence-building measures.

Alternative security proposals in the United States

Budgetary pressures for deficit reduction have provided an economic pretext for many recent alternative security proposals in the United States. Most prominent of these are the alternative security and defense budget proposals advanced by the Black Congressional Caucus led by Congressman Ron Dellums (Democrat from Oakland, Calif.) and his colleagues over the last several years.[21] Several basic principles are set forth to define a new defense policy which would substantially reorient defense budget priorities. First, reduction of the risk of nuclear war could be achieved by restrictions on new nuclear weapons funding, and encouraging real strategic arms reduction negotiations. Second, the adoption of a non-interventionist defense posture could be accomplished by restricting further growth in forces geared to intervention in the Third World. Third, a rollback in our forward-based forces and troops in Western Europe (specifically those which have been deployed for fighting an extended land war) should improve political stability during crisis situations and remove the military incentives for a preemptive nuclear strike by Warsaw forces. Finally, the implementation of an economic conversion and planning program is necessary in order to compensate militarily-dependent regions for economic dislocations due to cutbacks in defense programs.

Based on these principles of an alternative security policy, the Dellums budget reorients the missions and objectives of the military forces toward a less provocative and more defensive posture. It is important to realize that this realignment of US military policy is being advanced on a unilateral basis, and there is no explicit linkage of these measures to further bilateral and/or multilateral arms reduction agreements.

A collateral benefit of this defense footing is that it costs less, and it was originally projected to save about $200 billion between FY 1989 and FY 1993. The proposed strategic weapons cuts would have eliminated the next round of nuclear weapons modernization, principally additional funding for the MX missile, the Trident II missile, the Trident submarine, the air- and sea-launched cruise missiles, the Midgetman missile, the Stealth bomber, SDI research, anti-satellite weapons, biological and chemical weapons research, and any further nuclear warhead production. These strategic cuts cumulatively amount to between $93 and $108 billion over the period. Offsetting these reductions are about $3 billion in additional outlays to fund the development of new arms-reduction verification capabilities.

It is noteworthy that the complete elimination of further funding for atomic defense activities would include the end to all funding for the National Laboratories which perform much of the essential research functions for new strategic weapons development. This fact is passed over without comment by Congressman Dellums in his commentary on his proposed budget. Yet, such a policy would obviously have profound implications for the dynamics of the arms race. Furthermore, the end of funding for the production of fissionable isotopes used in the production of nuclear weapons implies a regime of forced gradual disarmament. The implications of such a shutdown of the nation's nuclear weapons production capacity are not commented on by Congressman Dellums; however, some disarmament advocates have suggested this approach as a means to accomplish controlled and measured nuclear disarmament.[22]

The proposed rollback in the US forward-based military posture would affect our conventional forces and troop deployments throughout the world, but especially in Western Europe and in our ability to intervene in the Third World. These weapons and troop cuts yield the balance of the budget savings. Congressman Dellums does argue for a unilateral withdrawal of two divisions of our NATO forces, with one decommissioned and the other relocated in the US. This gesture would serve as an opening move to further negotiated bilateral reductions with the Warsaw Treaty Organization. Furthermore, modernization of our land forces in Western Europe would be cut back, so as to reduce the tensions associated with such a provocative deployment.

Our naval forces would be curtailed in keeping with a non-interventionist posture. Two planned aircraft carrier battlegroups would be cancelled, and three of the existing 13 would be phased out. In addition, the Rapid Deployment Force would be eliminated altogether. These changes in the US military posture would help to limit the potential for global force projection. Congressman Dellums does not discuss how these measures might open the way for bilateral and multilateral limitations on interventionary forces, but such a unilateral move would clearly point the way for such negotiations.

Of the several other aspects of the Dellums defense budget proposal, economic conversion funding is perhaps the most important. Congressman Dellums proposes to fund conversion planning for militarily-dependent regions as an initial step towards a more comprehensive approach to planning for alternative civilian production for military contractors. Congressman Dellums correctly recognizes the extent of economic dislocation which is possible due to large-scale cutbacks in military contracts and pay. Moreover, he recognizes the economic inertia created by the self-perpetuating military procurement cycle, which requires the development of financial and institutional incentives to overcome. We will consider the magnitude of the economic conversion problem in greater detail in the concluding section of this chapter.

Overall, the proposals of Congressman Dellums offer an important interim strategy for reshaping our current military policy. Yet, this approach requires more elaboration of the precise character and goals of unilateral confidence building measures. Moreover, an explicit linkage of these unilateral steps to reciprocal reductions by the Soviets, leading to a series of bilateral and multilateral arms reductions and verification agreements, would make this approach more systematic and politically feasible. Finally, some consideration of possible regional accords to limit regional arms races and the arms trade with developing countries should also be considered in reshaping international security assistance.

Other proposals have recently been advanced by the Center of Defense Information (CDI),[23] a Washington-based independent research organization of former military officers who are critical of US defense policy, and by Paul Walker for the World Policy Institute (WPI) in New York.[24] Both proposals share a unilateralist approach which restructures US nuclear policy along the lines of a minimum deterrence strategy which is solely based on submarine-launched ballistic missiles. Each approach argues for deploying this deterrent on the new Trident submarine; but the CDI proposal is silent on whether such deployment would exclude the use of the Trident II D-5 missile. The significance of the D-5 is its accuracy and its potential use as a first-strike weapon. Obviously, such a force-restructuring would leave open the potential for an arms race in nuclear-armed nuclear submarines. In the absence of any coherent framework for arms limitation and test ban agreements, a new anti-submarine warfare race could develop into the next century. The presumed invulnerability of nuclear submarines assumed by CDI is just another thesis for the military planners and weapons scientists to disprove. It is for these reasons that Paul Walker proposes restricting the submarine force to only two Trident II carrying vessels, while the balance of the US fleet would carry the less accurate C-3 and C-4 missiles. In addition, Walker proposes that the US and Soviets seek to negotiate an anti-submarine warfare treaty to prevent the unfolding of a new phase of the arms race.

The scale and rationale of the proposals for realigning the balance of US forces differs in the CDI and WPI studies, but both do consider a substantial rollback of US forward-based forces and troops in Europe and the Pacific. The WPI analysis sees the initial unilateral withdrawal of US forces in Western Europe as a means to promote further formal withdrawals by NATO and Warsaw Treaty Organization forces. In addition, the WPI scenario sees the withdrawal of tactical nuclear weapons as a key goal to a bilateral disengagement process in central Europe. A parallel scenario is elaborated for Korea and the Pacific, leading to formal bilateral disengagement. The CDI scenario does not explicitly consider the implications for the NATO alliance except to note that our allies can adequately defend themselves and that the increased burden-sharing is both desirable and feasible.

Naval and interventionary forces would be severely curtailed under both scenarios, with each proposing drastic reductions in the numbers of aircraft carrier battlegroups from the current planned levels of 15 to 6 (with WPI proposing a further reduction to 4 by 1999). In addition, the number of air wings would be severely cut. Both of these measures would seriously restrict and reshape the potential interventionary missions of the military. Yet, only the WPI analysis explicitly incorporates the principles of non-intervention into its considerations.

Force and troop reductions proposed by each of these scenarios would yield tremendous budget savings over time. Only the WPI analysis presents long-term estimates, with potential savings amounting to $489 billion (in current dollars) less than the current Administration plans for the 1990–94 period, and $1375 billion to 1999. These cost savings are partially offset by a proposed $1 billion increase in allocations by the US government to the UN for its peacekeeping operations, thereby strengthening this international institution as a means of resolving conflicts.

These proposals would go far to redirect current military priorities, but the recourse to a submarine-based nuclear deterrent is the most objectionable feature because it leaves open the way for another phase of the arms race, especially if an anti-submarine warfare treaty isn't negotiated. Furthermore, neither approach is really a minimum deterrence posture; for example the CDI proposal allows for 3200 warheads, while the WPI proposal would allow nearly 3800 warheads. These levels of nuclear warhead deployment far exceed the destructive potential necessary to create the so-called nuclear winter effect.[25] More generally, each approach fails to explicitly link these defense postures to a set of bilateral and multilateral arms reduction and test ban agreements which might provide the concrete means to curb the technological and political potential for further rivalry. In addition, a non-interventionist posture must be complemented by a restructuring of the goals of international security assistance and official development aid to the developing world. Without multilateral agreements to curb the destabilizing effects of regional arms races, the transfers of arms and arms production technologies, and other instruments of 'low-intensity' conflicts, there is little doubt that these regional conflicts will continue.

All of the US alternative defense proposals reviewed here were directed to a post-Reagan Administration, with the hope that such an administration would be open to new thinking on defense policy. To date, the Bush Administration has been wholly unresponsive to such proposals. And while the Bush Administration has sought to advance a policy of 'beyond containment', there has been little substance to his initiatives. Indeed, the recently proposed 80 per cent bilateral reduction in chemical weapons only makes bilateral that which is already mandated by Congress.[26] Moreover, the proposal still would permit the modernization of US and Soviet chemical weapons. Yet, it is clear the Bush Administration is committed to negotiating a START type treaty. In this context, it makes sense to evaluate the implications of such a treaty, if only to think about how to orient a counter strategy for the peace movement.

BUDGETARY SAVINGS FROM PROPOSED ARMS LIMITATION AND DISARMAMENT AGREEMENTS

Against this backdrop it is worth considering the current prospects and budgetary implications of several proposed arms reduction agreements. The two most frequently mentioned possibilities are the so-called START treaty and various conventional arms reduction agreements for central Europe.

As noted in the Introduction, the currently proposed terms of a START-type treaty would allow the full range of strategic weapons modernization. There has been very little public discussion of the implications of such 'arms control as usual'. On the strategic side of the ledger, full modernization would mean that the next phase of the arms race would proceed apace. While the total number of nuclear warheads on the US side would be reduced by 30 per cent from about 13 000 to about 9000, and the Soviets' warheads would be cut by 35 per cent from 11 000 to 7000, such reductions would not preclude the deployment of remaining warheads on new delivery systems.[27] The Administration has advertised a 50 per cent reduction from 12 000 warheads to 6000, but this figure excludes various nuclear bombs which are excluded under 'special counting', principally because of difficulties in establishing clearcut verification procedures.[28] The total number of strategic nuclear delivery vehicles would be reduced from 2000 to 1600 for the US and for the Soviets from 2475 to 1600.

Many of the strategic nuclear delivery vehicles which would be phased out under these terms have already reached the end of their expected strategic 'life cycles', and were already scheduled for replacement under modernization plans. Thus, with replacement through modernization, there will be little real budgetary savings. These savings would be limited to the modest restrictions placed on deploying fewer Trident submarines, Trident II missiles and Advanced Cruise Missiles. One calculation made by Stephen Cain of the Defense Budget Project estimates these savings at roughly $7 billion for weapons procurement over the life of the treaty (in current dollars) and another $2 billion annually in operation and support outlays over the life of the treaty.[29] However, if modernization plans were curtailed under a more ambitious START treaty, Cain estimates the savings could be more substantial, perhaps amounting to $138 billion through the 1990s.[30]

Barry Blechman, the president of Defense Forecasts, has estimated the budgetary savings which could accrue from implementing a series of bilateral arms reduction treaties that have been under discussion within the arms control and disarmament community.[31] Four major proposed treaties are evaluated in his study, including: a START treaty which would permit a slightly restricted modernization program; a conventional force reduction agreement in central Europe, leading to a 50 per cent reduction in ground and air forces in the region; a bilateral agreement to reduce non-strategic naval forces by 20 per cent; and a bilateral agreement in Northeast Asia, which on the US side would call for the removal of the US Eighth Army from Korea and two tactical air wings. In addition, Blechman considers the implications of reaffirming adherence to the Anti-Ballistic Missile Treaty so as to prohibit the deployment of strategic missile defenses.

Blechman estimates that a START-type treaty would yield average annual savings for the US of $14 billion (in 1988 dollars); this assumes full modernization of US strategic forces with cancellation of only the rail garrison based MX missile and the B-2 Stealth. Meanwhile, all older strategic systems would be phased out. A ban on strategic missile defenses would add another $17 billion per year in budget savings. A treaty on conventional forces in Europe would average $15 billion per year, while a 20 per cent bilateral reduction in naval forces would yield another $15 billion in annual savings. Finally, a conventional force reduction agreement in the Far East would save $5 billion per year for the US. Total average annual savings would amount to $66 for the US, while the Soviet Union is estimated to save roughly $73 billion per year.

None of these calculations, however, accounts for the additional verification costs which would be required to implement either of these types of disarmament agreements. A comprehensive verification regime would involve: (1) the exchange of data before and after arms reduction took place; (2) on-site inspection to verify the data exchange on weapons systems and to observe the destruction of these systems; (3) on-site monitoring arrangements at production facilities and for remaining forces; (4) and the non-interference with national technical means of verification (i.e. satellite and remote sensing devices).[32]

In the case of the INF agreement, a study conducted by Greg Bischak and Michael Oden estimated that implementing the 13-year verification regime would cumulatively cost nearly $1 billion (in 1987 dollars) over the period.[33] Comparing these verification costs with the procurement and operation and support savings over the life of the Treaty yields a net cost savings of over $7.5 billion (in 1987 dollars). Clearly, a START-type agreement, as well as many of these other proposed treaties, would involve far more verification costs than the INF treaty, and therefore the net savings from implementing such treaties would be far less than has been estimated.

Cost alone, however, is a minor consideration when shaping an alternative security and disarmament policy for the US into the next century. More importantly, increased stability through the cessation of the technological dynamic of the arms race and the building of new international institutions is essential. In this regard, it is important to go beyond traditional arms control measures to explore the implications of real disarmament measures.

Test ban treaties and bans on fissionable materials production

An end to underground nuclear testing and a ban on further missile flight testing have often been advanced by peace activists as key elements of a disarmament program to end the strategic arms race. Implementation of these two test ban treaties, it is argued, would seriously curtail the technological forces propelling the arms race, while producing additional budgetary savings. Meanwhile, the end to the production of fissionable materials by the superpowers would halt one of the most environmentally destructive aspects of the arms race. In addition, all of these measures would build new institutions of verification and would enhance political and strategic stability.

A comprehensive nuclear test ban would require extensive investments for verification technologies to monitor compliance with the treaty. The exact costs of setting up such a verification system would depend on how low the detection threshold was set for identifying underground nuclear tests.[34] Perhaps the largest single investment would be for an 'in-country' seismic monitoring system coupled with a worldwide seismic system. The technical literature on the internal or 'in-country' system suggests that as many as 25 seismic arrays would be needed, with each array made up of a dozen seismometers, with tamper-proof instruments and communication links by satellite to relay data back to the US from the Soviet Union. One high-end estimate suggests that 25 seismic arrays might cost $250 million to build and install.[35] In addition to this cost it would be necessary to upgrade the existing worldwide seismic monitoring system. These seismic systems would have to be supplemented by other monitoring means to resolve ambiguous events through use of such technologies as: photoreconnaissance satellites; atmospheric monitoring; electronic surveillance; and on-site inspections to challenge suspicious events. Practically all of these supplementary monitoring means could rely on existing technologies and capabilities.

No overall cost estimate has been advanced for such a complete verification system, but it is likely that the annual investment, operation and maintenance costs would be far less than the current $1.9 billion spent on nuclear weapons research, development and testing by the US Department of Energy.[36] Indeed, a test ban would likely yield major cost savings in the long run, since no new nuclear warhead designs could be explosively tested, which would seriously restrict efforts to develop new generations of nuclear weapons. It should be noted, however, that in an era of supercomputers, science is quickly approaching the stage where computer simulations can be used to develop, refine and test new nuclear weapons systems. The need for actual testing may have been overstated by some, especially in light of the vast data base which has been accumulated from decades of testing. Moreover, elaborate test facilities have been constructed since the Partial Test Ban Treaty of 1963 which allow for testing of nuclear weapons effects without actual explosions. Such facilities would likely expand under a comprehensive test ban regime.[37] It is for these reasons that a missile flight test ban would be essential to complement a comprehensive nuclear test ban as disarmament measures to halt the technological dynamic of the arms race.

A missile flight test ban would be a far more pervasive measure for halting the modernization of strategic weapons systems, especially since assuring the reliability of new and existing ICBMs, SLBMs and air- and sea-launched cruise missiles requires extensive testing.[38] The implementation of a missile flight test ban would involve using existing capabilities to monitor compliance with the agreement. Since both the US and the Soviet Union already monitor military missile flight tests through the use of a wide array of technologies, there would be few, if any, new investments required. These technologies include: electronic early warning surveillance satellites and imaging satellites; ground, air and space-based radar; radio and communications facilities for intercepting and relaying data; computing facilities for analyzing missile telemetry; and other ground and sea-based tracking and control facilities. Indeed, since there would be only civilian missile flight tests to monitor (principally those missiles with suspicious trajectories), the annual requirements would probably be lower than they are now. In addition, outlays for US missile flight tests would be curtailed altogether, so there would be net savings overall. But, more importantly, the technological process of continual modernization would be halted, thereby enhancing the strategic stability between the US and the Soviet Union.[39]

The US peace movement has long backed a campaign for a comprehensive nuclear test ban, but little attention has been focused on halting missile flight testing of strategic delivery vehicles. The importance of considering these two treaties as part of an overall disarmament approach is that they are mutually reinforcing means of halting the technological and institutional forces propelling the arms race. Yet, most recently, leading elements of the US peace movement have shifted their focus from a campaign for a nuclear test ban towards efforts promoting a bilateral ban on further production of fissionable materials.[40]

The recent revelations about the breakdown of the nuclear weapons complex have made increased pressure around this issue especially important. Peace activists have recognized that a failure to intervene to stop the renovation and construction of the second generation of the nuclear weapons complex would permit the military planners and nucleocrats the means to fuel the next phase of the strategic arms race. It is for these reasons that some peace activists have called for a ban on further production of such fissionable materials as plutonium, highly enriched uranium and tritium.[41]

While activists are divided over the relative merits of including tritium in such a ban, there is general consensus on the goal of stopping further investments in new production capacities, which will seriously constrain future growth in nuclear materials inventories. Halting investments in new capacity will save the nation between $30 and $50 billion dollars over the next 25 years,[42] but it will not necessarily prevent the current process of strategic modernization. With the exception of tritium supplies, proponents of these bans on fissionable materials recognize that there are currently sufficient inventories to supply the modernization requirements set forth under the Reagan Administration's original plans. Nevertheless, adequate tritium supplies for current modernization needs could probably be assured by the negotiation of a START treaty.[43] Thus, a START treaty together with a fissionable materials ban (including tritium) could function as another round of 'arms control as usual' which could provide military planners with the means to continue the strategic arms race. Indeed, one could argue that, given the DOE's fiscal problems stemming from the environmental crisis of the nuclear weapons complex, a production ban and a START treaty could relax the fiscal constraints imposed on the DOE. Meanwhile the DOE could enhance its legitimacy among the general populace by endorsing another round of arms control.

It is precisely because arms control and limitation agreements have often functioned to economically rationalize the arms race, that some US peace activists argued for a more comprehensive approach to disarmament. Such a comprehensive disarmament approach would entail measures to halt the technological and political rivalries which give impetus to the arms race. Central to this approach is the construction of new international institutions to resolve conflicts and to enforce and monitor a multilateral disarmament process which would take place in a stepwise fashion over time.[44] The setting of such a serious disarmament agenda requires an examination of the more comprehensive bilateral and multilateral arms reduction and disarmament proposals put forward since 1962.[45] It is beyond the scope of this chapter to review these proposals here, but the historical record, together with the more recent draft treaties on comprehensive disarmament, provide, I believe, the conceptual basis for such a program.[46]

Yet all of these approaches to disarmament and alternative security face considerable political and economic opposition from the entrenched interests which support the current security policies in the United States. And while the traditional Cold War forces supporting current security policies may be weakening, the economic support for continuing business as usual remains formidable. Indeed, the economic impacts of adopting the more comprehensive alternative security and disarmament positions would be considerable. For this reason, many peace and disarmament activists have recognized that economic conversion planning would be necessary to mitigate the negative economic repercussions of adopting these policies.

DISARMAMENT AND ECONOMIC CONVERSION

For decades peace activists throughout the western world have argued for the need to address the economic repercussions of major disarmament initiatives, yet few have studied the economic implications of such disarmament and alternative security proposals. At most, peace researchers have focused on the budgetary savings that might accrue from adopting one arms limitation or reduction proposal. However, no one to date has examined the industrial and economic effects of adopting a wide-ranging set of disarmament or alternative security proposals. Examination of these economic impacts would reveal the scale and scope of the political and economic problems associated with advancing such a comprehensive disarmament and alternative security program. Indeed, the failure of current arms limitation negotiations to substantially curtail strategic and conventional weapons modernization, brings into question the underlying economic forces fueling the technological dynamic of the arms race.

Nowhere is this clearer than in the case of the proposed START treaty for strategic weapons limitation. As noted at the outset, it will permit practically the full range of strategic modernization, while cutting nuclear warhead deployments by about 32 per cent for the United States. Thus, such an arms limitation treaty would not constitute significant disarmament since it would give further impetus to the arms race, while protecting the economic interests which prosper from it. Indeed, the economic implications of the START proposals demonstrate why, to date, there has been so little interest among policymakers for concrete economic conversion planning.

In an effort to assess the approximate economic effects of arms control as opposed to disarmament, I examine the economic impacts of two fundamentally different strategic arms reduction proposals: one which permits full modernization; another which halts strategic modernization and instead charts a path to a minimum deterrence posture. I choose to examine this proposal because it highlights most dramatically the different implications of arms control versus disarmament. This is not to suggest that this proposal is necessarily the best or most comprehensive, or even on the agenda, but rather for purposes of calculating the economic effects, it is most readily detailed.

A START treaty with modernization

As noted above, the current negotiating proposals for a START treaty would permit the deployment of the next generation of ICBMs, SLBMs, strategic bombers and air- and sea-launched cruise missiles by the US and Soviet Union. According to the Congressional Budget Office (CBO), if the US adopted a fully modernized approach to implementing the START treaty it would mean that the budgetary savings would accrue primarily from retiring older systems and the resulting lower operation and support costs. The CBO estimates that such an approach would yield an annual average saving of about $2 billion (in 1988 dollars) in operations and support costs.[47]

In an effort to estimate the short-run costs of implementing such a START proposal, I develop estimates covering the 1991–94 period. I develop a variant of another CBO scenario, since it is clear that both the MX silo-based ICBM and MX rail garrison missile will be deployed.[48] Moreover, the deployment period for the B-2 Stealth bomber and the Midgetman mobile missile has been delayed into the late 1990s, and it is unclear whether or not they will be fully deployed. Nonetheless, both programs remain funded, albeit at slightly lower levels for RDT&E. The scenario for START is laid out in Table 5.2 and assumes that all systems currently planned will eventually be deployed, but during the first four years of treaty implementation, 1991–94, the B-1B, B-52H and Minuteman III missiles will be retained until the newer systems replace them in the last half of the decade. Limits on total warheads deployed are 6000 for each side, and the sublimits assume 4900 ballistic missiles, 3000 of which are ICBMs, with only 1600 strategic nuclear delivery systems (SNDVs) permitted. Moreover, sea-launched cruise missiles are not included in this scenario because they have not, to date, been included in the START negotiations. Under these assumptions, this scenario is examined for its budgetary and economic impacts over the 1991–4 period.

In Table 5.2, one should note that the imputed total number of strategic nuclear warheads (10 764) is based on the nominal capacity of each strategic nuclear delivery vehicle (SNDV) under the 'special counting' rules, which yields a number that is less than the estimated total of 13 275 strategic nuclear weapons. Moreover, while the B-1B counts under the 'special counting' rules as one SNDV, it is actually deployed in a penetrating role with 8 gravity bombs and 16 SRAM II missiles. Thus the actual number of nuclear warheads on all 90 B-1Bs is 2160 which raises the total number of deployed warheads to 12 834. In addition, in the scenario considered here the B-52H force is in a standoff role where it is assumed to be carrying only 12 externally mounted advanced air-launched cruise missiles (ACMs). However, a sufficient number of B-52H bombers may have already been modernized to permit the internal carriage of 8 additional ACMs, thereby raising each bomber's overall capacity to 20. Thus, putting aside the 'special counting' rules, the maximum number of deliverable nuclear weapons by bombers in the 1990 scenario may be as high as 4800. This raises the total number of nuclear warheads deployed in 1990 to about 13 554, which is higher than the stockpile estimate in Table 5.3. Thus, counting the maximum feasible load on the bombers in the 1994 scenario reveals that there may be as many as 3860 warheads on the strategic bomber force. This raises the actual number of warheads in 1994 to about 8746 which amounts to a real reduction by about 35 per cent over the 1990 levels.

Turning to the economic implications of this scenario, *outlays*,

Table 5.2   Interim US strategic force structures under proposed START
Treaty with full modernization

Kind of vehicle	1990 Force structure		1994 Force structure	
	SNDVs	Warheads	SNDVs	Warheads
ICBMs				
MX silo-based	50	500	50	500
MX rail garrison	0	0	50	500
Minuteman II	450	450	0	0
Minuteman III	500	1 500	250	750
Midgetman	0	0	0	0
Subtotal	1 000	2 450	350	1 750
Bomber				
B–1B (penetrate)*	90	90	90	90
B–52H (standoff)	90	1 080	85	1 020
B–52G (standoff)	70	840	0	0
FB–111A (standoff)	48	288	0	0
B–2	0	0	0	0
Subtotal	298	2 298	175	1 110
SLBMs				
Poseidon C–3	256	2 560	0	0
Poseidon C–4	192	1 536	32	256
Trident C–4	192	1 536	192	1 536
Trident D–5	48	384	168	1 344
Subtotal	688	6 016	392	3 136
Imputed Total	1 986	10 764	917	5 996
Nuclear stockpile estimate	–	13 275	–	–

* Penetrating bombers each count as one SNDV under 'special counting'
rules, whereas standoff bombers are counted as having their maximum
number of externally-carried cruise missiles.

Sources: Nuclear stockpile estimate is from 'Nuclear Notebook', *Bulletin of
the Atomic Scientist*, June 1989, p. 49. Other calculations from, *Nuclear
Weapons Databook, Vol. 1, U.S. Nuclear Forces and Capabilities*, T. Cochran,
et. al. (Cambridge, Mass.: Ballinger, 1984); *Modernizing U.S. Strategic
Offensive Forces: Costs, Effects and Alternatives* (Washington, DC: CBO,
November, 1987); *Strategic Defenses: Alternative Missions and Their Costs*
(Washington, DC: CBO, June 1989), Table C–1, p. 76.

rather than *Budget Authority* are used in estimating the budgetary effects, because it is actual spending which affects economic activity. The budgetary savings are estimated as the difference between projected procurement[49] and operation and support[50] (O&S) outlays without a START treaty versus procurement and O&S outlays with a treaty implemented over the period beginning in 1991. The projected baseline for strategic deployments is taken from the CBO.[51] The only procurement savings come from curtailment of modifications on the B-52H/G and the FB-111A strategic bombers. All other savings arise from lower O&S costs resulting from the retirements of most of these bombers and most of the Poseidon submarines. I estimate that the annual average savings over the 1991–4 period amount to $2.1 billion as measured in 1987 dollars. Over the life of the Treaty the annual average savings would likely be higher than this four-year estimate.

These reductions in O&S and procurement outlays were modeled as demand shocks resulting in lower purchases by the services from a specific mix of industrial sectors. The composition of industrial demands for operations and maintenance, personnel appropriations, and specific types of procurement were derived from the US Department of Defense's *Defense Translator*.[52] This weapons system translator breaks out the industrial proportions of demand for major weapons. The industrial aggregation of each weapon and O&M translator was adapted for use with the more highly-aggregated 39 × 39 industrial sectors of the RIMS II input–output multipliers.[53] By using these RIMS II multipliers for the appropriate industrial sectors in each translator one can model the direct, indirect and induced economic impacts on output, earnings and employment for all the major industrial and service sectors affected by the respective demand reductions. Since the RIMS II multipliers are for 1987, the spending reductions were deflated to 1987 dollars.[54]

The economic impacts from this method yield *static measures* of the *average annual impact* of these demand changes. While it would be better to use a dynamic input–output model to capture the marginal adjustments which would occur over time, this method provides a reasonable, relatively inexpensive, approximation of the overall effect.[55]

Table 5.3 summarizes the economic impacts of adopting a full modernization approach to implementing a START treaty. As one can see, the overall impact of these contract reductions is relatively modest, yielding a total average annual loss in output of over $5 billion, and over 108 000 jobs on an annual average basis during

Table 5.3 Estimated economic impacts of a full modernization approach to implementing a START treaty

	Impact on output (millions) ($1987)	Total employment effect (thousands)	Direct employment effect (thousands)
O&M spending reductions (−$1 120)	−$2 916	−49 291	−19 324
Personnel spending reductions (−$911)	−$2 105	−55 128	−26 820
Modification spending reductions (−$110)	−$373	−4 363	−970
Total	−$5 394	−108 782	−47 114

the period. Reducing these estimates by about 15 per cent provides a lower bound estimate of about $4.25 billion in annual losses in output and an average job loss of over 92 000.[56] Direct job losses comprise about 43 per cent of the total job losses, with the balance being comprised by indirect and induced job losses due to reduced purchases by prime contractors of intermediate goods and subcontracting services, as well as the reduced spending by workers.

These relatively small losses in output, earnings and jobs occur principally because of reductions in DoD personnel. Thus, the primary conversion and adjustment planning problem would come from reemploying civilian and military DoD personnel affected by these reductions. There may be some need for some regional economic assistance to adjust for the indirect and induced effects from these layoffs and the lower level of spending. However, these losses pale by comparison to those flowing from a disarmament approach to a START treaty.

A START treaty based on a disarmament approach

Adopting a disarmament approach geared to halting the technological dynamic of the arms race would result in an entirely different strategic force structure under a proposed START treaty. Instead of permitting full modernization, this alternative approach seeks to halt modernization of nuclear forces and achieve a real 50 per cent reduction in the size of the nuclear arsenal. In the longer run, this approach could replace the much-vaunted triad of strategic weapons – a primordial vestige of postwar inter-service rivalry, rather than strategic assessments – with a dyad based on ballistic missile submarines and bombers functioning in a standoff role. The archaic land-based ICBM could eventually be eliminated altogether (indeed, one might ask what is the purpose of deploying the rail garrison-based MX missile when it takes four hours to deploy for launch, according to Dr Lawrence Woodruff, Deputy Under-Secretary for Strategic and Theater Nuclear Forces).[57] Moreover, the structure of this approach could lay the basis for making a transition to a minimum deterrence posture for US and Soviet nuclear forces, culminating in an arsenal with perhaps no more than 2000 nuclear warheads on each side.[58]

The force structure under this START scenario is outlined in Table 5.4, which shows that the bulk of land-based ICBMs are eliminated by 1994, with only the silo-based MX missile remaining. Moreover, the Midgetman program is terminated. The B-1B bomber is deployed in a standoff role carrying 22 advanced air-launched cruise missiles (ACMs). The B-52H/Gs are phased out in their standoff role. In the arcane world of arms control and 'special counting' rules, the B-1B is counted as having more strategic nuclear warheads when deployed in its standoff role, while in its penetrating role – where it may actually be armed with 24 warheads – it counts as only one strategic nuclear delivery vehicle per bomber.

The ballistic missile submarine force is reduced by retiring half of the Poseidon submarines, particularly those carrying the older C-3 missiles. Meanwhile, the Trident submarines deployed with the newer D-5 missile are scheduled in this scenario to be backfit to accept the C-4 missile – a missile which is not considered to be a first-strike weapon. Thus, the funds originally allotted to backfit three of the C-4 carrying Tridents with the newer D-5 are instead used to backfit two of the D-5 Trident subs to carry C-4 missiles.[59] In addition, all scheduled outlays for building more Trident submarines are cancelled under this scenario, Thus, depending on how many nuclear warheads one assumes are actually deployed today (i.e. 12 654 versus 13 275), the strategic warhead count in 1994 may represent a real reduction under this START proposal of between 53 per cent and 55 per cent.

Table 5.4   Interim US strategic force structures under proposed START treaty without modernization

Kind of vehicle	1990 Force structure		1994 Force structure	
	SNDVs	Warheads	SNDVs	Warheads
ICBMs				
MX silo-based	50	500	50	500
MX rail garrison	0	0	0	0
Minuteman II	450	450	0	0
Minuteman III	500	1 500	0	0
Midgetman	0	0	0	0
Subtotal	1 000	2 450	50	500
Bomber				
B–1B (standoff)*	90	1 980	81	1 782
B–52H (standoff)	90	1 080	0	0
B–52G (standoff)	70	840	0	0
FB–111A (standoff)	48	288	0	0
B–2	0	0	0	0
Subtotal	298	4 188	81	1 782
SLBMs				
Poseidon C–3	256	2 560	0	0
Poseidon C–4	192	1 536	224	1 792
Trident C–4	192	1 536	240	1 920
Trident D–5	48	384	0	0
Subtotal	688	6 016	464	3 712
Imputed Total	1 986	12 654	595	5 994
Nuclear Stockpile Estimate	–	13 275	–	–

* The B–1 is counted as carrying 22 ACMs in its standoff configuration. Therefore, the imputed number of nuclear warheads in 1990 is higher in this scenario than in Table 5.2.

Sources: Nuclear stockpile estimate is from 'Nuclear Notebook', *Bulletin of the Atomic Scientist*, June 1989, p. 49. Other calculations from, *Nuclear Weapons Databook, Vol. 1, U.S. Nuclear Forces and Capabilities*, T. Cochran, et. al. (Cambridge, Mass.: Ballinger, 1984); and *Modernizing U.S. Strategic Offensive Forces: Costs, Effects and Alternatives* (Washington, D.C.: CBO, November, 1987); *Strategic Defenses: Alternative Missions and Their Costs* (Washington, DC: CBO, June 1989), Table C–1, p. 76.

Given these assumptions, the total projected budgetary savings in procurements, R&D, operations and maintenance, personnel costs, and military construction would amount to an annual average of $12.7 billion (in 1987 dollars) in outlays. These estimated savings are very conservative since they include outlays from Budget Authority allocated beginning in 1990 and do not include spendout from Budget Authority in prior years. Therefore actual savings in both outlays and Budget Authority would probably be much higher. Nevertheless, the majority of the savings come from procurement and R&D which comprise an annual average of $10.5 billion of the total, while reductions in operations and support costs account for $2.2 billion annually.

In order to evaluate the industrial impacts of these reductions in outlays, I present in Table 5.5 the economic impacts in terms of their effects on each of the 30 major industry groups analyzed in this study. While this presentation differs from that in Table 5.3, the bottom lines of each category are comparable. The virtue of this approach is that it allows one to see in some detail the industrial sectors which would be most affected by the implementation such a disarmament program.

As Table 5.5 shows, the impact on output would amount to an average of nearly $40 billion annually, with earnings reduced by nearly $11.1 billion on average. Job losses would be considerable, amounting to an annual average of nearly 510 000 over the period, with about 142 000 attributable to losses from direct layoffs, while the balance would be due to indirect job losses and induced job losses from lower levels of spending. While marginal economic adjustments would occur over time through reductions in overtime and fewer new hires by businesses in these industries, the overall impact of such a disarmament program would be considerable. Indeed, reducing these figures by 15 per cent yields a lower bound estimate of an annual average of over 433 000 jobs, and an average reduction in output of nearly $34 billion. However, as noted above, even without adjusting these estimates they are probably conservative because of the method used to project outlays savings.

As Table 5.5 shows, the direct impacts are especially concentrated within specific industries, such as the rest of transportation equipment sector, comprised by aerospace and shipbuilding; the electrical and electronic equipment industries; machinery; scientific instruments; and the chemicals industries. These industry groups would

Table 5.5   Industrial effects of a disarmament approach to a START treaty

Industry aggregate	Output effect (*$millions*)	Total employment (*thousands*)	Direct employment (*thousands*)
New construction	189.41	2 574	708
Maintenance and repair	125.26	1 848	649
Food and kindred products	45.60	484	60
Apparel	17.82	263	94
Paper and allied products	4.38	45	8
Printing and publishing	8.44	111	34
Chemicals and petrol	3 065.54	24 078	2 846
Rubber and leather products	6.70	76	22
Lumber and furniture	15.93	205	57
Stone, clay and glass	14.04	168	46
Primary metals	19.12	190	35
Fabricated metal products	212.93	2 411	614
Machinery, except elec.	1 197.12	13 777	3 312
Electrical and elec. equip.	8 922.98	108 502	28 843
Motor vehicles	197.38	1 836	218
Transportation equip.	19 941.55	231 967	50 367
Instruments and other	1 830.95	21 601	5 799
Misc. manufacturing	93.75	1 212	398
Transportation services	346.86	5 016	1 734
Communications, exc. TV	90.89	1 018	301
Utilities	34.82	262	36
Wholesales	75.97	1 090	388
Real estate	10.82	194	89
Hotels and lodging	26.68	478	219
Personal services	3.31	81	51
Business services	127.60	2 236	1 034
Eating and drinking	24.57	469	248
Health services	42.03	701	302
Misc. services	247.57	3 828	1 521
Households (includes govt. employment)	2 850.59	82 918	42 187
TOTAL	39 790.62	509 638	142 221

feel the most pronounced direct effects from major contract reductions. However, while the indirect and induced effects flowing from the reduced purchases would be partially felt within each of these industry groups, one should interpret secondary employment impacts (i.e. total employment less the direct employment effect) as the overall result of indirect and induced losses occurring from a shock to a particular industry, which in turn affects other industries. Thus, with the data presented here, one cannot determine how much of the indirect and induced effects occurs within a particular industry; rather, the secondary effects only show how much dislocation occurs as a result of a shock to a particular industry.

Geographical agglomerations of military industry within states and regions would undoubtedly amplify the impacts of these reductions in local economies. And while sub-contracting by prime contractors may disperse the effects of reductions on the prime contractors themselves, the existence of well-developed sub-contracting chains within states and regions tends to act as a centripetal force keeping these sub-contracts within the region. This phenomenon is reflected in the well-known agglomerations of military industry in such areas as Southern California, with its military aerospace and defense electronics corridor running from San Diego to Los Angeles. Massachusetts, Connecticut, Florida, Missouri and several other states exhibit similar regional agglomerations of military-serving industries. These regional agglomerations tend to amplify the effects of military spending reductions as the indirect effects of reduced purchases ripple out into the regional industrial economy, inducing further reductions in regional income and employment.[60]

It should be noted that this study of the effects of different approaches to a START treaty has not examined the ramifications of greatly-reduced activity within the nuclear weapons complex. Clearly, a treaty on the order of a scenario without modernization would have wide-ranging repercussions within the whole nuclear weapons complex.[61] Nor has this approach examined the implications of halting the deployment of nuclear armed sea-launched cruise missiles. Moreover, this study has not factored in the additional verification costs which would have to be incurred to implement either of these START scenarios. Obviously, such verification activities would partially offset the adverse economic effects of implementing any START-type treaty.

CONCLUSION

As the foregoing economic impact analysis shows, the implications of adopting a comprehensive alternative to the current US security and arms control policies would result in widespread economic dislocation within the manufacturing and service sectors of the economy.

These adverse effects would be far more pronounced in militarily-dependent regions and would require both regional and national economic conversion planning to mitigate. While compensatory federal and local spending may partially offset the aggregate effects of reductions in military spending, such compensatory policies would not necessarily redound to the benefit of the affected industries and regions. Moreover, using the savings from military cutbacks for deficit reduction would not stimulate the economy in the short run, nor would it directly compensate the affected sectors. Impacts of this scale and scope would require a comprehensive national framework for economic conversion planning on the order of the proposed legislation by Congressman Ted Weiss (Democrat, NY).[62] One of the main objectives of this proposed economic conversion legislation is to promote *decentralized* solutions to the economic dislocations resulting from reductions in military spending and disarmament initiatives.

While conversion legislation of this scope could address the economic effects of a fundamental restructuring of our security policy, the economic interests that would be affected by these changes are still wedded to business as usual. In order to overcome this opposition, it is critical that the peace movement advance a coherent analysis of the dimensions of a peaceful economy. In this regard, economic conversion analysis should be a key element of any alternative security and disarmament policies advanced by the peace movement. It is not sufficient to show that disarmament and alternative security policies will save the country money; instead, the movement must analyze the implications and alternatives to the militarized economy.

Significant changes in the character and direction of the internationalization of capital and the policies of 'actually existing socialism' should provoke a reexamination by political economists of the structural determinants of the arms race. Alternative conceptions of security and defense constitute an important area of research for the peace movement, and progressive political economists can contribute to this effort by examining the economic dimensions of a peace economy. Ignoring changes or resorting to habitual modes of analysis will only limit our capacity to stimulate popular pressure to end the arms race and begin the process of social and environmental reconstruction.

Notes

1. See *START and Strategic Modernization*, by Robert Norris, William Arkin, and Thomas Cochran, Natural Resources Defense Council, Washington, DC, December 1987, pp. 14–16.
2. See 'Warning: Military Spending May not be Bad For Your Economic Health: Some Thoughts on Conversion' by Juliet Schor, in *Radical America*, Vol. 21, no. 1, January 1987. Also see 'Capitalism and the Military Industrial Complex: the Obstacles to Conversion' by Michael Reich and David Finkelhor, *The Review of Radical Political Economics*, Winter 1973, Vol. 2, no. 4 and 'Converting Military Spending to Social Welfare: The Real Obstacles to Conversion' by Richard DuBoff, *The Quarterly Review of Economics and Business*, 1972.
3. See *Defense Without the Bomb*, by the Alternative Defense Commission, Taylor and Francis, London, 1983. Also see 'Alternative Defense Policies and the Peace Movement' by Ben Dankbaar in the *Journal of Peace Research*, Vol. 21, no. 2, 1984, pp. 141–55.
4. See *Gorbachev's Force Reductions and the Restructuring of Soviet Defense Forces*, Hearings before the Defense Policy Panel of the House Armed Services Committee, 100th Congress, 1st Session, 10 and 14 March 1989. Also see *New Thinking in Soviet Defense Policy: New Opportunities for US Arms Control Initiatives*, a report by the Committee for National Security Arms Control Task Force, May 1989, Washington, DC.
5. See 'U.S. Split Over Rise in Allies Loans to Soviets' by Clyde Farnsworth, *New York Times*, 21 October 1988, A-1.
6. See 'Cutting Arms in Europe: It's Down to the Details' by Michael Gordon, *The New York Times*, 9 March 1989, A-6.
7. See 'Bush Cuts '91 Military Plans' by Michael Gordon, *The New York Times*, 7 December 1989, A-19.
8. See *Making Appropriations for the DoD for Fiscal Year Ending September 30, 1990 and for Other Purposes*, Conference Report, House of Representatives, 101st Congress, 1st Session, pp. 35–56 and 57–95.
9. See *Environment, Safety and Health Needs of the U.S. Department of Energy, Vol. 1, Assessment of Needs, and Vol. 2, Site Summaries*, US DOE (DOE/EH-0079), December 1988. Also see *U.S. DOE Fiscal Year 1990 Budget Highlights*, Assistant Secretary of Management and Administration, Office of Comptroller, January 1989 (DOE/MA-0357) pp. 31–62.
10. See *New Technologies Across the Atlantic: U.S. Leadership or European Autonomy*, by Mario Pianta, Wheatsheaf Books, London, 1988, pp. 129–45. See also *Strategic Defenses: Alternative Missions and Their Costs*, Congressional Budget Office, June 1988, Washington, DC. Also see *Making Appropriations for the DoD for Fiscal Year Ending September 30, 1990 and for Other Purposes*, Conference Report, House of Representatives, 101st Congress, 1st Session, pp. 115–18, for details on cuts in the Star Wars programs.
11. See *Discriminate Deterrrence* by the Commission on Integrated Long Term Strategy, January 1988, Washington, DC, US GPO, p. 64.

12. Ibid.
13. See Dankbaar, 'Alternative Defense Policies', op. cit. for a good review of these discussions.
14. See 'The Soviet Proposal for European Security' by Dimitri Yazov, *The Bulletin of the Atomic Scientists*, September 1988, pp. 8–11. Also see President Mikhail Gorbachev's address to the United Nations, 7 December 1988, as reprinted in *The New York Times*, 8 December 1988, p. A-6.
15. See 'Nuclear Weapons Free Central Europe' by J. Goldblat in *The Bulletin of Peace Proposals*, Vol. 17, nos 3–4, 1986, Norwegian University Press, Oslo, Norway, pp. 415–18. Also see 'Nuclear Disengagement in Europe' by S. Lodgaard, *The Bulletin of Peace Proposals*, Vol. 17, nos 3–4, 1986, pp. 409–18.
16. See McGeorge Bundy, 'Nuclear Weapons and the Atlantic Alliance', *Foreign Affairs*, Vol. 60, no. 4, pp. 753–68.
17. See Dankbaar, 'Alternative Defense Policies', op. cit.
18. For a discussion of the NATO Follow-on Forces Attack doctrine and AirLand battleplan, see 'Defending Post-INF Europe' by Jeffery Record and David Rivkin, in *Foreign Affairs*, Vol. 66, no. 4 1988, pp. 735–54. Also see Dankbaar, 'Alternative Defense Policies', op. cit.
19. See 'The Concept of Common Security' by Frank Blackaby, et al. in *The Bulletin of Peace Proposals*, Vol. 17, nos 3–4, pp. 395–408.
20. For a discussion of the framework first advanced by Clarke and Sohn see Chapter 4 of *The Conquest of War* by Harry Hollis, Averill Powers and Mark Sommers, Westview Press, Boulder, Colorado, 1989, pp. 38–53. For a detailed exposition of the framework proposed by Marcus Raskin, see *Draft Treaty for a Comprehensive Program for Common Security and General Disarmament*, by Marcus Raskin, Institute of Policy Studies, Washington, DC July 1986. Also, see *An Introduction to Disarmament* by Robert Krinsky, National Commission for Economic Conversion and Disarmament, Washington, DC, May 1988.
21. See 'Toward Increased Defense Sense' by Ronald Dellums and Daniel Lindheim, in *Winning America*, edited by Marcus Raskin and Chester Hartman, South End Press and Institute of Policy Studies, 1988, pp. 302–15.
22. See *The Tritium Factor* by the Nuclear Control Institute, Washington, DC, December 1988. For a short overview, see 'The Tritium Factor' by Paul Leventhal and Milton Hoenig in the *New York Times*, 4 August 1988.
23. See 'What is Ours to Defend?' by Gene La Rocque, in *Harpers*, July 1988, pp. 39–50.
24. See *American Priorities in A New World Era* by the World Policy Institute, New York, 1989, especially pp. 10–20 and the technical appendix. For an earlier version, see 'A Post-Reagan Military Posture' by Paul Walker, in *Post-Reagan America* by the World Policy Institute, New York, 1987.
25. See *The Aftermath: The Human and Ecological Consequences of Nuclear War* edited by Jennie Peterson for *Ambio*, Pantheon Books, New York, 1983, pp. 74–93. Also see 'New Models Confirm Nuclear Winter' by

Alan Robock, *Bulletin of the Atomic Scientist*, September 1989, pp. 32–35.

26. See 'Bush Offers to Slash Chemical Weapons by 80% if Soviets Accept Cap on Total' by Michel McQueen, *Wall Street Journal*, 26 September, 1989, p. A-26.
27. Norris, *START*, op. cit. p. 13.
28. Ibid.
29. See *The START Agreement: Strategic Options and Budgetary Savings* by Stephan Alexis Cain, Defense Budget Project, Washington, DC, July 1988, p. 3.
30. Cain, *The START Agreement*, op. cit.
31. See 'A $100 Billion Understanding' by Barry Blechman and Ethan Gutmann, *SAIS*, Vol. 9, no. 2, Summer/Fall, pp. 73–99.
32. For a discussion of these aspects of an arms limitation treaty see 'The INF Treaty and the United States' Experience: The Industrial, Economic and Employment Impacts' by Gregory Bischak and Michael Oden, Working Paper No. 11, Disarmament and Employment Programme, International Labour Office, Geneva, April 1989, pp. 1–12.
33. Ibid, pp. 10–12.
34. For a discussion of the importance of threshold requirements for verification procedures of a comprehensive test ban see *Toward a Comprehensive Test Ban* by Steve Fetter, Ballinger, Cambridge, MA, 1988, pp. 107–58.
35. Ibid, p. 116.
36. See *U.S. Department of Energy Budget, FY 1990, Budget Highlights*, Comptroller, January 1989, Washington, DC, p. 24.
37. See *Nuclear Weapons Databook, Vol. II, U.S. Nuclear Warhead Production*, by Thomas Cochran, et al., Ballinger, Cambridge, MA 1987, pp. 51–6. Also see 'Test Ban Fever' by William Arkin, *Bulletin of the Atomic Scientist*, October 1986, pp. 4–5.
38. Ibid.
39. Ibid.
40. See, *The Tritium Factor*, op. cit. Also see Senate Bill 1047, 101st Congress, 1st Session, *International Plutonium Control Act*. In addition see testimony before the Senate Budget Committee, March 1989, by David Culp, Coordinating Director of the Plutonium Challenge. Finally, see *International Plutonium Control Act: The U.S. Has Little to Lose and Much to Gain*, by David Albright, Federation of American Scientists,̈ Washington, DC, 30 June, 1989.
41. Ibid.
42. Ibid.
43. Ibid.
44. Krinsky, *Introduction to Disarmament*, op. cit.
45. Ibid.
46. Raskin, *Draft Treaty*, op. cit.
47. See *Modernizing U.S. Strategic Offensive Forces: Costs, Effects, and Alternatives*, Congressional Budget Office, US Government Printing Office, Washington, DC, November 1987, p. 43.

48. See, *Strategic Defense: Alternative Missions and Their Costs*, Congressional Budget Office, US GPO, June, 1989, Appendix C, Table C-1, p. 76. Also see '50 MX Missiles to be Shifted to Trains in 7 States' by Bernard Trainor, *The New York Times*, 30 November 1989, p. A-1. The scenario in Table 5.2 assumes that each B-1B is armed with 8 SRAMS and 16 gravity bombs; that each B-52H/G is armed with 12 ALCMs; that there are 16 Poseidon subs carrying 16 C-3 missiles on each sub; that there are 8 Poseidon subs carrying 16 C-4 missiles on each sub; that eight of the Trident subs are carrying 24 C-4 missiles and that two Trident subs are carrying 24 D-5 missiles.

49. Projected procurements are taken from the Congressional Budget Office report *Selected Weapons Costs From President Reagan's 1990–1991 Program*, 17 April 1989, Washington, DC, US CBO. The projected procurements for the B-2 Stealth bomber were taken from *CRS Issue Brief: B-2 Advanced Technology Bomber*, by Dagnija Sterste-Perkins, Foreign Affairs and National Defense Division, Congressional Research Service, Library of Congress, 21 August 1989. All other outlays figures were taken from the Department of Defense's *Procurement Program (P-1)* and *Research, Development, Testing and Evaluation (R-1) for Fiscal Years 1990–91*, US Department of Commerce, National Technical Information Service, Springfield, Virginia, January 1989. All costs were deflated to 1987 dollars as derived from the *National Defense Budget Estimates for Fiscal Year 1990/91*, Office of the Assistant Secretary of Defense (Comptroller), Washington, DC, March 1989, Table 5–8, pp. 52–3.

50. Operation and support costs for the US Air Force's strategic systems are derived from *U.S. Air Force Cost and Planning Factors* (AFR-173-13), 9 March 1988, National Technical Information Service, Springfield, Virginia, Table 7-2, and from the September 1986 edition, Tables 7-4 and 7-7. Trident submarine O&S costs were derived from *Trident II Missiles: Capabilities, Costs and Alternatives*, Congressional Budget Office, Washington, DC, July 1986, Table 4. Poseidon costs were taken from *The Nuclear Weapons Databook Vol. 1, U.S. Nuclear Forces and Capabilities*, Thomas Cochran, et al., Ballinger, Cambridge, Mass, 1984, p. 135.

51. Projected strategic deployments were taken from *Modernizing U.S. Strategic Offensive Forces: Costs, Effects, and Alternatives*, Congressional Budget Office, US Government Printing Office, Washington, DC, November 1987, Tables C-1 through C-5, pp. 81–7.

52. *The Defense Translator*, Prepared for the Secretary of Defense, Director of Program Analysis and Evaluation, by W. Thomas, M. Sheridan, P. Richanbach and David Blond, of The Institute of Defense Analysis, Alexandria, Virginia, June 1984.

53. See *Regional Multipliers: A User's Handbook for the Regional Input–Output Modeling System (RIMS II)*, US Department of Commerce, Bureau of Economic Analysis, May 1986, Washington, DC for a discussion of the input–output model and multipliers. These multipliers were updated with the 1987 multipliers for the United States economy

which are available for a charge from the US Bureau of Economic Analysis, Regional Economic Analysis Division, Washington, DC.

54. All outlay data was deflated to 1987 dollars using deflators derived from the *National Defense Budget Estimates for Fiscal Year 1990/91*, Office of the Assistant Secretary of Defense (Comptroller), Washington, DC, March 1989, Table 5-8, pp. 52–3.

55. Comparison of dynamic input–output estimates of a one-billion dollar demand shock to the rest of transportation equipment industry group using the REMI FS-53 input–output model (see 'The TFS Regional Modeling Methodology' in *Regional Studies*, 19, 1985 by George Treyz and Ben Stevens, pp. 547–62 for documentation of this model) yields estimates of 34 460 jobs for the base year 1987. The RIMS II estimates for the same industrial aggregation and base year yield estimates of 39 700 jobs from a one-billion dollar shock. Thus, there seems to be about a 15 per cent difference between static and dynamic estimates in this case.

56. Ibid.

57. See Hearings on *National Defense Authorization Act for Fiscal Years 1988/89, HR 1748, and Oversight of Previously Authorized Program*, before the Committee on Armed Services, House of Representatives, 1st Session, 100th Congress, 3–25 March 1987, p. 328.

58. A thorough discussion of the logic and structure of the minimum deterrence posture is outlined in 'Reducing U.S. and Soviet Nuclear Arsenals' by Harold Feiveson, Richard Ullman and Frank von Hippel, *Bulletin of the Atomic Scientist*, August 1985, pp. 144–50. For an even more far-reaching approach see *Blundering Towards Disaster* by Robert McNamara, Pantheon Books, New York, 1986, p. 143.

59. For an analysis of the projected backfitting costs for converting C-4 capable Trident subs to D-5 missiles capabilities see *Trident II Missiles: Capabilities, Costs and Alternatives*, Congressional Budget Office, Washington, DC, July 1986, p. 31.

60. Bischak and Oden, 'The INF Treaty', op. cit. part IV.

61. For an examination of the effects of disarmament treaties on the nuclear weapons complex, see Bischak and Oden, ibid. Also see 'Facing the Second Generation of the Nuclear Weapons Complex: Renewal of the Nuclear Production Base or Economic Conversion?' by Greg Bischak, in *Making Peace Possible*, edited by Lloyd J. Dumas and Marek Thee, Pergamon Press, London, 1989, pp. 111–37.

62. See HR 101, *Defense Adjustment Act*, 101st Congress, 1st Session, 1989.

6 Towards a New National Needs Agenda for Science and Technology Policy: The Prospects for Democratic Science and Technology Policymaking

Joel S. Yudken and Michael Black

INTRODUCTION

As a new decade dawns, the United States faces the challenges of increasing global competitiveness, mounting environmental problems and a rapidly changing international security situation. All of these factors have contributed to the reexamination of how and where the US government should invest its public science and technology resources to meet a growing number of critical national needs, especially in an era of increasing austerity.

In this chapter we examine these issues and recent proposals for instituting a new set of national technology and industrial initiatives which would promote special interests under the rubric of national security and economic competitiveness. We argue that such a policy would be a suboptimal solution to the nation's economic and social problems. Instead, we posit the foundations of a new national needs-oriented policy for applying and developing the nation's science and technology resources. In the first section we present an overview of this proposed marriage between military agencies and civilian high-technology policy and provide an assessment of its economic, political and social implications for our society, especially in relation to the large number of national needs which are not being addressed. In the second section we build an argument to show that proposals centered exclusively on national security and competitiveness criteria will yield suboptimal solutions because they will inhibit technology transfers, narrow the science and technology base, and retard effective demand for basic research and critical technologies necessary to meet social, as well as economic needs. In the last section of this chapter, we advance the elements of a National Needs Agenda for Science and Technology which would guide science and technology policymaking towards solving a broader range of economic, social and environmental problems and democratically involve all segments of society.

THE NEW INDUSTRIAL POLICY DEBATE

For some time now, Congress has deliberated over the kinds of federal support that should be given, if any, to promote the development of high-definition television (HDTV) in the United States. It has conducted hearings, and the Executive has issued reports evaluating the potential importance of HDTV to the nation's economy and its competitiveness in the global marketplace. Industrial organizations and government bureaucrats have joined forces to argue the case for substantial federal private-sector aid for the creation of a new HDTV research and development (R&D) consortium, and for other incentives that are needed to create a viable national HDTV industry. They claim that if the federal government doesn't act soon, the US will lose whatever competitive edge it has in its semiconductor, computer and telecommunications industries, suffering serious economic losses in the coming decades. In the midst of these deliberations, the Department of Defense's (DoD) flagship R&D agency, the Defense Advanced Research Projects Agency (DARPA) has started its own initiative, providing over $30 million in funds to US firms for HDTV R&D.

The push for a HDTV policy has not gone unopposed. A significant backlash has erupted among conservatives in the Bush Administration. They quite correctly perceive HDTV to be a stalking horse for a movement to institute a new type of industrial policy in the US, one in which the federal government would play a much more active part in domestic industrial development. As Susan Walsh Anderson observes, 'HDTV has become the bellweather for U.S. readiness to meet the challenge of a new generation of information technologies.'[1] The opponents' criticisms, that the federal government should not be in the business of 'picking technological winners and losers', are reminiscent of attacks on industrial policy by Reagan Administration laissez-faire ideologues, earlier in the decade.

What is unusual about the current debate is that the main protagonists are themselves high-ranking government officials and industrial leaders, drawn mostly from two powerful, disparate interest groups in the US – the high-tech industrial sector and the military–industrial complex. These leaders argue that a new government–business partnership is needed if the US is going to remain competitive in the global marketplace. In one of their main proposals, which some have labeled 'industry-led policy', industry leaders would identify the economically strategic technologies and industries that the government would target for various forms of support, such as R&D subsidies, tax incentives, relaxed anti-trust laws, trade protections, and regulatory reform. This position has garnered bipartisan support in Congress and even received backing from Commerce Secretary Robert Mosbacher.

All this talk of 'industrial policy', promoted as it is by leading members of government and industry, may cause 'liberal Democrats' to wonder, as Robert Reich recently wrote, 'if they've died and gone to industrial-policy heaven'.[2] A number of liberal academics and Congresspeople have indeed come out in favor of this program, apparently with the hope that this is a wedge for eventually legitimating a broader industrial policy in the US.

Ironically, the roots of the present-day initiative can be traced back to attempts by President Reagan to undercut the industrial policy drive led by the Democrats, as part of their 1984 election campaign. President Reagan sought to upstage this effort by establishing a Commission on Industrial Competitiveness, headed up by fellow Republican, Hewlett-Packard CEO John Young, and comprised of leading members of the private sector.

The subsequent Commission report, however, received a very cool reception from the Reagan Administration. It drew national attention to the fact that the US position in the global economy was in serious decline. The United States not only was losing its markets in basic manufacturing industries such as textiles, steel and autos – the primary stimulus for the Democrats' industrial policy proposals – but it was also being threatened in its most advanced high-tech industries, such as semiconductors, computers, telecommunications and advanced materials. More significantly, the report argued that macroeconomic measures are necessary, but not sufficient means to cope with the growing problem, and suggested that the federal government play a leadership role in maintaining US competitiveness.

The main warnings and arguments of this report have since been reiterated and amplified by a slew of other reports and studies produced by groups and individuals from the private sector, academia, and the government itself. Their central concern is the rapid erosion in the competitive advantage of US technology over the last decade. From a surplus in 1980, the US manufacturing trade balance declined to a record deficit in 1987 of $137.7 billion, and from a very large surplus in 1981, the trade balance in high-technology goods descended to a deficit in 1986 of $2.6 billion.[3] These figures reflect the general drop in productive performance of the US economy since the 1970s, and the declining market shares of US high-technology industries over the last five years, in particular. The US consumer electronics industry was an early casualty, its market share shrinking from nearly 100 per cent in 1970 to less than 5 per cent today. Since 1980, however, other major US high-technology industries such as semiconductors and semiconductor manufacturing equipment, machine tools, and pharmaceuticals have also seen large bites taken out of their market shares by foreign competitors, particularly by the Japanese.[4]

It is doubly painful that in most of these industries, the key technologies were originally pioneered in the United States. As *The New York Times* observes, in an article about the potential sale of the last US-owned maker of highly-sophisticated chip manufacturing equipment to a Japanese firm, the 'story of how the United States has gradually withdrawn from the semiconductor equipment business is a familiar one for America's high-technology industry'. Although in industry after industry the technology was first developed in the United States, it writes, 'the American advantage was eroded and eventually eliminated'.[5]

Many reasons have been given to explain the drop in US performance, from the trade and business practices of competitor nations, to the high cost of capital to US firms, exacerbated by the large federal budget deficit. Shortsighted and outdated management practices common to US businesses, also contribute to the malaise. But there seems to be widespread agreement that a principal cause of economic decline is the failure of the US to invest sufficiently in civilian R&D and technological development.

The US private sector has lagged significantly behind its corporate competitors in Europe and Japan in support of long-term R&D, most of which, in the United States occurs in universities and government laboratories. Until the 1980s, the US corporate sector has taken a back seat to the federal government in support of basic research. As a

Congressional Office of Technology Assessment (OTA) report explains, 'pressures for near-term profits have forced many larger U.S. corporations away from basic research'. It notes that only 'a few hundred companies account for the lion's share of industry-funded R&D – three firms (IBM, AT&T, General Motors) for more than 15 per cent'.[6] The recent wave of corporate mergers has also contributed to the decline of US corporate R&D levels since 1985.[7]

Specifically, the separation of corporations from the principal centers of basic research in the US has been a major obstacle to quick and efficient technology transfer of innovations to commercial products and processes. In addition, US corporations have not paid adequate attention to investing in the technology transfer process, and particularly in R&D, that leads to improvements in manufacturing process technologies, a by-product of their preoccupation with short-term profitability. Finally, corporations have difficulties working cooperatively on R&D efforts. As the Massachusetts Institute of Technology (MIT) Commission on Industrial Productivity reports, 'underdeveloped cooperative relationships between individuals and between organizations stand out in our industry studies as obstacles to technological innovation and the improvement of industrial performance'.[8]

A more general problem is the fragmentation of US S&T policy. Several agencies have initiated R&D programs relevant to advancing economically strategic technologies for manufacturing productivity and industrial competitiveness. The DoD has the largest number and most significant of these efforts. Yet, there is no national commitment or coherent policy for enhancing the nation's industrial competitiveness. Nor is there any single office or agency in the federal government with the responsibility for coordinating the many different programs in this area scattered across the different agencies.

Meanwhile, both Japan and nations in Western Europe have embarked on major government-subsidized R&D initiatives in critical technological areas such as high-performance computers, superconductors, advanced aircraft, biotechnology and telecommunications. They aim to strengthen their own capabilities in *both* basic science and technology and stimulate a new wave of innovations for increasing their competitive edge in commercial technology markets.[9] With all this investment, it has been predicted that Japan's science will catch up with its technology within one or two decades.[10]

Significantly, Japan and Western Europe outspend the US in commercial R&D and have policies that support cheaper and easier capital for private investment. This, in turn, makes it easier for their corporations to make long-term R&D investment in competitive technologies without regard to short-term profitability. At first glance US R&D spending appears to be much larger than that spent by Western Europe and Japan. But if the portion of the federal R&D budget devoted to national defense is deducted, US spending on civilian R&D equals only around 1.8–1.9 per cent of US GNP, while Japan's proportion of non-defense R&D spending of its GNP is about 2.8 per cent, and West Germany's is about 2.6 per cent.[11]

Not surprisingly, US high-technology industrial leaders have turned to the federal government for leadership and support, calling for new policies which will preserve US technological advantage in economically strategic industries. As reported by the MIT Commission on Industrial Productivity, 'There is an overwhelming consensus that science and technology policies should be accorded high priority in rejuvenating U.S. international competitiveness.'[12] However, lacking both a coherent S&T policy and a designated federal body to approach for support, US industrial groups have been forced to go to the DoD, particularly DARPA, to get what they need.

For its part, the DoD has been undergoing a fundamental change in its relation to the domestic economy over the past decade. The DoD's huge investment in R&D, products and services has been called, by some critics, a *de facto* industrial policy. The DoD R&D budget, which has grown to over $40 billion per year, represents two-thirds of the total federal R&D budget and approximately one-third of the total private and public expenditures on R&D in the US today. Hence, for almost forty years military objectives have been the predominant 'demand pull' governing the nation's overall R&D agenda. Indeed, since the Second World War a number of important technologies – jet aircraft, integrated circuits, computers, satellites, and advanced materials – have 'spun-off' into the civilian sector as a result of DoD procurement and R&D investment policies. DARPA, in particular, has forged an unusual track-record, within the DoD, of fostering successful technology transfer into the commercial sector.

Nevertheless, the general position of the DoD *vis-à-vis* the civilian economy has been largely laissez-faire, its investment decisions dictated by military needs rather than economic consequences. In recent years, this position has shifted. The DoD, and DARPA in particular, is now being touted, as *Science* magazine observes, as the 'federal government's central agency for keeping high-tech industries competitive'.[13] Competitiveness now appears to be an explicit part of the DoD's mission. For example, the Defense Science Board recently called for the creation of an industrial policy board under DoD control.[14] Similarly, an inhouse DARPA strategy document states that the agency's objectives include developing technologies 'that will help the U.S. maintain qualitative superiority in defense systems, and to retain its competitive position among the industrialized nations'.[15]

Subsequently, the DoD, especially DARPA, has become the self-appointed principal bankroller of several commercially important technology projects and R&D consortia in the US. DARPA's budget has doubled since 1985, rising to $1.3 billion in fiscal 1989. Much of this growth is a result of the agency taking on support for major research projects and industrial R&D consortia in a variety of technologies it deems critical to both civilian and defense industries. For example, the agency spends $100 million per year in support of the semiconductor industry's consortium, Sematech[16] and is the principal sponsor of another consortium, the Microelectronic and Computer Technology Corporation (MCC), which conducts a variety of advanced computer and microelectronics research. DARPA is also one of the largest federal sponsors of superconductivity research, doling out over $30 million million-per-year to several institutions and three consortia,[17] and is the only federal sponsor of HDTV research.[18] In addition, the agency laid much of the foundation for the nation's computing and information-processing capabilities, and accounts for more than two-thirds of all federal funding for advanced computer R&D.[19]

With all this commercially-relevant R&D activity, some DARPA officials have even begun to believe that their agency is playing a role equivalent to that of the Ministry of International Trade and Industry (MITI) in Japan. A program manager contends, for example, that 'MITI was modeled after [DARPA]. . . . It's in that sense that DARPA was started, and is very interested in applying the same sort of strategic thinking and planning for national competitiveness for manufacturing.'[20]

The DoD/DARPA move into the civilian technology sector is the product of internal and external pressures that have been forcing the Pentagon to rethink its military force postures and organizational operations. First, the Gramm-Rudman-Hollings bill to put a cap on federal spending raised the specter of defense R&D programs being the most likely targets for early reductions in the DoD budget. Given the recent events in Eastern Europe and the Soviet Union, large cuts in the DoD budget, particularly military R&D, have now become a certainty rather than just a possibility. Hence, one can't rule out bureaucratic instinct as an important motivation for DARPA's foray into the commercial sector, as the military rationale for its R&D budget has diminished.

But the DoD and DARPA also seem to be responding to a reevaluation of national security policy brought about by the relaxation of East–West tensions. Increasingly, even within the Pentagon, economic security is being equated with national security – a view that just a few years ago was voiced only by nuclear disarmament and conversion advocates. The principal threat to US long-term security appears to derive more from its economic competitors than from its long-time military adversary, the Soviet Union.

Less generally, a number of military industrial officials are worried about the perceived deterioration of the defense industrial base. They cite the growing dependency of military systems on foreign sources for critical technologies and components,[21] which they believe is a serious threat to US military preparedness. The next generation of weapons technology – such as 'smart' weaponry, automated battlefield management, survivable command and control systems – is especially dependent on the same types of advanced technologies that many consider critical battlegrounds for economic competitiveness (semiconductors, high-performance computers, machine intelligence and neural nets, HDTV and telecommunications technologies, superconductors and advanced materials). Hence the convergence of the military's interest in rebuilding the defense industrial base with the civilian high-technology sectors' concern with maintaining the competitiveness of their industries in the global marketplace.

Some Congresspeople, civilian executives and academics have been uneasy with the growing DoD/DARPA penetration into the civilian industrial sector. Expressing a view shared by others, Robert M. White, president of the National Academy of Engineering, noted in a recent speech that the DoD has become the 'nation's de facto Ministry of Technology by default'. But, he states, 'while we need to be thankful that some agency is taking the lead, the Defense Department is not where it should be'.[22]

The question is, what should be in its place? Some leaders, such as Senator John Glenn, have pushed the notion of a civilian equivalent of DARPA. However, while a dedicated civilian technology agency may be desirable, it appears that the DoD, as defense analyst Jacques Gansler notes, 'is the most politically acceptable and available organization to do it'.[23] And, as science policy writer Daniel S. Greenberg writes, 'Given the absence of an alternative bankroll, that's where they are bound to remain.'[24]

The convergent military–civilian high-tech program is clearly the emerging S&T policy approach to the competitiveness problem in the United States today. Attempts by groups such as Rebuild America to package this agenda as 'industry-led' policy is an obvious attempt to blunt the opposition of laissez-faire conservatives, many of whom have a knee-jerk reaction against anything that smacks of 'industrial policy'. This effort seems to have failed, however, as officials in the Bush administration have taken the offensive, severely criticizing DoD and DARPA for their extensive involvement in private-sector projects. There have even been calls for cuts in funding for Sematech and HDTV – although that is unlikely to happen – which has set in motion a bipartisan counterattack in Congress, reaffirming the importance of DARPA to the nation's high-tech competitiveness strategy. For example, *The New York Times* reports that a letter, 'signed by Representatives Richard A. Gephardt of Missouri and Mel Levine and Norman Y. Mineta of California, all Democrats, and Senator John Heinz, Republican of Pennsylvania' said that eliminating these programs would be 'economic insanity'.[25] As of this writing, this debate is unresolved.

Regardless of the outcome of this debate, however, we feel the results will be problematical. If the laissez-faire ideologues succeed in stifling the military–civilian high-tech agenda, the US will face a huge policy void. Without federal government guidance and support, the existing fragmented S&T policy system may seriously retard advanced S&T development, precisely at a time when the US's foreign competitors are picking up the pace of development in strategic technology areas.

Even more troubling is the growing trend of foreign, particularly Japanese, penetration into the US domestic industrial base. Some US firms, and even research universities, are looking overseas for sources of capital and R&D funds because of difficulties in acquiring sufficient domestic support. In one recent example, General Electric and Pratt & Whitney have submitted applications for research money from MITI as part of a Japanese Government-financed project to design a 'hypersonic' commercial aircraft. As a senior US aerospace executive was quoted in *The New York Times*, 'Funding for America's own projects is pretty chancy. . . . We need as many different sources as we can find.'[26]

Even more disturbing are the recent overtures by the Perkins-Elmer Corporation to a Japanese firm regarding the possible sale of its semiconductor manufacturing equipment unit, because it couldn't find a US buyer. This unit is the last major maker of sophisticated semiconductor tools of its type in the US.[27] Universities too, have been going to foreign sources for research funds. Japan tops the list of foreign funders for domestic university research. As noted in *Business Week*, nobody 'blames universities for accepting money [from Japan]. In view of the decline of federal and state funding, universities must find funds elsewhere'.[28]

Lacking a civilian alternative, DARPA's role as 'venture capitalist' for critical high-technology initiatives is perhaps preferable to nothing at all. DARPA's track-record, both in supporting state-of-the-art university research, and working closely with business firms in spinning-off technology into commercial markets, has been relatively good in certain areas. Despite this administration's official opposition, the military–civilian high-tech industry 'marriage' remains the most viable option for keeping the US in the international competitiveness game, at this time.

Nevertheless, we argue that this trajectory is inadequate for meeting the nation's actual economic and social needs in the coming decades. First, we question the ability of the competitiveness proposals put forth by the military–civilian high-tech 'coalition' to succeed on their own terms. We believe that a DoD/high-tech industry-dominated S&T policy will constrain and distort the process of technology transfer of basic innovations to commercializable products. The divergence between military and commercial technology requirements, and the military's control of vital S&T resources will inhibit efforts at applying technological advances for products needed in the civilian economy.

In addition, the military–civilian high-tech program doesn't sufficiently address how government policies can affect internal corporate practices which hinder the processes of technology transfer and innovation within industrial firms. In particular, only lip-service is given to the key role of workforce participation in shopfloor innovation. The high-tech industry and the Pentagon have also been notorious for their anti-labor practices.

Our second major concern is that the military–civilian high-tech agenda will significantly narrow the nation's fundamental science and technology base, which is the foundation for all future economic growth. The combined DoD emphasis on applications development with the corporate focus on short-term profits will crowd out basic research and narrow the nation's research agenda, creating significant gaps in the S&T base.

Finally, because this policy reflects only the narrow interests of a small elite group of corporate executives and military bureaucrats, we believe it will preclude much-needed support for basic research and technology development in critical areas of national need. There are several pressing national problems – environmental protection, modernization of public infrastructure and the manufacturing base, renewable energy, mass transportation, and affordable housing – which require significant S&T investments for their solutions, and will not be addressed by the military–civilian high-tech program.

Below, we elaborate on these three principal shortcomings of the emerging military–civilian high-tech industrial program, and try to show why it will be deficient for meeting the US's long-term economic, social and environmental needs. In the section that follows, we sketch a *National Needs Agenda in Science and Technology* as an alternative strategy for S&T development which would target national needs rather than a select number of industries or technologies. This proposal attempts to reconceptualize a new policy framework for more adequately and equitably allocating the nation's critical S&T resources, built around an agenda of national needs and formulated through an open democratic process.

A 'SUBOPTIMAL' INDUSTRIAL STRATEGY

Although it may appear to be the 'only game in town', the convergent military–civilian high-tech program is suboptimal for addressing the nation's economic and social needs on three grounds. By suboptimal, we mean that it only partially satisfies a given set of criteria and desired outcomes.

First, it may inhibit and distort the process of *technology transfer* from basic S&T innovations to commercializable and socially useful products. We are skeptical that this 'marriage' will be able to even meet its own objectives of enhancing US domestic corporate productivity and performance.

Second, it may narrow rather than expand the nation's *science and technology* (S&T) *base* – that is, the advancement of long-term fundamental research along the boundaries of science and engineering disciplines – which is the seed-corn for all future technological, economic, and social evolution.

Third, and most importantly, it may inhibit *effective demand and create opportunity costs* with respect to the development and application of S&T innovations to other vital economic and social needs (e.g. environmental, public infrastructure, energy, transportation).

Inhibition of technology transfer

The most critical problem for US competitiveness is technology transfer: the ability to exploit and transfer knowledge and innovations generated in the S&T base to commercializable or social utilitarian applications. US basic science research has been the envy of the world for four decades. Yet, as we noted earlier, US industry has not capitalized on its own strong S&T base as swiftly and effectively as have foreign competitors. Caught up in the drive for short-term profits, it has failed to invest sufficiently in the transfer of R&D innovations to new product and process technologies. Most US industries – with the notable exceptions of the semiconductor and computer industries[29] – have simply not maintained links to the science and technology base, either by supporting research in universities or funding their own long-term research.

Equally important has been the failure of the private sector to sufficiently invest in what Kenneth Flamm and Thomas McNaugher call 'middle-ground' research, which they describe as 'an ill-defined but critical no-man's land' between generic research and product development, 'in which basic science is first translated into practical new concepts for products and processes'.[30] In many cases, US firms have preferred to move off-shore, to exploit cheaper labor costs and increase short-term profits, rather than invest in new R&D.

By contrast, the Japanese and Western European nations, until recently, targeted most of their R&D investments primarily to middle-range civilian R&D, rather than to generic S&T research, especially during the 'catching-up' phase of their development in the sixties and seventies. Ironically, these same nations greatly benefitted from the federally-sponsored fundamental research, which was accessible through the open scientific literature.

While the US's economic competitors have been hitching their commercial technology transfer wagons to the US S&T engine – and now increasingly to their own – the US has spent most of its efforts on harnessing this base to its military needs. Over the last decade, defense science and technology base spending was roughly halved, while applications development spending saw dramatic gains. The DoD's R&D programs have increasingly emphasized accelerating the transfer of S&T research to military missions and applications. Given the predominance of DoD R&D in the total federal R&D budget, most of the federally-funded mid-level R&D appears therefore to be dominated by DoD objectives and missions.

But, as Kenneth Flamm notes, 'given the growing importance of advanced technology to U.S. economic performance and the still dominant role of military support in many fields of applied research, the extent to which commercial application of new technologies is affected by military sponsorship of research is a significant issue'.[31] Two major aspects of this movement which may hinder civilian technological development. First, military sponsorship may reinforce the already considerable divergence between military and civilian technology requirements. Second, it may increase the diversion of scarce R&D resources away from technology development relevant to civilian needs.

Diverging design and performance requirements

The divergence of military and civilian technologies has been addressed in many writings. For example, a Berkeley Roundtable on the International Economy (BRIE) study found that as defense R&D became oriented towards esoteric weapons development, the civilian impacts of military R&D have been either negative or neutral.[32] Depletionist writers such as Melman, Dumas, and Ullmann have long argued that the incompatibility of military and civilian design and performance characteristics has greatly curtailed the success of military spinoff.[33] As Ullmann writes, 'the highly specialized nature of military technology gives few real opportunities for successful transfers. Thus fewer than one percent of the 8,000 patents resulting from Navy research and available for licensing are actually licensed, compared, for instance, to 13 percent of Department of Agriculture patents.'[34] Similarly, an OTA report observes, that as 'the defense sector has grown apart from the rest of the U.S. economy', military R&D spending 'has less impact' on commercial innovation, while other nations are focusing 'more of their resources, both public and private, on commercial technologies'.

Military scientists and engineers operate in an environment which emphasizes high performance regardless of costs. Commercial designers try to achieve high performance and quality at the lowest possible costs. The divergence in the military and civilian design 'cultures' has been intensified in recent years by the Pentagon's emphasis on full-scale development of large complex weapon systems which have required increasingly specialized components, processes, and materials.[35] Thus, fewer commercially relevant technologies emerge in military R&D projects than ever before, and the diffusion of those with commercial potential has appreciably slowed.[36]

Military diversion of R&D resources

The divergence of military and civilian technology fuels the military's diversion of critical R&D resources from the civilian economy. Depletionist writers argue that US military R&D and production employ a disproportionate fraction of the science and technology workforce, relative to its contribution to industrial output.[37] In addition, the shift within the DoD's R&D budget towards development projects and away from technology base support contributes to the diversion problem. There are now fewer dollars and people devoted to the generic and middle-ground research that would have greater potential civilian applications. Plus, as weapons systems R&D is concentrated in the larger military industrial firms, there has been correspondingly less in the smaller innovative firms from which commercial spinoffs would be more likely.[38] In short, coupling the military's diversion of R&D resources with the dearth of corporate R&D investment has led to a very serious shortage of resources available for domestic technology development.

This problem, of course, has been a core concern of the DARPA entrepreneurs, Pentagon reformers, and 'industry-led' policy advocates from the beginning. Hence, they are, on the one hand, pushing for a reform in military design that emphasizes using state-of-art, commercial components in their systems development, and on the other, advocating a much stronger Pentagon role in developing national competitiveness. In line with the 'industry-led' policy strategy, this includes subsidizing R&D consortia in dual-use technologies for civilian and defense industrial needs.

In theory, industrial consortia appear an ideal instrument for developing generic and middle-ground innovations with high dual-use potential. In practice, consortia face a number of difficult challenges. For example, problems can arise between partners in a cooperative venture – especially if they are competitors – over setting R&D agendas, sharing technologies and business information, controlling costs and determining intellectual property rights. In addition, there is a tendency for participating firms to focus their internal efforts on shorter-term work, and pushing the cooperative's agenda towards applied rather than basic research.[39] Given these limitations, the emphasis on consortia seems overblown. Consortia may be a good way to accelerate some areas of technology, but Robert E. Gomory, vice-president for science and research at IBM, reminds us that 'they are only a small part of the competitiveness effort'. Yet, he warns 'they are being confused with the whole thing'.[40]

The participation of defense-related firms within major consortia and DoD/DARPA's role as the primary federal bankroller for most of these initiatives, also raise troubling questions. Will civilian technology needs be subordinated to the specialized requirements of the military industrial participants? Is it reasonable to assume that the DoD's heavy hand will not leave its mark on the fragile working relationships existing within consortia resulting in outputs of marginal commercial potential?[41]

Worker participation and technology transfer

Another issue unaddressed by the military–civilian high-tech alliance is the role of worker participation in the innovation process. It is widely acknowledged that any national competitiveness initiative will greatly depend on active workforce cooperation. As former Secretary of Labor Ray Marshall notes, workers are not 'likely to go all out' in a new technology production system 'unless they have some ways to protect their interest in the process. . . . Since workers are so important to seeing to it that the technology gets maintained and developed, then their interests should be represented in whatever kinds of policies get put together.'[42]

At best, the current-day industrial competitiveness proposals have given this notion lip-service. Their main emphasis is on technological solutions *per se*, which can blind people from seeing that labor is integral to the innovation process. We believe it is just as essential to 'target' work organization and managerial strategies as technologies. The design of products and processes does not take place in a vacuum. Technologies applied in the design of products and processes are selected and modified to fit into specific organizational and economic contexts. Hence, as an OTA study notes, the nation's technology base encompasses the 'intuitive rules and methods that lie at the heart of technological practice', many of which are tacit rather than formally codified. Progress in industrial production 'depends heavily on experience and empirical know-how'. But, it concludes, 'reluctance among American engineers and managers to learn from shop-floor employees hurt productivity and competitiveness'.[43]

Attention to this aspect of design and production is therefore crucial for innovation to take place. Corporate labor practices will have to change a great deal if they are going to reap the full benefit of new industrial technologies. Numerous experiments in worker-participation schemes and quality circles over the last few years indicate that some corporate leaders are interested in exploring this new thinking. On the other hand, labor unions remain skeptical, for good reasons, about many of these efforts. They have witnessed many instances where corporate management utilized work partici-pation schemes as means to undermine union autonomy. To be truly effective, workforce participation in productivity efforts must be non-exploitive, offering workers a measure of real decision-making power in technology and production planning.[44]

Narrowing the science and technology base

A strong science and technology base is necessary for a productive economy, and is one of the US's principal assets. We are concerned, however, about the possibility that the adoption of the military–civ-ilian high-tech industrial program as the nation's S&T policy will distort and narrow the research allocation process in the United States, especially in the context of the federal budget deficit.

For the first time in recent history the US science and engineering community is faced with a zero-sum game in its budgets for funda-mental research. This has made the problem of how to best distribute science resources to support a well-balanced, stable and adequately-funded research base very difficult. For over forty years the research community has benefitted from an implicit 'social contract' with the federal government in what Robert Rosenzwieg, President of the Association of American Universities, has called a 'Faustian bar-gain'. In exchange for giving researchers latitude to follow their own pursuits, the federal agencies obtained the work they needed for furthering their own mission objectives. Until recently, the majority of scientists probably found this system of patronage to be satisfactory. As Rosenzweig notes, 'what's made the system work as well as it has, is that every year . . . there has been more money than there was before. You lubricate a lot of problems by having money to spread around.' On the other hand, he adds, 'my concern is that we appear to be going into a period in which that may [no longer] be true'.[45]

Researchers now find themselves confronting potentially serious reductions in their S&T research budgets. The costs of doing research and of training new researchers continue to escalate. As a field advances, it gets more expensive to make each new step. This has caused concern among researchers that R&D resources will not be able to keep up.

There is also a distribution problem. While some fields and sub-fields of science are well-funded, others are experiencing difficulties obtaining all the funding they need.[46] A related issue is the problém of 'big vs. little' science. Some researchers have complained that individual and small-group research are being systematically squeezed out to fund 'big ticket' projects, such as the $6 billion Superconducting Super Collider, which are often supported less on merit than on pork-barrel politics.[47] The problem of adequacy and distribution of funding in science has been likened to a 'have' versus 'have not' situation. As aptly stated at a recent meeting of the American Association for the Advancement of Science (AAAS), 'on the one hand, we have a story of a rich city, if you want, but we have a number of homeless cases developing'.[48]

A primary obstacle to overcoming this difficulty is the fragmentation of the federal S&T budget process. The United States lacks a means for setting priorities for allocating its increasingly scarce S&T resources; an issue raised by a recent report of the National Academy of Sciences,[49] which we also discuss in a later section. Our first concerns, however, are the impact of the Department of Defense (DoD) on S&T research, and the potential overcommercialization of research objectives.

DoD and the direction of fundamental research

Now commanding more than two-thirds of the $60 billion federal R&D budget, Defense Department R&D grew more than 80 per cent (in constant dollars) between fiscal 1980 and 1988, while civilian R&D fell by one-quarter.[50] Universities, which train most of the nation's scientists and engineers, are especially dependent on federal patronage. Over 60 per cent of all basic research is performed in universities, 70 per cent of which is government-supported. The DoD is second only to the National Institute of Health in support of academic R&D.[51] Certain academic disciplines, such as aeronautics and astronautics, electrical engineering and computer science rely on the DoD for between 60 to 70 per cent of their R&D funding.[52]

There have been many critics of DoD involvement in R&D, especially regarding the impacts on fundamental research.[53] Generally, they argue that the substantial role of the DoD in funding S&T research distorts the direction of the research, inhibits advances in its scientific foundations, threatens intellectual freedom, and even limits the potential for much-needed research 'spin-off' for commercial and other social uses.[54]

The actual impact of the DoD on S&T research, however, is not that clear-cut. Part of the problem is terminology. For example, fundamental or basic research in science seeks to discover new knowledge and insights about phenomena in the universe. Technology research – or applied research – is concerned with discovering new ways of doing things that may have applications in the real world. In reality, the boundaries between these categories are often blurred. One researcher's 'applied research' may be another's 'basic research'. Nevertheless, for scientists concerned with the advancement of knowledge, it is problematic when support for applied research undercuts fundamental inquiry. Moreover, it is argued, most technological innovation today is dependent on progress in basic research.

Hence there are at least two related problems: how DoD's emphasis on mission and applications in its R&D programs, is crowding out long-term basic research; and how the imbalance in funding sources for S&T research causes a *de facto* selection of research problems in only those areas congruent with the Pentagon's missions, creating gaps in the S&T base relevant to other economic and social needs.

(i) Applications crowding out basic science

In his classic work, *Science: The Endless Frontier*, Dr Vannevar Bush noted that 'there is a perverse law governing research: under the pressure for immediate results, and unless deliberate policies are set up to guard against this, applied research invariably drives out pure'.[55] Although Bush was referring to research in the private sector, Kenneth Flamm and Thomas McNaugher, of the Brookings

Institution, suggest a corollary for the public sector. In mission agencies, 'stringent budgets have typically meant cutting back on longer-term, more speculative research in favor of delivering the functioning systems that commanders, or department heads or mission specialists are clamoring for. The project most distant from clear or immediate missions are sacrificed – and this too means development is favored over research'.[56]

Flamm's and McNaugher's view describes the current predicament in federal R&D funding. Due largely to the DoD's investment in weapons programs, the balance of Federal R&D funding has been channelled away from the research base and towards exotic development projects. Within the R part of R&D, there is also ample evidence that applied, mission-oriented research is growing faster than basic. Even the NSF has focused its recent efforts on building up applied, experimental research areas.

In part, this is due to Congressional pressures on the agencies to make programs more directly relevant to their missions and to the needs of society (e.g. competitiveness, AIDS research). As former DoD research director William Perry recently observed, generalized support in Congress for basic science research exists, but it does not always translate to specific programs.[57] Consequently, program managers have increasingly 'packaged' their programs to appear relevant to mission or national needs.[58] In addition, some leading members of the science community have complained that DARPA is 'micromanaging' more of its contracts and demanding more 'deliverables' with faster results, than it did in previous decades.[59] For example, Michael Dertouzos, director of the Laboratory for Computer Science at MIT, observes that DARPA has 'become more bureaucratic and more attuned to the military and short-term needs.'[60]

Another effect is on the training of the nation's future research workforce. As Lewis M. Branscomb, Director, of the Science, Technology and Public Policy Program at Harvard University points out, there are serious concerns that 'the U.S. is neglecting the fundamental science from which new ideas emerge and through which advanced students of science and engineering are professionally trained'.[61] The extent to which applied research and development crowds out support for basic research, correlates with the rising domestic shortage of scientists and engineers. Thus, Branscomb adds, 'while we are thinking about how to rebuild our industrial technology, the Japanese are giving priority to their basic science. We must keep our leading technical asset healthy.'

(ii) Funding and the direction of fundamental research

DoD's applications-orientation also affects the direction of basic research in more subtle and indirect ways. A central question is, how do the mission-priorities of major sponsors of science and engineering research influence the choice of areas of generic research and types of problems worked on, within and across disciplines? Despite much anecdotal evidence on either side of the debate, systematic research and analysis has only recently been undertaken. The 'loosely-coupled and complex' relationship that exists between funding agencies, researchers and their employing institutions makes definitive study of the problem very difficult.[62] To evaluate it, we need to look at the nature of science research activity itself, and its relationship to the research funding process.

When a mission agency funds research it usually has some short- or long-term objective in mind, congruent with its mission. But it is common to think of the process of laboratory research as separate from the process of turning innovations into useful applications. The process of research innovation is a 'black box'. Funding provides the opportunity for innovations and their applications but is independent from the process that actually produces them. Some argue, therefore, that scientists, not their funding agencies, determine the direction of research. For example, MIT's Michael Dertouzos contends that history has shown 'that the source of computer science funding and its objectives and aspirations are quite independent of the ultimate payoffs. Science, especially the science yet to be discovered, isn't too happy going where we want to go. It goes where it wants to go.'[63]

In our view, the science funding–research relationship is more complex. The direction of science research is actually the product of an interplay between two processes, 'technology push' and 'demand' or 'user pull'. 'Technology push' refers to the process by which basic innovations make new applications possible. For example, microelectronics research discoveries led to whole new classes of applications in industry and the military. In contrast, 'demand pull' refers to how an emphasis on applications in research can stimulate basic discovery and innovation.

For example, in applications development, the first step is to identify desired technological capabilities and specifications. These are then translated into detailed technical requirements, which, in turn, define specific areas of knowledge that need to be researched in the hope of generating new discoveries that help solve practical problems. For example, the Japanese magnetically-levitated train (Maglev) program supports basic research on superconductors, which is expected to lead to new technical breakthroughs that aid in the development of transportation technologies. Hence, new research directions and exciting synergies can sometimes be set in motion or 'pulled' along by a prior emphasis on specific ends.[64]

The 'science-goes-where-it-wants-to' view appears to stress 'technology push' as primary in the relationship between basic research and applications development. We argue that the 'demand pull' process is equally important in shaping the direction of research activities. Specifically, the 'demand pulls' created by mission agencies exert a bias on the direction of the research activities they support, through their ability to influence the areas and types of problems researchers choose to work on. As J. C. R. Licklider, a computer scientist at MIT and a former DARPA official, notes, regarding the relationship between research goals and eventual results, 'there are many choice points that one passes in traveling through research. And if there's just a little shading and biasing of one to the right or to the left, you wind up in a pretty different place after you go through 1000 more choice points.'[65]

More to the point, funding agencies are able to exert this influence on research choices through their control over the allocation of research resources. No research or applications development could occur without a commitment of resources by agencies seeking to achieve their objectives. Thus, a 'demand pull' created by strong mission objectives and backed by resources, constitutes a 'filter' through which areas of research, types of problems, and even methods and approaches, are selected in order to achieve a given objective. From this process, new basic discoveries may emerge, providing the foundations for a new 'technology push' which, ironically, may or may not satisfy the original goal.

Most federal R&D agencies supporting generic research do so with specific ends in mind. A look at research funding patterns for a given field would show a range of different types of research under contract, reflecting the goals of the different mission agencies.[66] In an ideal R&D funding world, observes Kenneth Flamm, 'diversity in funding sources and in research has a positive value'.[67] That is, multiple funding sources representing a diversity of missions and research goals encourages an optimum mix of problems and approaches, while guaranteeing support for researchers from the widest range of disciplines and subdisciplines. Put another way, if the funding 'portfolio' for a field is not sufficiently diversified (i.e. it is dominated by one or two founders) it is probable that certain lines of inquiry and types of approaches will be emphasized over others.

In this way, we believe that the DoD's preeminence in several strategic areas of science and technology contributes to a narrowing in the range of problems worked on, in the areas of research explored, and in the types of discoveries that have been produced. Moreover, the dominance of the defense 'demand pull' filter over any other social or economic goals in the federal R&D agenda may preclude critical areas of innovation for commercial development, much less for meeting a host of vital social needs.

For example, an OTA study notes that 'gaps and holes in the [industrial] technology base emerge particularly in fields that federal agencies – DoD, DOE, NASA – view as too far from their missions, and that, in the view of corporate managers will not yield financial returns in the short or medium terms'. Some of the industrial technologies consequently neglected by government and corporate investors include construction technologies, advanced steel processes, railway technology, combustion processes (which affect environmental pollution), and corrosion and wear processes.[68]

(iii) The commoditization of science research

DoD dominance is not the only problem for maintaining a strong S&T base. With the emphasis on competitiveness, universities are increasingly being brought within the orbit of entrepreneurial high-tech corporations through industrial subsidies to special R&D centers and individual academic researchers, or involvement in joint industrial R&D ventures and consortia. While this may be necessary for improving technology transfer possibilities, there is also a danger that growing ties between corporations and universities will further push academic research programs towards applied activities at the expense of basic research and education. Corporations often have shorter horizons and narrower goals than the DoD. As one noted theoretical computer scientist found to his 'dismay', his 'industrial sponsors are much tougher task masters [pushing for results] than even the hardest mission oriented [federal] agencies'.[69]

An equally important issue is the growing number of scientists caught in a conflict of interest between their commercial and academic commitments. Referring to the rise of 'academic entrepreneurialism', science writer David Dickson argues that this movement towards 'knowledge as commodity', threatens 'the integrity of university research . . . by raising barriers to the open exchange of information, . . . and disrupting the social relations of the laboratory.'[70] Similarly, *Business Week* reports that 'the profit motive has swept the campus far more than anyone has dreamed it would just a few years ago', causing critics to worry 'that campus capitalism may skew the research and educational mission of the universities'.[71]

Effective demand and opportunity costs in civilian markets

A DoD-dominated civilian industrial policy inevitably creates difficulties for finding support for other needed civilian technologies which may not fall within the definition of what Pentagon or the high-tech sector consider 'strategic'. One reason is the lack of effective demand created either in the private or the public sectors, comparable to national defense for 'pulling' up the S&T base and for developing new products to apply to these social needs. Government policies can stimulate effective demand directly by procurement and R&D subsidies, or indirectly, by providing incentives to the private sector for investing in technologies and production in these areas, and for finance and venture capital to invest their resources in new start-ups in socially useful technologies. We therefore question the implicit notion that the benefits of the 'industry-led' technology policies, which will help only a few industries, will automatically 'trickle-down' through the market process to non-targeted industries, communities, and workers.

David Dickson aptly characterized the narrowing effect of the military–civilian high-tech industrial program, in this passage written a few years ago:

> The implication of the new agenda, placing military strength and international competitiveness in high technology at the top of the priority list, is that planning for science is now almost exclusively based – whether in the short, the medium, or the long term – on the needs of the military and the marketplace; social objectives (such as protection of health or the natural environment) have been displaced as the principal focuses of research planning and are accepted only to the extent that they are compatible with increased military strength or commercial profits.[72]

S&T needs of basic industries

Almost all US industries have science and technology needs. It is important for the nation's economic wellbeing that its manufacturing industries, in particular, be targeted for significant levels of support. High-technology should not be considered a panacea for economic development and job-creation in regions decimated earlier by plant shutdowns in traditional industries.

But R&D investments for basic industries are difficult to come by. As a *New York Times* article observes, 'obtaining financing for consortiums is by no means a given. . . . In industries of less strategic concern, or which are not under siege, it may be more difficult to obtain Government backing for cooperative ventures.'[73] Similarly, Ray Marshall notes, 'if you are in a declining industry you are going to have a hard time getting funds for R&D, to maintain your position in industry'.[74] The steel industry backed away from R&D investments to modernize its plants a long time ago and the large integrated steel companies are technologically backward.[75] The textile industry has also been neglected. Japan has heavily funded research for new technologies in that industry, while the US has provided very little.[76] Even civilian industries closely allied with high technology and defense industries, such as machine tools, shipbuilding, commercial aircraft and consumer electronics, suffer from inadequate R&D support – a factor in the loss of major portions of their markets.

To resurrect these industries, new infusions of R&D funding will be needed, targeted especially to manufacturing process technologies. Unfortunately, there are only a few government policies which attempt to address this need. Of added concern is that the DoD is the principal sponsor of many of the critical technology programs which most directly relate to manufacturing capabilities. This includes, for example, machine tools, numerical controls, robotics, advanced materials, lasers, artificial intelligence, and computer-aided-design, manufacturing, and engineering.

The role of the Air Force's numerical controls program in the decline of the US machine tool industry has been amply illustrated.[77] The MIT Commission on Industrial Productivity acknowledges that there was a 'mismatch between the way the technology developed [under DoD auspices] and the needs of most potential users'. This can also apply to almost all other technological areas. While the DoD tries to push these technology programs in directions that suit their special needs – often pressuring for short-term results and premature applications – the Japanese look towards the long-run and provide steady, predictable funding which ties their R&D initiatives to commercial objectives.

Social needs and the new technologies

In the meantime a number of pressing national needs such as environmental protection, renewal of the public infrastructure, new and improved mass transportation, rebuilding the nation's merchant fleet, renewable energy, affordable housing and accessible health care go begging. Not surprisingly, there are gaps in the knowledge base for addressing this range of problems. Similarly, we need to produce many new technologies, products and applications in these areas. As Stanford economist Nathan Rosenberg writes, 'in certain areas, such as alternative energy or anti-pollution technologies, industry may simply lack sufficient R&D resources or the necessary market-generated incentives. In many industries and areas of substantial social need, we simply do not have the basic knowledge of scientific and technical phenomena to proceed intelligently.'[78]

Unfortunately, government programs have been greatly cut back in these areas, especially since 1980. For example, the Environmental Protection Agency's R&D budget was cut 40 per cent between 1980 and 1983, after Reagan got into power, though it has begun to recover somewhat. The non-defense energy budget was also decreased over that decade, and the solar program virtually gutted. Similarly, the R&D budgets of several other agencies which address various public needs, including the Urban Mass Transit Administration, the Consumer Product Safety Commission, and US Fish and Wildlife Service, for example, dropped in constant dollars over the last ten years. In any case, their R&D spending levels are all so small that combined they only make up a tiny fraction of the DoD's R&D budget.[79]

Consequences for workers

A final problem with the military–civilian high-tech program is its general lack of attention to problems of the workforce. It's not clear the extent to which it would actually benefit US workers. According to the 'trickle-down' view, if US industries are made more competitive by modernizing their production technologies, then any job displacement caused by new technologies will be offset by new production. This assertion is true in the aggregate, provided the modernization occurs in an expanding economy.[80] However, the employment impacts of new technologies are very uneven across and within different industries and occupational groups. New technologies tend to restructure production and jobs, change skill requirements and make it harder for some individuals to find jobs, often aggravating ongoing local unemployment.[81]

In addition, many critics have pointed to a number of negative impacts of new technologies on the quality of work.[82] This includes: reduced control of workers on the jobs; deskilling; increased anonymity and social isolation; reduced physical mobility; job dissatisfaction and stress; more monotony and boredom; and new occupational health and safety hazards.[83]

Another matter is *where* new jobs are created. It will not benefit US workers if commercial semiconductor firms respond to productivity gains by expanding their operations offshore, as they have done in the past. Advancing communications technologies are now creating mobility even among white-collar office jobs, as service-sector firms in insurance, publishing, telecommunications and software development find it easier to move to offshore sites, and take advantage of lower wage rates in places like Jamaica, Barbados, South Korea, China, and the Philippines.[84]

Thus, we feel it is as vital to target the nation's human resource base as it is to subsidize the investments of a select group of industries. As Reich writes, 'Our economic future, as well as our national security, is better served by developing a large corps of technologically sophisticated workers within the nation than by boosting the profitability of America's global corporations.'[85]

TOWARDS A NATIONAL NEEDS AGENDA IN SCIENCE AND TECHNOLOGY

Above, we argued that the marriage of military and civilian high-technology interests is suboptimal for national wellbeing. An enormous commitment of public resources is being proposed for pursuing a strategy of commercial and military dominance in the world, but from which we may get neither economic nor national security.

The possibility of large cuts in the defense budget presents the US with new challenges and opportunities regarding the distribution of an expected 'peace dividend' to non-defense social needs. Unfortunately, given the prevailing laissez-faire mood of the Bush Administration, and the recent slap at DARPA for its 'civilian' projects, there exists neither leadership nor a coherent policy at the federal level to guide an efficient, balanced reallocation of the S&T resources freed up by a defense retrenchment.

The problem is compounded by a fragmented federal S&T budget process which is spread across several federal offices, funding agencies and Congressional committees.[86] Civilian R&D, in particular, suffers from this fragmentation. In the Congressional budget process civilian S&T budgets are handled separately from military R&D programs. Instead, they are pitted against funding for other basic social programs such as housing and community development. A juxtaposition which, as National Academy of Sciences President Frank Press observes, 'tests political reality'.[87]

Unless the United States adopts a better way to distribute its S&T resources, pork-barrel and special interest politics will increasingly dominate the S&T policy agenda with deleterious consequences for the nation's S&T capabilities. A more 'optimal' approach is required for directing national policies towards meeting the nation's science and technology needs. For example, the Japanese strategy for promoting an economic or social objective is to make a national commitment – usually government-led in collaboration with industry and universities – to mobilize resources towards the specified goal through a coordinated set of policies. The US needs a comparable commitment to achieve its own goals, beyond the narrow objectives of the Defense Department or high-tech corporations.

Below, we sketch a *National Needs Agenda in Science & Technology*, as an alternative strategy for national S&T development. This proposal reconceptualizes a new policy framework for guiding the nation's allocation of R&D commitments – a S&T *perestroika*, if you will – keyed to an agenda of national needs determined by open democratic deliberation.

At this time we can only foreshadow what a full-blown National Needs Agenda would be. More work is required to produce an actual package of policy and legislative recommendations. In any case, such an Agenda would consist of several national policy initiatives, each comprised of a coordinated set of policies, designed to mobilize the nation's scientific and technological resources to achieve specific national objectives. The formulation and execution of these initiatives would be guided by the following five principles or criteria.

(i) Each initiative would target a national need, providing a 'filter' for selecting which industries and technologies would receive R&D resources and assistance.

(ii) Each initiative would create a demand-pull on S&T development, that is, by creating an effective demand for socially-needed products and technologies, it would simultaneously direct R&D activity towards a specific social need and facilitate the transfer of technological innovations to socially useful products, while 'pulling-up' fundamental advances in the science and engineering disciplines.

(iii) All the initiatives would be governed by the larger goal of increasing national productiveness, a more inclusive notion than competitiveness or productivity, which stresses social and environmental objectives, as well as efficiency, profits and market share.

(iv) The agenda would seek a balance across and within the initiatives regarding the allocation of resources for R&D and technology transfer.

(v) The agenda would emphasize democratic participation and public access in the making and execution of S&T policies at every level.

While earlier industrial policy proposals wanted to 'target industries' for federal support, and current-day competitiveness efforts 'target technologies', the new initiatives would 'target national needs'. In one sense, we agree with the laissez-faire argument that the federal government should not 'target' specific industries or technologies over any other in its policies. It is precisely our concern that the military-civilian high-tech agenda represents only a very narrow set of interests within society.

On the other hand, we do not agree that the market mechanism is sufficient for making the necessary choices for guiding the nation's future S&T investments. Part of the problem has been a failure of the market to give signals and incentives to the private sector for investing in modernizing technologies to improve productive capability, much less in middle-ground and long-term generic R&D. In addition, the market alone is not able to stimulate effective demands for products, services, and R&D investments in a number of critical areas of social need. We therefore believe that the federal government, working in partnership with business, labor, and the non-profit sector, should take the lead in initiating national commitments to address real, pressing social and economic problems.

Policy initiatives which target national needs in such areas as environmental restoration, industrial renewal and retention, public infrastructure renewal, mass transportation, sustainable energy, affordable housing, sustainable agriculture, and accessible health care, for example, would create 'demand pulls' for guiding the nation's S&T resources towards the development of products, applications, and solutions to problems which address those needs. Specifically, in each initiative the federal government would actively create effective demands for key industries through direct procurements and policies which mobilize market resources to achieve the desired social ends. The initiative would directly subsidize or create incentives for industries in the specified needs areas to conduct basic research, improve technology transfer, produce desired products, and create new jobs, while maintaining health, safety and environmental standards. Consequently, rather than competing with social programs for funding in the budget process, S&T programs would be coordinated consciously to incorporate instruments for achieving social policy goals. Social programs and the nation's S&T base would develop in tandem, mutually reinforcing each other.

Precedents and examples

The premier precedent for a large-scale 'demand pull' effort in the United States, of course, is the Department of Defense R&D program. For the last forty years, national security has been the predominant filter guiding much of the US S&T development. Another notable US precedent was the Apollo Program in the 1960s, directed by NASA. Its goal was not only to land a person on the moon, but build up the overall US civilian, military and scientific capabilities in space.

Large-scale national initiatives are more commonly instruments of policy in Japan and Western Europe. Often, a specific industry or technology is targeted for development, such as the European Airbus (commercial aircraft), RACE (telecommunications), ESPRIT (information technology), and BRITE (manufacturing) programs, and Japan's Fifth Generation Computer Program, the counterpart to DARPA's Strategic Computing Program.[88]

Having a broader scope are the European Eureka Program, with applications targeted to commercial products, manufacturing, transportation, health, environmental problems, and other areas, and the Japanese Human Frontier Science Program which focuses on human biological functions and their artificial applications with the goal of stimulating advances in biotechnologies, diagnostics, instrumentations and pharmaceuticals.[89]

Allocation issues, productiveness and balance

A major step in the formulation of each national needs initiative would be the identification of critical industries, technologies and special problems for targeting policies and incentives. This includes compiling a comprehensive 'critical technologies list' similar to the DoD list created on a request from Congress.[90]

For example, an initiative for rebuilding the public infrastructure would target key industries associated with waste treatment, mass transportation, and heavy construction for bridges and highways for investments and incentives in R&D and production, much of which must come from the government. A critical technologies list would include new materials, design technologies and product innovations for making more efficient, safer, inexpensive, and functional systems for public use. In an industrial renewal initiative, selected basic manufacturing, extractive and service industries would be targeted for R&D investments, for developing new products and process technologies, such as in advanced steelmaking, or automated sewing and clothing manufacturing.[91]

Conversion of military industries presents a special set of problems. Research is needed to identify and develop alternative products and technologies that can be adapted in the conversion of military industries such as shipbuilding, missiles and aerospace, electronics now threatened with cutbacks. An R&D program for conversion would be incorporated into a special conversion initiative, instituted through legislative acts (such as Rep. Ted Weiss's (D–NY) Defense Economic Adjustment Act). A National Needs Agenda, it should be noted, would increase conversion opportunities by creating effective demands in a variety of social needs areas, for the first time.

Cross-cutting strategic industries and technologies which are critical for more than one initiative needs area also should be identified, as they may be accorded priority in the allocation process. For example, some high-technology industries like microelectronics, computers, telecommunications, advanced materials, robotics and machine tools may be considered strategic, as they are crucial to the economic performance of other industries and for addressing a wide range of national needs. These initiatives would downplay the predominant military–corporate objectives currently guiding programs in these technologies, and strengthen support for neglected areas of inquiry, innovation, and applications for meeting civilian commercial and social objectives. For example, R&D programs in high-performance computing, advanced materials and optoelectronics can be designed to complement technology initiatives in steel processing, mass transportation, alternative energy, environmental modeling, and pollution control.

An especially important cross-cutting criterion for developing these ideas and allocating R&D resources is productiveness. The MIT Commission on Industrial Productivity recognized that criteria like competitiveness and productivity are too narrow for guiding policies that target technological development. The Commission adopted the term 'productive performance' which, they write, is 'compounded of [a firm's or industry's] productivity and of various other factors that tend to be ignored in most economic statistics, like quality, timeliness of service, flexibility, speed of innovation, and command of strategic technologies'.[92]

Our notion of productiveness adds to their criteria goals relating to the needs of workers, consumers, and the general public. For example, job security, good wages, a healthy and safe work environment, meaningful work and skill-enhancement, would be key productiveness objectives; as would be product quality, consumer health and safety, and environmental protection. Ideally, the Agenda's initiatives would be coordinated across several industries and social needs areas to achieve the highest levels of national productiveness.

Specific technologies and problem areas which satisfy productiveness criteria would be especially favored for support. Quality of worklife, for example, would be valued as much as economic efficiency. Research on skill-based automation would be supported as well as that on productivity-enhancing automation. According to Frank Emspak, Director of Massachusetts Center for Applied Technology, 'skills-based automation is centered on the notion that workers also set the criteria for design and that their criteria are of equal weight with other business related criteria'.[93]

A second major allocation criterion is balance. A balanced framework is required for deciding S&T priorities, to satisfy the many competing interests for these resources, while linking them to broad social objectives. The Agenda would seek a balance in the allocation of resources across needs initiatives, industries, technologies, R&D budgets and performers. Ideally, all deserving projects, performers, technological areas and research disciplines would receive the resources and assistance they need.

For the science research community, the balance of funding across different categories of R&D (basic research, applied research, and development) is especially problematical. Scientists are understandably concerned about the apparent swing towards instrumental research activity by their funding sources. But this is perhaps unavoidable in the zero-sum federal budget environment, which is putting great pressure on Congress and federal agencies to tie investments of public money to clearly-observable ends of public utility. Both the public and Congress seem willing to support a certain amount of fundamental science research as an intrinsic social good, but only up to a point. Hence, while some scientists may bridle at political considerations being brought into any scientific research decision, tight public monies will necessitate setting R&D priorities.

Institutional issues and democratic participation

Therefore, budget priorities must be determined at the Congressional and Executive levels, as recommended by a recent report of the National Academy of Sciences.[94] Guided by the critical industries and technologies lists, such a process would attempt to assign an appropriate mix of needs within given budget constraints, balancing the roles of the various agencies, and the resource allocations across and within needs areas.

A major issue is which federal agency (or agencies) should be the principal 'champion(s)' to coordinate the initiatives. It is essential that civilian agencies have the principal responsibility for this function, as a counterbalance to DARPA. A new independent civilian technology agency may eventually be necessary, its potential political problems notwithstanding. The Agenda may provide a more appropriate context for creating such an agency, however, giving it a stronger mandate and political base to lobby for funding and implement its programs.

Joint-agency committees, modeled on the existing Federal Coordinating Committee on Science and Technology (FCCSET),[95] may also be appropriate means for coordinating cross-cutting initiatives and S&T programs. A FCCSET-type body would seek representation from all relevant federal agencies to coordinate activities and responsibilities for the various components of an initiative under their jurisdiction.

In any case, as initiatives are divided up among different agencies, there would be concomitant increases in their R&D budgets, resulting in a diversified portfolio of funding sources for critical areas of research. That is, by tying basic research programs to demand-pull initiatives, a multiplicity of funding sources focusing on a range of different types of programs within basic as well as applied areas would be created. This would help diminish the dependency of some fields on only one or two agencies for primary funding, such as the reliance of computer science on the DoD. There would then be several possible funders interested in overlapping, but still different types of approaches in a field, reflecting the variety of problems with which they are concerned. This, in turn, would stimulate a wider range of areas of inquiry and approaches to scientific problems.

Perhaps the most important challenge for the Agenda will be to establish mechanisms of democratic participation and public access at every level of the S&T policy process. Without this, its broad social mandate would be significantly curtailed. An important step would be to broaden the R&D advisory process for Congress, the Executive, and the Federal R&D agencies, to include inputs from public interest (e.g. environmental, industrial retention groups), labor, local and state government, and constituency (minorities, women) groups. One possibility is to establish a National Citizen's Science and Technology Advisory Board as an adjunct to the National Research Council. Usually comprised of scientific experts from academia and the private sector, research advisory boards often wield a great deal of influence over policymakers and agency bureaucrats, providing input about the content of R&D programs, desired budgeting levels, regulatory issues and other matters.

Beyond the advisory boards, it is essential to have broad-based representation in all critical areas of S&T decision-making in government and industry: to guarantee the establishment of social quid-pro-quos; to help create accountability for corporate and political interests that get special benefits; and to broadly distribute the outcomes leveraged by these benefits in a socially equitable way. Inclusion of labor and community representation in the formation of consortia and joint industry–university ventures might be considered as a policy condition. On the whole, however, there are as yet few S&T policy mechanisms, at any level of government, where these interests are adequately represented.

The S&T policy process would also need to be decentralized, involving the participation of regions, states, and communities. This would encourage a diversity of viewpoints and approaches to problems, and flexibility to tailor policies to the needs of specific locales, as well as increase outlets for public access to resources and especially to S&T educational opportunities. The nation needs not only to expand the supply of faculty, engineers and science researchers, it must target minorities, women, underemployed and displaced workers, and other disenfranchised people for education and training which prepares them for employment in the emerging high-tech industrial epoch.

Agenda initiatives might support community-based technology projects and science in the public interest centers around the nation,[96] a technology extension service, and technical assistance centers, to foster fruitful interactions between academic research laboratories and local businesses, labor and communities. In many cases local industries need technical assistance, not advanced R&D for upgrading their operations, as the National Apparel Technology Center, in Raleigh, NC, for example, has discovered.[97]

A high priority of the Agenda would be to increase the participation of the nation's workforce in S&T programs applied to problems of industrial production and workplace design. As the Cuomo Commission report argues, we need a 'new view of technology', in which technology derives not only from academic and industrial laboratories, but directly from the manufacturing process. 'Often technology is born on the factory floor', the report observes.[98] Tacit and experiential knowledge gained in the act of production, therefore, is critical to innovation. Yet, despite widespread agreement, including within management circles, on the importance of workforce participation for improving US industrial performance, labor remains, at best, a junior partner in the corporate S&T system.

CONCLUSION

In the 1940s, Senator Harley Kilgore (D–WV), a New Deal populist, led attempts to establish a nationally coordinated postwar S&T program keyed to civilian needs, headed by a NSF-type agency. Playing off the growing anti-New-Dealer feeling, Vannevar Bush led the opposition to this program, fighting for, and eventually succeeding in getting a scaled-down version of Kilgore's proposed agency established, which supported only basic science research and education. Though this resulted in the formation of the National Science

Foundation, it left the DoD as the only major government agency capable of promoting large-scale R&D efforts in the nation; thus beginning the hegemony of DoD over the nation's R&D program, which has prevailed to the present day.

The nation is now at another crossroads, as the DoD role in R&D begins to be scaled back and economic performance now dominates the S&T policy discourse. Since the 1970s, industry after industry in the US has been losing its competitive edge. In response to this crisis, however, our purpose in proposing the National Needs Agenda is not to espouse a kind of technological nationalism, as has often been resorted to in this debate.[99] Transnational, multi-polar relations have replaced East–West bi-polar relations in governing international political and economic affairs.[100] The US must learn to adapt to this new geopolitical reality. It can no longer assume its former position of economic and military dominance.

Within this new global order the development and control of science and technology have become paramount concerns. Thus, we propose a strategy which emphasizes the goal of national productiveness over the narrow nationalistic notion of competitiveness. We seek to harness the nation's science and technology resources in a way that couples enhanced economic performance with the efforts to solve our many looming environmental and social problems. Moreover, many of the initiatives we propose will require cooperative science and technology endeavors across international boundaries if they are going to be relevant to the emergent human ecological issues confronting all societies.

Perhaps most important, we seek to demystify, demilitarize, and return science and technology – which for so long in world history have been the handmaidens of powerful and aggressive forces – once again to a human level. In this way they can play the vital and positive role in human evolution that they should, as our principal tools for enhancing the quality of life on our planet.

Notes

1. Susan Walsh Sanderson, *The Consumer Electronics Industry and the Future of American Manufacturing* (Washington, DC: Economic Policy Institute, 1989) p. 20.
2. Robert B. Reich, 'Members Only', *The New Republic* (26 June 1989).

3. US Department of Commerce, *United States Trade Performance in 1987*. Reported in Susan Walsh Sanderson, ibid., pp. 4–5.
4. Council on Competitiveness, *Picking Up the Pace: The Commercial Challenge of American Innovation* (Washington, DC, 1988).
5. David E. Sanger, 'Key Technology Might Be Sold to the Japanese', *The New York Times*, 17 November 1989.
6. US Congress, Office of Technology Assessment, *Commercializing High-Temperature Superconductivity*, OTA-ITE-388 (Washington, DC: US Government Printing Office, June 1988), p. 21.
7. Industry Studies Group, Division of Science Resources Studies, National Science Foundation, 'Economic Outlook and Corporate Mergers Dampen Growth in Company R&D', *Science Resource Studies Highlights* (NSF 88-311) (Washington, DC, 11 March 1988).
8. Michael L. Dertouzos, Richard K. Lester, Robert M. Solow, and the MIT Commission on Industrial Competitiveness, *Made in America, Regaining the Productive Edge* (Cambridge, MA: The MIT Press), p. 94.
9. See Mario Pianta, 'Technology, Economic Change and Transatlantic Relations', Paper for the panel on 'Technology and Political Order in Europe II: technology, economy and political change,' at the Convention of the International Studies Association, London, 28 March–1 April 1989, unpublished, National Research Council, Institute for studies on research and scientific documentation (CNR-ISRDS), Via De Lollis 12, 00185 Roma, Italy; and, 'High Technology Programmes: For the Military or for the Economy', *Bulletin of Peace Proposals*, 19:1 (1988), pp. 53–79.
10. Francis Narin and J. Davidson Frame, 'The Growth of Japanese Science and Technology', Vol. 245, *Science* (11 August 1989), pp. 600–605.
11. Council on Competitiveness, 'Picking Up the Pace', op. cit., p. 28.
12. Dertouzos et al., *Made in America*, op. cit., p. 306.
13. Daniel Charles, 'Reformers Seek Broader Military Role in the Economy', *Science*, Vol. 241 (12 August 1988), pp. 779–81.
14. Defense Science Board, *Industrial Deterrence: Meeting National Security Needs Through Industry and Technology, Final Report of 1988 Defense Science Board Study of the Defense Industrial and Technology Base, Volume I*. Chairman, Robert A. Fuhrman, Vice-Chairman, William A. Anders. (Washington, DC: Office of the Under-Secretary of Defense for Acquisition, October 1988).
15. Dated 14 June 1987.
16. Charles, 'Reformers', op. cit.
17. G. Christopher Anderson, 'Superconductivity Consortia Proliferate Despite Scientific, Economic Questions', 3, 14, *The Scientist* (10 July 1989).
18. Andrew Pollack, 'America's Answer to Japan's MITI', *The New York Times*, 5 March 1989.
19. See the two studies by Kenneth Flamm, *Targeting the Computer* (Washington, DC: The Brookings Institution), 1987; and *Creating the Computer*, (Washington, DC: The Brookings Institution), 1988. See

also Joel S. Yudken and Barbara Simons, 'Federal Funding in Computer Science: A Preliminary Report', *SIGACT News*, SIGACT, Association for Computing Machinery, 19, 1 (Fall 1987), pp. 53–62.

20. Interview conducted by Yudken, June 1988. See also Pollack, 'America's Answer', op. cit.

21. See: Defense Science Board, *Industrial Deterrence*, op. cit.; Office of the Under-Secretary of Defense (Acquisition), *Bolstering Defense Industrial Competitiveness, Preserving Our Heritage/ The Industrial Base/ Securing Our Future, Report to the Secretary of Defense by the Undersecretary of Defense (Acquisition)* (Washington, DC, 15 July 1988).

22. Reported in, Daniel S. Greenberg, 'Casting the Pentagon as Guide for U.S. Industry Begs for Calamity', *The Los Angeles Times*, 10 January 1989.

23. Ibid.

24. Ibid.

25. John Markoff, 'Cuts Are Expected for U.S. Financing in High-Tech Area', *The New York Times*, 16 November 1989.

26. David Sanger, 'Assurance By Japan on Jet Deal', *The New York Times*, 4 December 1989, p. C–1.

27. David Sanger, 'Key Technology Might Be Sold to the Japanese', *The New York Times*, 27 November 1989.

28. Leslie Helm et al. 'On the Campus: Fat Endowments and Growing Clout', *Business Week* (11 July 1988), p. 70.

29. The spectacular entrepreneurial growth of these industries since the 1970s can be attributed to their proximity to major research universities in Silicon Valley around Stanford University, and Boston's Route 128 around MIT.

30. Kenneth Flamm and Thomas L. McNaugher, 'Rationalizing Technology Investments', In John D. Steinbrunner (ed.), *Restructuring American Foreign Policy* (Washington, DC: The Brookings Institution, 1989), p. 135.

31. Flamm, *Targeting the Computer*, op. cit., p. 15.

32. Jay Stowsky, 'Beating Plowshares Into Double-Edged Swords: The Impact of Pentagon Policies on the Commercialization of Advanced Technologies' (Berkeley: Berkeley Roundtable on the International Economy (BRIE), April 1986); Michael G. Borrus, *Competing for Control: America's Stake in Microelectronics* (Cambridge, MA: Ballinger Publishing Company, 1988); US Congress, Office of Technology Assessment, *Commercializing High-Temperature Superconductivity*, op. cit.; Jacques Gansler, *Affording Defense* (Cambridge, MA: The MIT Press, 1989); Lenny Siegel and John Markoff, 'High Technology and the Emerging Dual Economy', in David Bellin and Gary Chapman (ed.), *Computers in Battle* (New York: Harcourt Brace Jovanovich, 1987), pp. 259–82.

33. See for example: Seymour Melman, *Profits Without Production* (New York: Knopf, 1983); Lloyd J. Dumas, *The Overburdened Economy* (Berkeley: University of California Press, 1986); John E. Ullmann, *The Prospects of American Industry Recovery* (Westport, CN: Quorum Books, 1985).

34. John E. Ullmann, 'Economic Conversion: Indispensable for America's Economic Recovery', Briefing Paper Three (Washington, DC: National Commission for Economic Conversion and Disarmament, April 1989), p. 17. Ullmann cites the bibliography in Michael Dee Oden, *A Military Dollar Really is Different*, (Lansing, MI: Employment Research Associates, 1988); and A. Etzioni, *The Moondoggle* (Garden City, NY: Doubleday, 1964); S. Melman, *Our Depleted Society* (New York: Holt, Rinehart and Winston, 1965).

35. See Gansler, *Affording Defense*, op. cit., pp. 215–38 and endnotes for evidence and discussion of these points.

36. See Leslie Bruechner and Michael Borrus, 'Assessing the Commercial Impact of the VHSIC (Very High Speed Integrated Circuit) Program', *BRIE Working Paper* (Berkeley, CA: Berkeley Roundtable on the International Economy (BRIE) December, 1984), p. 5.

37. Between 11 per cent and 14 per cent of all manufacturing output while employing between 27 per cent and 32 per cent of all scientists, engineers and technicians. See Office of the Assistant Secretary of Defense, Comptroller, *National Defense Budget Estimates for FY 1988/89* (Washington, DC, April 1988 Tables 6–11 and 6–12. See also Michael Oden, *A Military Dollar Really Is Different*, op. cit., and Lloyd J. Dumas, *Overburdened Economy*, op. cit., p. 201.

38. See Jacques Gansler, *Affording Defense*, op. cit., p. 221. He writes in a footnote (n. 25): 'For an extensive discussion of the benefits of smaller size in achieving innovation and growth, see F. M. Scherer, *Innovation and Growth: Schumperterian Perspectives* (MIT Press, 1984), especially pages 224 and 237.'

39. US Congress, Office of Technology Assessment, *Commercializing*, op. cit., p. 135.

40. Quoted in Lawrence M. Fisher, 'Need for High-Tech Consortiums Stressed', *The New York Times*, 12 January 1989.

41. See Michael Borrus, *Competing for Control*, op. cit., p. 252.

42. Telephone interview by Joel S. Yudken, 30 January 1989.

43. US Congress, Office of Technology Assessment, *Commercializing*, p. 37.

44. For an interesting review of different participation efforts in different industrial situations, see Lowell Turner, 'Three Plants Three Futures', *Technology Review*, Vol. 92, no. 1 (January 1989), pp. 39–45. For different views of worker participation, their effectiveness and labor impact see also: 'The Payoff from Teamwork', *Business Week* (10 July 1989), pp. 56–62; 'The Economic Forces Behind Participation', *Economic Notes*, Vol. 55, nos. 7–8 (New York: Labor Research Association, July–August 1987).

45. Panel on 'Federal Funding and Academic Physical Sciences', Dr Barbara Simons, Chair, Annual Meeting of the American Association for the Advancement of Science (AAAS), San Francisco, CA, 17 January 1989.

46. See US Office of Technology Assessment, *Commercializing*, p. 133, n. 2; Joel S. Yudken and Barbara Simons. 'Federal Funding in Computer Science: A Preliminary Report', *SIGACT News*, SIGACT, As-

sociation for Computing Machinery, 19, 1 (Fall 1987), pp. 53–62.

47. Phil W. Anderson, '"Super" Science Squeezes "Small" Science', *The New York Times*, 5 February 1988.

48. Panel on 'Federal Funding and Academic Physical Sciences', Dr Barbara Simons, Chair, AAAS Annual Meeting, San Francisco, CA, 17 January 1989.

49. Barbara J. Culliton, 'Science Budget Squeeze and the Zero Sum Game', *Science*, Vol. 241 (6 May 1988), p. 713.

50. National Science Foundation, Division of Science Resources Studies, *Federal Funds for Research and Development, Federal Obligations for Research by Agency and Detailed Field of Science/Engineering: Fiscal Years 1967–1989.*

51. Between fiscal 1980 and fiscal 1988, DoD support for academic R&D grew 96 per cent in constant dollars, while NSF funding rose only 25 per cent and DOE support increased 15 per cent. NIH accounts for 47 per cent of total Federal R&D funding to academic institutions in fiscal 1988, over 90 per cent of which goes to the life sciences. The DoD share is about 16 per cent. Albert H. Teich and Kathleen M. Gramp, *R&D in the 1980s: A Special Report, R&D Budget and Policy Project* (Washington, DC: American Association for the Advancement of Science, Office of Public Sector Programs, September 1988).

52. See Joel S. Yudken and Barbara Simons, 'Preliminary Report', op. cit.

53. See the collected works of Professors Seymour Melman, Lloyd J. Dumas, and John Ullmann, for example.

54. Thomborson, Clark (formerly Thompson), 'Military Direction of Academic CS Research', *Communications of the ACM* 29, 7 (July 1986): 583–5.

55. See Vannevar Bush, *Science: The Endless Frontier, A Report to the President on a Program for Postwar Scientific Research* (GPO, 1945), p. 77. Cited in Flamm and McNaugher, 'Rationalizing', op. cit., p. 134.

56. Ibid., p. 135.

57. Banquet keynote address, COSEPUP, AAAS, at 1989 AAAS Annual Meeting, San Francisco, CA, January 1989.

58. See Joel S. Yudken and Barbara Simons, *A Field in Transition: Current Trends and Issues in Academic Computer Science, Final Report of the Project on Funding Policy in Computer Science*, for the Science Policy Committee, SIGACT, ACM (Stanford, CA: 1990 forthcoming).

59. Based on interviews of researchers and academic computer science department and laboratory chairs, conducted by Joel S. Yudken, January 1987 through January 1988.

60. Quoted in Andrew Pollack, 'America's Answer', op. cit.

61. Quoted in Susan L. Sauer (ed.), *R&D in the New Administration, Change & Continuity, Colloquium Proceedings*, 13 and 14 April 1989 (Washington, DC: Committee on Science, Engineering, and Public Policy, American Association for the Advancement of Science, 1989), p. 64.

62. See Edward J. Hackett, 'Funding and Academic Research in the Life Sciences: Results of an Exploratory Study', *Science & Technology Studies* 5:3/4 (1987), pp. 134–47.

63. Dwight B. Davis, 'Assessing the Strategic Computing Initiative', *High Technology* (April 1985), pp. 41–9.
64. See Joel S. Yudken and Barbara Simons, *A Field in Transition*, op. cit.
65. See Dwight Davis, 'Assessing', op. cit.
66. For a discussion of this regarding computer science, see Joel S. Yudken and Barbara Simons, *A Field in Transition*, op. cit.
67. Kenneth Flamm, *Targeting the Computer*, op. cit., p. 188.
68. US Congress, Office of Technology Assessment, *Commercializing*, op. cit., p. 91. See also: *Directions in Engineering Research: An Assessment of Opportunities and Needs* (Washington, DC: National Academy Press, 1987).
69. Richard Karp, Professor of Computer Science, University of California, Berkeley. Panel on 'Federal Funding and Academic Physical Sciences', Dr Barbara Simons, Chair, AAAS Annual Meeting, San Francisco, CA, 17 January 1989.
70. David Dickson, *The New Politics of Science* (Chicago: University of Chicago Press, 1988), p. 57.
71. 'Million-Dollar Professors: Should the Ivory Tower Be a Gold Mine?', *Business Week* (21 August 1989), pp. 90–92.
72. David Dickson, *The New Politics of Science*, op. cit., p. 18.
73. Lawrence M. Fisher, 'Need for High-Tech Consortiums', op. cit.
74. Telephone interview with Ray Marshall, by Joel S. Yudken, 30 January 1989.
75. See Seymour Melman, *Profits Without Production*, op. cit., Dertouzos, et al., *Made in America*, op. cit., for discussions on steel industry R&D.
76. Telephone interview with Ray Marshall, by Joel S. Yudken, 30 January 1989. See also Richard Kazis, 'Rags to Riches? One Industry's Strategy for Improving Productivity', *Technology Review*, Vol. 92, no. 6 (August 1989), pp. 42–53.
77. See: David Noble, *Forces of Production* (New York: Knopf, 1984); Seymour Melman, *Profits Without Production*, op. cit. See also Dertouzos, et al., *Made in America*, op. cit., p. 239.
78. Nathan Rosenberg, *Inside the Black Box: Technology and Economics* (Cambridge: Cambridge University Press, 1982), p. 236.
79. See National Science Foundation, Division of Science Resources Studies, *Federal Funds*, op. cit.
80. See Wassily Leontief and Faye Duchin, *The Future of Automation on Workers* (New York: Oxford University Press, 1986); George T. Silvestri and John M. Lukasiewicz, 'Occupational employment projects: the 1984–95 outlook', *Monthly Labor Review* (November 1985), pp. 42–57.
81. US Congress, Office of Technology Assessment, *Computerized Manufacturing Automation. Employment, Education and the Workplace* (OTA-CIT 235) (Washington, DC, April 1984), p. 104. The Machinists Union, for example, has witnessed large numbers of its aerospace members losing jobs in metalworking, drafting, inventory control, tools and production planning as a result of Pentagon-sponsored automation. Phone interview with Richard Greenwood, Special Assistant to the President, International Association of Machinists, Washington, DC, 31 January 1989.

82. The literature on this is enormous. For a good overview of the deskilling literature, see Barbara Baran and Carol Parsons, 'Technology and Skill, A Literature Review', prepared for the Carnegie Forum on Education and the Economy, Berkeley Roundtable on the International Economy, January 1986. On worker control see Harley Shaiken, *Work Transformed: Automation and Labor in the Computer Age* (New York: Holt, Rinehart and Winston, 1985).

83. Many health problems, for example, have been reported by semiconductor employees due to toxic chemicals used in chip fabrication process, and by aerospace workers due to new composite materials they work with. Interview with Richard Greenwood of the International Association of Machinists, 31 January 1989.

84. John Burgess, 'Exporting Our Office Work, New technology is sending white-collar jobs abroad', *Washington Post National Weekly Edition*, (1–7 May 1989), p. 22.

85. Reich, *The New Republic*, op. cit.

86. Barbara J. Culliton, 'Science Budget Squeeze', op. cit., p. 713. See also National Academy of Sciences (NAS), National Academy of Engineering (NAE), Institute of Medicine (IOM), *Federal Science and Technology Budget Priorities, New Perspectives and Procedures, A Report in Response to the Conference Report on the Concurrent Resolution on the Budget for Fiscal Year 1989* (H. Con. Res. 268) (Washington, DC: National Academy Press, 1988).

87. Ibid.

88. ESPRIT, the European Strategic Programme of Research in Information Technology, is funded by $800 million of EEC funds; RACE is the acronym for R&D in Advanced Communications for Europe, and BRITE, is Basic Research in Industrial Technologies for Europe. See Mario Pianta, *Bulletin of Peace Proposals*, op. cit.

89. Ibid.

90. See Martin Tolchin, 'Critical Technologies: 22 Make the U.S. List', *The New York Times*, 3 March 1989; Michael Mecham, 'U.S. Pressed by Allies on Critical Technology Research, Pentagon Says', *Aviation Week & Space Technology* (3 April 1989) pp. 52–5.

91. For textile industry example, see: Richard Kazis, 'Rags to Riches?', op. cit.

92. Dertouzos, et al. op. cit., *Made in America*, p. 33.

93. Frank Emspak, 'Going on the Offensive: Technology and Labor,' *Dollars & Sense*, 1989, pp. 8–10. For early European examples of worker-centered technology projects, see Ake Sandberg (ed.), *Computers Dividing Man and Work, Recent Scandinavian Research on Planning and Computers from a Trade Union Perspective*, Arbetslivcentrum (March 1979).

94. See National Academy of Sciences, et al., *Federal Science and Technology*, op. cit.

95. See, for example, *Report of the Federal Coordinating Council on Science Engineering, and Technology Panel (FCCSET) on Advanced Computer Research in the Federal Government*, Robert E. Kahn, panel chairman, June 1985 (released 15 November 1985).

96. Such as those once supported by the National Science Foundation, Science for Citizens Program, terminated by the Reagan administration. Rachelle Hollander, 'Institutionalizing Public Service Science: Its Perils and Promise', in James C. Petersen (ed.), *Citizen Participation in Science Policy* (Amherst: The University of Massachusetts Press, 1984), pp. 75–95.
97. Richard Kazis, 'Rags to Riches?' op. cit.
98. The Cuomo Commission on Trade and Competitiveness, Lee Smith, Director and Editor, Lewis B. Kaden, Chairman, *The Cuomo Commission Report, A New American Formula for a Strong Economy*, (New York: Simon & Schuster, A Touchstone Book, 1988), p. 119.
99. See for example, David H. Brandin and Michael A. Harrison, *The Technology War, A Case for Competitiveness* (New York: John Wiley & Sons, 1987).
100. For an interesting discussion of this see: John Zysman, 'Redoubling the Bet: Power, Wealth and Technology', *BRIE* Working Paper no. 38, (University of California, Berkeley, CA: Berkeley Roundtable on the International Economy, forthcoming).

7 Constituencies and New Markets for Economic Conversion: Reconstructing the United States' Physical, Environmental and Social Infrastructure

Jonathan Feldman

INTRODUCTION

The close of the 1980s has brought renewed opportunities for the adoption of a national conversion policy in the United States, the Soviet Union and certain European nations like Italy and West Germany. These opportunities have been created by a seemingly disparate chain of events: expanding trade and budget deficits in the US; 'economic restructuring' in the Soviet Union; and the declining industrial competence of both superpowers. The inability of both the Soviets and the US to sustain rapidly-expanding military budgets has resulted in a military pullback by the Soviets and a slowdown of military spending by the US. In January 1989, the director of the Soviet National Institute of the Economy said that the real Soviet budget deficit was $165 billion and described it as the most important economic problem facing the country.[1] Such economic pressures have promoted President Gorbachev's overtures to Western Europe and the United States for agreements to mutually reduce their military programs.

The Gorbachev initiatives, together with the fiscal constraints on US military spending, have created a political opportunity for international disarmament negotiations and domestic efforts to convert the US military economy to civilian purposes. However, the tremendous political power of the warmaking institutions in the US, coupled with the economic dependency created by long-term military spending, have created barriers to conversion. So extensive is this dependency that more than 26 million Americans are either directly or indirectly dependent on military spending, according to an estimate by the National Commission for Economic Conversion and Disarmament.[2] The extensive influence of the military economy underscores the need to organize those constituencies that support new federal budget priorities to advance a national conversion program based on major military budget reductions, economic planning and new investments in needed civilian goods and services.

The political constituencies for a national conversion policy can be identified by the political and economic groups which have been adversely affected by the contradictory effects of the military economy. Many of these political constituencies recognize that military spending retards productive investment, diverts budgetary resources from the welfare state and leads to economic dislocation of military workers and their communities during downturns in military spending. The distinctive ways in which the military economy affects the structure of industries and the workplace, the national budget priorities, and the economy as a whole indicates which constituencies could be served by a comprehensive national conversion policy. It is the purpose of this chapter to show how such a national conversion policy for the US could bring together a progressive coalition to advance a program of major military budget reductions, economic expansion through civilian conversion, economic redistribution and an innovative agenda to promote industrial redevelopment and environmental protection. Indeed, it is the thesis of this chapter that the only way in which all the outstanding social, environmental and financial deficits can be addressed is by building such a coalition.

In order to examine why and how such a coalition and political mobilization could come into being, it is important to address the contradictory impacts of the military economy on the state, society and civilian industry. In particular, it is necessary to show how the requirements of the military economy have imposed fundamental social and economic trade-offs on broad segments of our society, while extracting a high cost in terms of lower overall economic performance in the civilian economy. Moreover, it is necessary to understand how persistently high levels of military spending block the political agendas of progressive social movements and numerous other constituencies. Indeed, to understand the political–economic function of military spending in the post-Reagan era, one must examine how the state was restructured under the Reagan Administration and how that has led to the current fiscal crisis of the state.

THE NEW FISCAL CRISIS OF THE STATE

President Reagan entered office promising to reduce wasteful federal spending, cut taxes, turn over control of many federal programs to state and local governments, and to revive America's political and military might. Supply-side economists for the Administration promised that these actions would stimulate economic growth and thereby eliminate the fiscal crisis of the state which had grown as federal expenditures had continued to outstrip tax revenues throughout the 1970s. While the Reagan Administration did succeed in cutting taxes, reducing many social welfare programs and turning the control of many other programs to state and local authorities, these measures did not stimulate sufficient growth to pay for the increased military programs. Nor did these military programs enhance the overall rate of accumulation through technological spin-offs and their demand-pull effects on the rest of the manufacturing economy. Indeed, as is widely recognized today, the Reagan Administration opted for a strong-dollar policy to attract the foreign savings necessary to finance the military buildup and to cover the shortfall in federal revenues. The results are written in the red ink that measures the doubling of federal debt since the accession and departure of Reagan from office.

The legacy of the Reagan Administration is a deepening of the fiscal crisis at all levels of government. The persistence of the federal deficit has meant even more austerity for already hard-hit social programs. Nowhere has this austerity been more graphically reflected than in the steep reductions in federal grants-in-aid to state and local governments. Table 7.1 summarizes the cumulative impact of these cuts in several programs, which amounted to nearly $60 billion over 1981–88.

Meanwhile, the social and human toll of these cutbacks has become increasingly visible throughout the United States, as homelessness, drug abuse and public health crises mount. The burden of these problems, and the cutbacks which contributed to them, have fallen disproportionately on the working poor and those 'weak client' groups that are not represented by powerful interest organizations and lobbies. Today, however, the consequences of these social de-

Table 7.1   Cumulative cuts in federal urban grants-in-aid, 1981–88
(billions of 1982 dollars)

Item	Amount
Primary and secondary education	−7.7
Employment and training	−26.8
Housing and community development	−9.2
Urban mass transit	−8.4
Public health	−4.5
Social and community service block grants	−2.7
TOTAL	−59.3

Source: Table 1 in *A Shift in Military Spending to America's Cities* (Lansing, MI: Employment Research Associates, 1988), p. 6.

ficits are also affecting a broader spectrum of society, especially at the state and local levels, where the deterioration of the social and physical infrastructure is most evident. Many other constituencies are affected by the curtailment in programs for employment and training, health care, education, drug-abuse prevention and treatment, urban mass transit, environmental protection, and those programs that serve the wider community.

These social deficits and problems have been aggravated by regional economic dislocations due to the decline in the domestic manufacturing base, the erosion of industrial productivity, the worsening of terms of trade in agriculture because of the overvalued dollar. But for the first time, those regions and industries which have been the primary beneficiaries of the military buildup face similar regional dislocations because of the contraction of military spending.

In the face of rising social demands and deficient tax revenues, where is the money going to come from with which to address these needs? Indeed, is there a feasible political economic program which can forge an alliance among those who have suffered most from this new fiscal crisis of the state? As suggested earlier, the answers to these questions lie in understanding which groups have lost the most because of the Reagan legacy, and how a reversal of our national priorities and a program of economic conversion could chart the way to social and environmental renewal. In order to identify where the potential support lies for such a progressive program, it is necessary to examine the extent of the social deficits created by Reagan's attack on the social welfare institutions, and identify those social groups which were most affected.

Income maintenance and redistribution

The deep cutbacks in programs designed to promote income maintenance and redistribution have affected the unemployed and those citizens who must depend on income maintenance programs such as Aid to Families with Dependent Children (AFDC), Food Stamps, Medicaid and other social welfare programs. The curtailment of these 'needs entitlement' programs and the tightening of eligibility requirements came at a time when the recessionary trends of the early 1980s and the economic decline in manufacturing trends in the mid-to-late 1980s increased the demand for these services.

The slowing of economic expansion in the early 1980s hit many states especially hard and led several states to restrict eligibility for unemployment insurance (UI) programs as financing them became increasingly difficult. The tendency to cut back such programs was exacerbated by federal policies initiated in 1981 which imposed greater costs on those states which were depending on the federal government to assist the financing of their basic programs. In the 1970s, extensions of unemployment benefits for 13 weeks were granted to help state and local governments cope with recessionary forces; but early in the Reagan Administration worker access to such extended benefits was sharply restricted by the federal government. While Congress eventually took steps to reverse these policies, a 1987 study reported that 'aggregate expenditures for basic state UI in the 1982–1984 period were 30% to 40% less than they would have been under the previously prevailing policies, and . . . the corresponding reduction for extended benefits was more than 50%'.[3]

Clearly, workers in the manufacturing and service sectors suffered the most because of these policies, with blue-collar workers in the manufacturing sectors bearing the brunt of layoffs, curtailments in Trade Adjustment payments, and denial of extended unemployment benefits.

Meanwhile, cutbacks have also occurred in food and nutrition programs; but these reductions actually began under the Carter Administration. In 1979, several steps were taken to limit both eligibility and benefits and led to large reductions in 1981. As a result, while 68 per cent of the poor participated in the Food Stamps program in 1980, only 59 per cent of a much larger population participated in 1985.[4]

Exacerbating these declines in social welfare assistance were the cutbacks which occurred in Social and Community Service Block

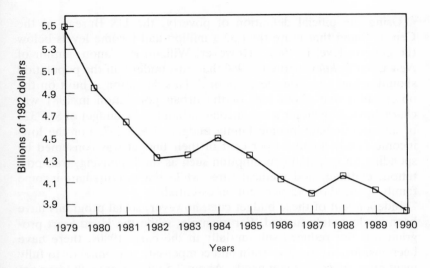

Figure 7.1   Social Services Block Grants, federal grants to state and local governments, 1979–90
Source: *Historical Tables, Budget of the United States Government, FY 1989,* Table 6.1, pages 122–31.

Grants. The Social and Community Service Block Grant programs provide federal funds for state and local governments to set up the delivery systems for a broad range of social services, including such things as child day-care, foster care, child protective services, legal services and nutritional programs for the young and old. As Figure 7.1 illustrates, all Social Service Block grants declined from $5.5 billion in 1979 to a projected low of $3.7 billion in 1990, as measured in inflation-adjusted dollars.[5]

These cutbacks have occurred at the same time that changing demographic patterns within the workforce have increased the need for social programs. A 1989 report by the Ford Foundation analyzed the impact of these changes, showing that:

More than half of the children born in America today will live in single-parent homes before age eighteen. Single parents find it much more difficult to manage work and child care and to link up with the opportunities and protections of the traditional labor market. For this and other reasons, nearly 25 percent of America's children under six now live in poverty.[6]

Using the official definition of poverty, the US Bureau of the Census found that more than 32.5 million had income levels below the poverty level in 1987.[7] However, William B. Canon, author of *New Class Politics*, wrote in 1986 that 'just under half the population should actually be considered poor'.[8] This definition is built on the observation that about half of the urban population in 1981 was characterized by either a low-income urban family budget of $15 323 or an intermediate-income family budget of $25 407. For the low-income family about 80 per cent of their budget was consumed by spending on essential consumption such as food, housing, transportation, clothing, and medical care, while the intermediate-income family spent about 75 per cent on essentials.[9]

Independent of these budget cuts, however, social programs have been inadequately funded. For example, while the Head Start program was not reduced substantially in the early 1980s, there have been insufficient funds to train and compensate personnel or to fully meet program constituent needs. About 2.5 million poor children are eligible for the program; however, funding limits have meant that only one in five of these children is currently enrolled. Meanwhile the cost of mounting a comprehensive child-care program is increasing. For instance, the Democrats' 1975 child-care bill would have cost $7 billion in 1975, but now it would cost about $15.5 billion (in 1988 dollars).[10]

The size of the social welfare deficit has been documented by the Ford Foundation's report, *The Common Good*. As shown in Table 7.2, if the Special Supplemental Food Program for Women, Infants and Children (WIC) were made an entitlement program, and all the people participated who were eligible, based on income criteria, the program's costs would increase by between $1.5 billion and $2 billion annually. To serve half the eligible population for the Head Start program would cost $2 billion annually.

The Ford Foundation study recommended an expansion of the Earned Income Tax Credit (EITC) program by adjusting benefit levels to recipient family size so that additional funds would be received for each dependent. Other recommendations are that the nation's Unemployment Insurance (UI) program could be changed to move beyond income maintenance to encompass training and retraining for new jobs. For unemployed persons who could not find jobs in existing labor markets, public service jobs could serve as a means to enter the job market. As Table 7.2 shows these reforms would cost $5.3 billion annually.

Table 7.2 A new social welfare budget

Government outlay increases for proposals to help children

Program	Recommended increases (billion dollars)	New recipients
WIC	1.7	3.4 million
Head Start	2.0	0.9 million

Government outlay increases for proposals to help working-age adults (first year) (billion dollars)

Program		
EITC expansion	2.3	
Retraining and UI reform	1.0	
Public-service jobs	2.0	

Projected costs of reforms in programs for the elderly (billion dollars)

Program initiative		
Raise SSI benefits	2.5	
Ease SSI asset test	0.1	
Subsidize long-term care	7.2	
Total costs of reforms	$18.8 billion	

Source: Ford Foundation Project on Social Welfare and the American Future, *The Common Good*, (New York: Ford Foundation, 1989).

Programs for the elderly are another area in which the Ford study proposed much-needed reforms. The study recommended an increase in Federal Social Security Insurance (SSI) to assure minimum poverty-line incomes for those in need. Indeed, the study found that in 1984, 62 per cent of elderly single black women and 28 per cent of elderly single white women were living in poverty. The report suggested easing restrictive limits on asset tests to qualify for SSI benefits. Finally, the study recommended the use of federal subsidies to ensure the spread of private long-term care insurance so that no one would be left uncovered. The projected costs of the reforms would amount to $7.8 billion annually.

The overall costs of such social welfare reforms would amount to $18.8 billion annually. Clearly, in a time of fiscal austerity, financing such reforms can come either from cuts in military spending, new taxes or both. In order to protect and renew vital social welfare institutions, however, the unemployed, the clientele of social welfare agencies, the trade unions, and other crucial constituencies will have to be mobilized to advance these reforms, while opposing further increases in military spending.

ENVIRONMENTAL AND ENERGY PROGRAMS

The close of the 1980s has brought greater attention to a series of environmental problems related to pollution of the air, water and land. Numerous statistics attest to growing environmental problems and the huge capital, labor and technological resources that must be marshalled to confront them. For example, a report of the first national survey of cancer risks from toxic air pollutants from industry found that there are 'more than 200 plants that pose risks at least 1,000 times higher than the federal government considers acceptable'.[11] These plants extended to 37 states, far beyond the petrochemical and oil refinery complexes of northern New Jersey, Texas and Louisiana that are traditionally associated with toxic air pollution.

Water pollution is also a major problem. An article in *The New York Times* on 3 August 1986 entitled 'Aging of Water Systems a Northeastern Epidemic' described how aging metropolitan water systems, outdated water-treatment plants and chemical and industrial pollutants have increasingly threatened the safety of water supplies. In response to these concerns, the Environmental Protection Agency has proposed rules that would mandate the filtration of all surface-water supplies. However, in New York State alone, 'more than 7 million of the 9 million people who drink water drawn from surface sources get water that is unfiltered'.[12] Groundwater supplies from Maine to Delaware are threatened by leaks of gasoline, pesticides and other industrial byproducts.

Other aspects of the environmental crisis reveal that billions of dollars will have to be spent by corporations and government to clean up or reverse past environmental damage. For example, the Environmental Protection Agency estimated in 1989 that between $16 billion and $33 billion will have to be spent over the next 20 years to reduce acid-rain-causing emissions by 50 per cent.[13] The total cost for cleaning up ten of the Great Lakes' dirtiest areas could reach $3.4 billion, according to a 1989 report.[14]

To address such environmental disasters will require increased governmental regulation and efforts to reduce pollution at the source. Indeed, pollution control efforts which focus solely on cleanup rather than source reduction threaten to produce a pattern in which public funds merely subsidize the health hazards created by negligent corporations. However, independent of regulatory enforcement and source reduction efforts, the need for increased federal expenditures is still considerable. Federal intervention is needed to clean up past environmental disasters and to fund or otherwise subsidize environmental infrastructure projects including reforestation, renewable energy systems, sewers and water filtration systems. In addition there is a need to develop alternative transportation systems such as light rail and high-speed trains in order to reduce urban air pollution and congestion.

In the area of hazardous waste cleanup there is a pronounced deficit in federal and private efforts. In 1988, estimated total spending for control, prevention and cleanup of hazardous wastes was $16 billion. Of this amount, $7 billion was spent by public sources and $9 billion by private sources.[15] However, Table 7.3 shows that excluding DoD and DOE sites the total bill for cleaning up the hazardous waste problem could reach as high as $73 billion. Despite this funding gap, the Environmental Protection Agency (EPA) has not significantly increased funding for its Hazardous Waste treatment program, which has averaged on $114 million over the last four years.

In the case of the Department of Energy and Department of Defense, the environmental legacy of the Cold War is marked by the huge environmental cleanup problem stemming from the nuclear weapons complex and the other hazardous-waste sites caused by military operations. According to estimates prepared by these agencies (see Table 7.3), the cost of addressing these problems could total between $126 billion to $145 billion over the next 25 to 35 years. To meet these costs will require that scarcity be imposed on other areas of the budget.

Indeed, the politics of scarcity has already affected the regulatory practices of the EPA, making them inherently unattainable. For instance, federal clean-water standards require state and local governments to invest in new primary and secondary sewage treatment systems; however, the cutback in federal grants-in-aid to assist state and local governments in building these systems has made meeting the standards infeasible. One commentator has noted that 'federalism has come to mean that the federal government is going to

Table 7.3   Cleanup costs for various programs

Program	No. of potential sites	Estimated cost in billions of dollars
Superfund sites	60 000	50
Sites of RRCA cleanups*	2 400	23
State-funded cleanup sites	22 000	45
Defense Department sites	7 200	11–15
Department of Energy sites	NA	115–130

NA: Not available
* Sites linked to the 1976 Resource Conservation and Recovery Act (RCRA) and its 1984 amendments.
Sources: General Accounting Office, 'Dealing with Problems in the Nuclear Weapons Complex Expected to cost over $100 billion', Washington, DC, July 1988, GAO/RCED–88–197BR; Salomon Brothers, Inc., Wertheim Schroder & Co., Smith Barney and Harris & Co. compilations as published in *Engineering News Record* 9 March 1989.

write all these laws and tell everybody how to do it, and then leave it up to the state and local governments to figure out how they're going to pay to implement all these programs'.[16]

The politics of scarcity has also affected the regulatory capacity of the EPA to enforce its standards. For example, in the case of drinking-water standards, the federal and state authorities have failed to enforce health standards for drinking water used by hotels, schools and other non-municipal water systems. The director of the EPA's office of drinking water explained that 'with 200,000 public water suppliers out there, there is no way we can have an enforcement program that deals with every violation. Nationwide, we have only 45 people to enforce the water programs.'[17]

The contradictory nature of federal policies is also evident in the failure to coordinate the nation's environmental policies with its energy policies. Federal funds are needed to develop technologies that promote clean and efficient energy systems. Yet, federal energy policy has not encouraged such environmentally sound energy development. Indeed, according to Michael Renner of Worldwatch Institute, 'in the 1984 fiscal year, out of total federal energy subsidies of $46.7 billion, renewables and energy efficiency combined received barely $2 billion, even though every single dollar devoted to them yields 80 times as much energy as a dollar subsidy to nuclear power'.[18]

Meanwhile, federal nuclear power programs receive $352 million a year, but only $35.5 million is spent on photovoltaic research. The Bush Administration wants to cut this further to $25 million, while West Germany is spending $60 million and Japan $40 million on solar research.[19] However, the development of a sustainable energy system may require public intervention to develop solar power industries because, 'Exxon Corp., Shell Oil Co., and Motorola Inc. have gotten out of the business and ARCO, the world's largest maker of solar cells, is planning to sell its solar subsidiary.'[20]

A lack of coordination among federal policies and the lack of financial resources have blocked serious efforts to enforce the existing environmental regulations. Meanwhile, 80 per cent of the public polled in July 1989 by *The New York Times* agreed that 'protecting the environment is so important that requirements and standards cannot be too high, and continuing improvements must be made regardless of cost'.[21] Thus, if public policy is to reflect the public's will, the political battle will increasingly be over setting new budget priorities which can provide the resources necessary to regulate and clean up the environment.

HOUSING AND COMMUNITY DEVELOPMENT

The need for federal intervention to address the housing crisis can be seen in statistics which show a significant homelessness problem, rising rent burdens, large waiting lists for public housing and the sizeable capital costs of new construction. Median rents rose 30 per cent for households with incomes below $3000 between 1978 and 1980. In New York City, 200 000 persons are on the public housing waiting list. Sixty thousand wait in Miami, 44 000 in Chicago, 23 000 in Philadelphia, and 13 000 in Washington, DC.[22] The social deficit in housing was also documented in a 1988 study prepared by the Harvard Joint Center for Housing Studies, which showed that since 1980 over five million renters and four-and-a-half million home-owners live in substandard housing, and that the stock of affordable homes has dramatically dwindled over the decade.[23] Meanwhile, those living below the poverty-level are competing for a dwindling supply of unsubsidized low-cost housing.

These deficits have been exacerbated by both federal cutbacks and rising rental and housing costs. As Figure 7.2 illustrates, Housing and Community Development Block Grants were severely cut over the

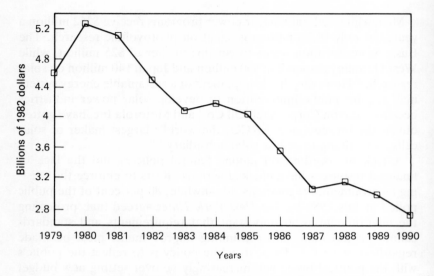

Figure 7.2   Housing and Community Development Grants: federal grants to state and local governments (1979–90)
Source: *Historical Tables, Budget of the United States Government, FY 1989*, Office of Management and Budget, Executive Office of the White House, Washington, DC, Table 6.1, pages 122–31.

years 1979–90, falling from a high point in FY 1980 of nearly $5.3 billion (in 1982 dollars) to a low of just over $2.7 billion in FY 1990. The reduction in these federal grants has seriously curtailed the ability of state and local governments to address the problems of homelessness and the supply of low-cost housing.

Federal intervention into the housing market is particularly necessary to meet the needs of those who cannot afford the housing provided by the private market. The affordability problem is compounded by the deficient supply of housing provided by the private sector. The Institute for Policy Studies Working Group on Housing has analyzed the effects of these shortcomings in the private sector supply of new housing construction:

The federal Housing Act of 1968 set a goal of producing 26 million units over a ten-year period, or 2.6 million units a year. Only 21.5 million units were built. The industry's all-time-high production figure came in 1972, with 2.4 million units. By 1981 the annual total was down to 1.1 million units; it rebounded to 1.8 million units by

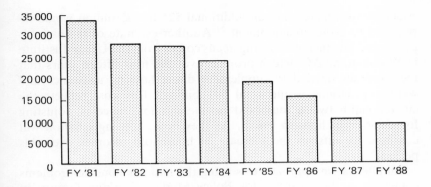

Figure 7.3   Units completed of Public and Indian Housing (1981–88)
Source: Public and Indian Budget Division, Department of Housing and
Urban Development, Washington, DC, 21 December 1988.

1986 before starting another descent, down to 1.6 million units in
1987, 1.4 million in 1988. Not suprisingly, the government has now
officially abandoned the embarrassing task of surveying national
housing needs and setting production goals.[24]

The Working Group also reports that virtually no new subsidized
housing units are being produced, and federal budget authority for
low-income housing dropped from $32.2 billion in FY 1981 to $8.4
billion FY 1988.[25] These data confirm the trends reported by the
Housing and Urban Development Administration (HUD). HUD
data depicted in Figure 7.3 shows a drastic decrease in the number of
Public and Indian Housing completed, with a drop in the total
number of units from 33 631 in FY 1981 to 9146 in FY 1988. In this
period, only 168 420 units were completed.[26]

These declines in public and low-income housing construction have
been compounded by the fact that half a million low-income housing
units are lost each year due to conversion, abandonment, inflation,
arson and demolition.[27] It is against this backdrop that one must
measure the rise in homelessness. HUD estimated that there were
between 250 000 and 300 000 homeless persons on an average night
between December 1983 and January 1984. By contrast, the Community for Creative Non-Violence estimated that during the winter
of 1983–84 as many as two to three million were homeless each
night.[28]

In order to modernize the nation's public housing stock ABT

Associates estimates that an additional $21 to $25 billion would be required to avoid abandonment.[29] Another estimate of the nation's public and low-income housing needs comes from the Urban Institute in Washington, DC, which projects over the next fifteen years that the subsidies needed to supplement direct housing assistance and welfare programs would total $41 billion. This cost reflects the current gap between household income and housing costs, adjusting for inflation of housing prices. As they note, housing inflation will continue to outstrip the increase in household incomes over this period.[30]

An alternative approach to solving the nation's housing problems comes from the Institute for Policy Studies Working Group on Housing, which has advanced a comprehensive new policy to restructure home ownership and the renovation and building of housing. Such a housing program would include incentives for the conversion of private rental and homeowner units into 'social ownership'. Social ownership refers to arrangements for land banking and tenant cooperatives which would take large numbers of housing units out of the private market and place them under public community trust. The main incentives for adopting such social ownership would be refinancing schemes for private homeowners who face bankruptcy and eviction, and financing for modernizing and rehabilitating existing subsidized and converted units. New housing construction could be financed through such social ownership policies. New methods are also proposed for providing operating subsidies for these types of social ownership. The cost for the first year of this comprehensive housing program was estimated to be $54.9 billion in FY 1988.[31]

The housing crisis is most simply a crisis of affordability. To address this problem would require increasing incomes or lowering housing costs. But cost reduction is not likely to be spontaneously generated by the housing market, because of the influence of powerful interests like real estate developers, construction firms, attorneys and others who benefit from the inflation of housing as it is sold and resold to consumers. The other side of this market logic is growing homelessness, abandonment, and the dwindling supply of affordable housing. This crisis has led to the formation of a coalition which planned the large housing march in Washington, DC in October 1989.[32] This coalition has explicitly linked progress on affordable housing with the curtailment of the military budget, thus forging a link in the movement for economic conversion.

HEALTH CARE

The deficits in housing, social welfare, environmental renewal, and education represent a threat to the maintenance of decent standards for public health. These deficits contribute to increasing poverty, pollution, homelessness, and the spread of drug abuse and disease, which in turn places greater demands on the public health care system. These trends are compounded by the rising cost of health care services, the increasing share of the elderly in the total population, a shortage in nurses, and the AIDS and drug crises. These factors not only strain the existing capacity of the health care delivery system, but also demand increased outlays on preventive medicine and public health education.

While the need for such services has increased, the federal government has failed to make a major commitment to address these problems through a comprehensive national health care policy. The United States stands alone with South Africa as the only western industrialized countries without a National Health Program that makes access to health care a basic right for all.[33] The social deficit in health care can be seen in the picture presented by health-care expert Vicente Navarro:

From 1980 to 1985, more U.S. children died of poverty, hunger and malnutrition than the total number of U.S. battle deaths in the Vietnam War.

The number of people without health coverage increased by 5 million from 1982 to 1984.

Thirty-eight million people do not have any form of health insurance coverage, public or private; 36 percent of them are children.

Twenty years after the establishment of Medicare (the insurance program for the elderly) senior citizens still have to pay more than 20 percent of their health expenditures.

In 1980, 19.3 percent of two-year olds had not been fully immunized against polio. By 1985 this figure had jumped to 23.3 percent, or nearly one child in five.[34]

Despite such deficits, the Reagan Administration had cut back needed health care programs. While overall federal budget outlays for health rose from $28.5 billion in 1981 to $36.3 billion in 1988 (in constant 1982 dollars), numerous cuts took place in Public Health Block Grants which provided services for the elderly, maternal and child care, disease control, drug and alcohol abuse treatment and so on.[35] A report in 1989 noted that Medicare represents 7 per cent of all federal expenditures, but it received 12 per cent of all federal cutbacks.[36] But while Medicare was cut back, rising numbers of hospitals have been forced to close primarily because Medicare no longer pays hospitals as much as it costs to treat elderly patients. A June 1988 report noted that a record total of 150 community hospitals had closed over the 1986–87 period, while few hospitals opened at that time.[37] Community health centers and the National Health Service were also cut, and the Reagan Administration sought to reduce federal support for biomedical research on cancer, heart disease, arthritis, immunology, cell biology, molecular genetics, neurological disorders and strokes.[38]

One estimate for the costs of reversing these policies has been made by the Congressional Budget Office for Senate bill 1265, a mandated health-care bill. This bill would affect 51 million people, 23 million of whom were not previously insured. It would add $27.1 billion in incremental costs to employment-based health plans, $17 billion of which is already being spent on providing care to uninsured people. Thus, the net cost of this mandated benefits approach would be $10 billion.[39] However, other national health insurance proposals, such as the National Health Program proposed by former presidential candidate Jesse Jackson, would have provided increased health services at lower costs. The projected cost difference (or savings) in 1989 between the Jackson plan and the current health system would be $69.3 billion. This differential is based on projected savings in such areas as insurance overhead, hospital and nursing home administration, physicians' billing, advertising and health industry profits.[40]

Some health-care analysts argue that new federal funds would not be needed if the health industry could be successfully restructured to cut waste, overcharges and administrative overhead. However, in the short run, federal intervention is urgently needed to address the health crisis. Political mobilization around this crisis has led to calls for new government spending as the Congress has been slow to come up with a reform for restructuring the health industry. Federal intervention is needed to provide new funding to ease the shortage of nurses. A report in 1988 found that there were 137 000 vacancies for registered nurses in hospitals and nursing homes.[41] The percent of total full-time nursing positions vacant each year increased from 4.4 per cent in 1983 to 11.3 per cent in 1987. The nursing shortage has led to temporary closings of emergency rooms and intensive care units and delays of elective surgery. Government funding is needed to pay reimbursement costs for recruiting and training nurses, financial aid for students in nursing schools and increased wages in order to attract more people into the profession.

The AIDS crisis is another area requiring immediate federal intervention. The number of people infected by this disease, and the resulting deaths, are growing dramatically. By July 1989, the total number of persons diagnosed with AIDS had passed 100 000 and the total number of deaths had reached 59 391.[42] The costs of addressing the AIDS burden are also significant. In 1986, direct health care costs for AIDS were more than $1 billion. A Rand Corporation study estimated that the AIDS epidemic 'could cost $37 billion for the care of 400 000 victims between now and mid-1991'.[43] These estimates were made before recent findings confirmed that the drug AZT could delay the onset of AIDS in people with only minor symptoms. The drug costs as much as $8000 a year for persons with AIDS. For those with the virus who have not yet developed its symptoms, the costs may be less, perhaps $3600 a year. Richard Burzon, a scientist at the Institute of Medicine in the National Academy of Science, has estimated that the combined cost of AIDS testing and giving AZT to those who need it would amount to several billion dollars a year.[44]

The limitations on health-care coverage and the expansion of health-care costs are rooted in the profitmaking nature of the health-care industry. Indeed, the potential for profit is considerable. A review of the profits for the major segments of the health-care industry in 1983 reveals that the drug and pharmaceutical segment garnered $5.6 billion, the medical and surgical equipment suppliers $1.8 billion, the insurance and financial institutions $2.1 billion, and hospitals and other health-care institutions yielded $2.8 billion.[45] Clearly, in order to curb the rising costs of health care there will have to be some regulation of market power and profits in these key sectors.

Corporations outside the health-care industry have begun to recognize the need for structural reform of health care, and some corporate leaders are even beginning to discuss the need for national health care. Nonetheless, the predominant method used by corporations to cope with rising health-care costs has been to shift them on to the workers. For instance, from 1985 to 1987, the amount of the annual cost borne by a company in a typical plan for health expenses increased 35 per cent, while the amount borne by an employee increased 58 per cent.[46] These disproportionate cost increases tell only part of the story, as firms try to reduce or eliminate health-care benefits for their workers.[47] This in turn has led to a political reaction by labor. A report in August 1989 described management and union disagreements over health-care costs in the contract talks involving the American Telephone and Telegraph Company, four large steel companies and several supermarket chains on the West coast. Proposals to shift health-care costs to workers have been at the center of two strikes of regional phone companies and the United Mine Workers strike against the Pittston Coal Group.[48] Such contention between management and labor, together with the rising costs of health care, especially for the elderly, are sure to increase support for federal intervention to develop a comprehensive national health-care policy. Yet, for such a policy to be realistic, there must be a plan for funding it.

EDUCATION AND EMPLOYMENT AND TRAINING

The nation's educational system has suffered from federal cutbacks, underinvestment, mismanagement and a failure to compensate teachers in a manner necessary to attract and retain high-quality instructors. A study by the US Department of Education found that 16.4 per cent of all students who were sophomores in 1980 failed to graduate from high school two years later. Other estimates suggest that about one in four teenagers leaves high school before receiving a diploma.[49] There is a growing divergence between the skill-levels required by new jobs in the workplace and the ability of schools to produce students competent in working at such jobs. The Reagan Administration was able to politically exploit the deterioration of the nation's education system, and shift the focus away from the critical socio-economic issues underlying the crisis. As education scholar Leon Botstein has commented,

> Playing upon the widespread fear of federal meddling in local school affairs, Reagan and [former Secretary of Education William] Bennett, in the name of higher standards and rigor, have gained political credit for the continuing deterioration of American

schools. . . . Bennett framed the issue as one of will, respect for tradition, and discipline, managing to pull the focus away from funding.[50]

However, funding remains an essential part of the crisis. Chapter 1 of the Education Consolidation and Improvement Act of 1981 funds compensatory education programs for educationally deprived and low-income students. While this program has had a favorable impact on student performance, as the Ford Foundation study has noted, 'the proportion of children served by Chapter 1 fell from 75 percent in 1980 to 54 percent in 1985'.[51] A survey of educators at thirty-one schools in Detroit, Denver, Indianapolis, New Orleans and Rochester gave evidence of deficiencies in staff-levels and school equipment. Seventy-five per cent of these educators said that resources like teaching materials and equipment were inadequate and more than 85 per cent said their schools did not have enough staff. Rundown school buildings and overwhelming workloads have hurt teacher performance.[52] Such conditions reflect both a failure in federal budgetary commitments and the inadequate and discriminatory financing mechanisms used by state and local governments to fund their school districts. School districts which are dependent on the property tax base for financing face austerity as property owners reject tax-increases.[53] Clearly, both tax reform and federal assistance will be central to solving state and local educational financing problems.

The nation's system of higher education is not insulated from these fiscal woes. While tuition has surpassed the average rate of inflation in recent years, colleges and universities face a physical infrastructure crisis. Universities and colleges have deferred expenses for maintenance, leading to an estimated bill of $20 billion required for repairing and modernizing buildings, equipment and utilities, according to a report issued in 1988. This study entitled, *The Decaying American Campus: A Ticking Time Bomb*, said that the potential cost for addressing these infrastructure problems could total $70 billion.[54]

Employment and training programs are another crucial area of educational investment which have suffered from the Reagan Administration's restructuring and cutbacks. These programs provide training and retraining services in both on-the-job and classroom situations so that the young, the unemployed, the unskilled, and those workers who need to acquire new job-skills can find and hold new jobs.

Employment and training grants have fallen the most of all federal grants-in-aid, from $6.7 billion (1982 dollars) in 1981 to a low of $2.5 billion in 1988.[55] Congress, recognizing that the cutbacks came at time when state and local governments were struggling to cope with the dislocation caused by the recession of the early 1980s and the loss of manufacturing jobs, restored some of these monies with the passage of the Emergency Jobs Act of 1983. Yet, these temporary measures did not address the longer-term employment and training needs that had developed as a result of the growing trade deficit, declining competitiveness and economic restructuring. Indeed, the Reagan Administration's Job Training Partnership Act (JPTA) which replaced the Comprehensive Employment and Training Act (CETA) had not been well designed to address the problems of plant closings, mass layoffs and regional economic dislocation which had disproportionately affected manufacturing industries. According to the Bureau of Labor Statistics 1984 estimate, under Title III of JPTA only 6 per cent of the 2.2 million workers who had lost their jobs due to plant closures were enrolled in the job training program.[56] The passage of the Economic Dislocation and Worker Adjustment Assistance Act of 1987 replaces Title III of JPTA, and provides more financial assistance to hard-pressed regions in the nation's industrial heartland. Yet more needs to be done to reverse the damage inflicted on the nation's workforce. Moreover, there is the special problem of dislocation from military cutbacks which needs to be addressed.

In an era of intensified international competition, employment and training programs become essential for maintaining and upgrading the skills of the workforce so that jobs can be retained and increased. Educators, employers, trade unions, the unemployed and the economically disadvantaged all are increasingly demanding more federal investment in these critical human resources which hold the key to the economic future.

PHYSICAL INFRASTRUCTURE

The physical infrastructure made up by the national stock of roads, bridges, sewers, mass transportation systems and other vital public investments is another area which has suffered massive disinvestment over the last 21 years.[57] Estimates published in 1982 found that nearly 45 per cent of the nation's bridges needed major repairs or total replacement and that nearly 25 per cent of the country's bus and

Table 7.4   Annual capital investment requirements, 1983–2000 (billions of 1982 dollars)

Item	JEC Study	CBO Study
Main highways and bridges	40.0	27.2
Other transportation	9.9	11.1
Sewage systems	9.0	6.6
Water systems	5.3	7.7
TOTAL	64.2	52.6

Sources: Table 4.9 in Joint Economic Committee of Congress, *Hard Choices: A Report on the Increasing Gap Between Infrastructure Needs and Our Ability to Pay for Them*, (Washington, DC: U.S. Government Printing Office, 1984), p. 57; George Peterson, et al., Infrastructure Needs Studies: A Critique, a paper prepared for the National Council on Public Works improvement, The Urban Institute, Washington, DC, 1 July 1986 as cited in *Fragile Foundations: A Report on America's Public Works*, (Washington, DC: National Council on Public Works Improvement, February 1988).

subway systems should be replaced. Pat Choate, senior policy analyst for TRW, Inc., warned in 1982 that from $2.5 to $3 trillion would be needed just to maintain the present level of service on public facilities over the next ten years.[58] The Joint Economic Committee (JEC) and the Congressional Budget Office (CBO) of the Congress have carried out their own assessments of infrastructure needs. Table 7.4 summarizes the projected annual capital investment requirements estimated by these two studies for the seventeen-year period examined. The JEC estimated a serious shortfall between the total projected needs and expected revenues for each of the four main infrastructure areas examined. A deficit of $265 billion was expected for highways and bridges, $88 billion for other transportation, $41 billion for water systems and $49 billion for sewer systems over the period 1983 to 2000.[59] The CBO study found a projected deficit in public infrastructural investment amounting to $52.6 billion annually.

Increasingly, policymakers are recognizing that these deficits in public infrastructural investment tend to slow overall economic productivity and growth. Research by David Alan Aschauer of the Chicago Federal Reserve Bank has shown a strong direct relationship between non-military public infrastructural investment and aggregate economic performance in the US and other leading western industrialized nations.[60] The clear lesson is that the composition of public investment *does* matter when considering economic performance. In the past, economics of the Keynesian persuasion have often been about what kind of government investment is made, instead of focusing on the effects of government spending on aggregate demand.[61] Today, it is clear that not only the level, but the qualitative aspects of government spending must be considered in evaluating the effects of public finance.

A program of public non-military capital investment could play a critical role in forging a national coalition for an economic conversion policy. A broad range of interests could benefit from such a program, including trade associations of heavy construction and architectural concerns, manufacturers, state and local officials, trade unions, especially workers throughout the manufacturing and construction trades, and numerous other potential constituents.

BEYOND THE POLITICS OF SCARCITY: RENEWAL OF THE SOCIAL WELFARE STATE AND THE PUBLIC INFRASTRUCTURE

The accumulated deficits we have described above, together with the vast diversion of labor, capital, and technological resources into the military have taken their toll on productivity and economic growth. But economic decline, whether viewed as a consequence of regional deindustrialization or a failure in production competence, is creating a new interest in expanding public investment in infrastructure, civilian technological development, education, employment and training and other social and human needs. Yet the drive to renew the nation's social welfare institutions and convert the national budgetary priorities from military to civilian production must overcome the political and economic obstacles which are the legacy of the Reagan years.

The sizeable social deficits chronicled here have produced a politics of scarcity in which Reagan-style federalism has been used to play one particular interest group off against another. The division of interest groups has succeeded because the Reagan style of federalism has shifted responsibility for program funding on to under-capitalized state and local governments. Together with decentralization of control over social programs and tax reductions – which were partly designed to subvert further increases in funding social programs – these changes in federalism weakened the base for large-scale federal spending in the civilian sector. The net result has been a politics of scarcity in which social groups battle over limited resources, and are thereby divided and conquered. In large measure the Reagan approach to federalism was a counter-attack on federal initiatives of the 1960s and 1970s which had been successfully organized by numerous progressive constituencies to redress problems in education, social welfare, environmental protection and other issues.[62]

Today, the opponents of Reagan-style federalism are slowly drawing together, but to achieve their political objectives they must confront the budgetary legacy of the Reagan era. Basically, Congress, the executive and the political media have presented the public with three immediate ways to deal with the fiscal deficits: raise taxes; cut social programs; or cut defense spending. But these options fail to take measure of the sizeable social deficits and the need to confront the socio-economic challenges that they pose to society. However, while Democrats and Republicans alike have traditionally favored huge military budgets, both parties face resistance to further cutting of social programs. On the other hand, both parties' leaders view new taxes as politically risky. In the last two political campaigns, the Republicans have been able to politically exploit the Democrats' call for new taxes, hence the recent political jockeying for new tax-cuts. The evidence suggests that these tax-cuts will not stimulate growth enough to solve the financial deficit, let alone finance the programs which are necessary to address the numerous social deficits. While these programs could be funded by increased corporate taxes and increased progressive tax proposals, such proposals seem unlikely at this stage. Thus, the final budgetary option is to reduce military expenditures.

The military spending reduction option is increasingly likely. In fact, a poll in May 1989, showed that 'fully three-quarters of those participating said that the Defense Department's budget should not grow at all for five years, or should be reduced by 3 percent in each of the next three years'.[63] The National Governors' Association at its July 1989 meeting warned that the federal government needed to spend more on transportation and education to keep from falling behind other nations. A report by a group led by Illinois governor James R. Thompson noted that the United States ranked 55th in the world in capital investment for public infrastructure.[64] Meanwhile, even such traditionally conservative political groups as the National Association of Counties' board of directors have called for both defense cuts and tax increases to help prevent further cutbacks.[65]

In addition, many public policymakers are beginning to recognize that demographic forces alone are likely to result in an expansion in welfare state expenditures. The Ford Foundation found that the increasing share of retired persons in the population will mean that there will be fewer workers to support those entering the retirement system, thereby adding additional stress to the already overburdened social security and medical care systems.[66] It is for these reasons that the Ford Foundation has advocated its wide-ranging set of social welfare reforms in order to rationalize the system.

But for Congress to respond to these diverse political pressures will require a coherent political solution backed by the support of a coalition of interests capable of forcing its way on to the political–economic agenda of the day. However, is it credible to suggest that military budget reductions could finance a comprehensive program to address the nation's social deficits? Table 7.5 draws up a preliminary estimate of the cost of what we shall call 'The Save America Budget'. Such a program would amount to $173.3 billion in the first year. Clearly, this is a formidable sum of money. While such an alternative set of budget priorities might be able to mobilize a broad set of constituencies, is it feasible to argue that military reductions could finance something on this scale?

Table 7.5   The Save America Budget: estimated annual federal outlays needed for selected public works and services

Environmental repair

   $17.5 billion   First year of ten-year program for cleaning up radioactive waste and atomic bomb plants.

   $10.0 billion   First year of ten-year program for cleaning up toxic wastes costing $100 billion according to Office of Technological Assessment estimates.

   $6 billion   Annual cost to cut sulfur dioxide emissions by 8–12 million tons/year in the United States to combat acid rain.

Infrastructure

   $26 billion   The difference between needs and available revenues required for repair of roads, bridges, water and sewer systems from 1989 to 2000.

   $10 billion   First year of a ten-year program costing $100 billion to prepare the nation's rail system for electric power propulsion.

Education

   $30 billion   One year of Department of Education spending for public education with a 50% increase in expenditures over and above current annual allocations by the federal government.

$10 billion   Annual cost of a full preschool education entitlement, with adequate salaries for teaching staff.

$2.2 billion   A restoration of President Bush's proposed cuts from the compensatory education program.

$4.4 billion   An addition to Head Start Program so that all eligible children could be served.

$1.0 billion   To restore Bush's proposed cut of financial assistance to needy students.

$8.0 billion   The first year of a ten-year program to address deferred maintenance at colleges and universities.

$1.1 billion   The first year cost of a two-year program to purchase 77 000 school buses needed, each costing $30 000.

Housing
$30 billion   The annual cost of a comprehensive housing program to address the housing shortage and homelessness problem.

Health
$5.1 billion   The annual cost of providing pre-natal care for the poorest mothers.

$.1 billion   The first year cost of a five year program to construct waters and sewers for 100 000 residents along the Texas/Mexico border.

$1.0 billion   Restoration of proposed Bush cuts in supplemental Social Security assistance for the blind, elderly and disabled.

$9.6 billion   Restoration in the proposed Bush cut in Aid for Dependent Children.

$7.3 billion   Cost of providing food stamps to eligible persons who are not receiving them.

Total estimated cost of a Save America Budget: $173.3 billion

Sources: see note 67.

As a starting point for discussion, Table 7.6 illustrates that the lion's share of these program investments could be funded by major military budget reductions totalling between $100 to $120 billion annually. (Since there is some degree of overlap among these proposals, the range of possible savings from these proposals has been adjusted for double counting, etc.) These reductions could be made even without a major international arms agreement as they depend on scaling back unnecessary programs or waste within the military procurement system. Nonetheless, there would probably be substantial political and economic opposition to mounting such a program. The political opposition would likely center on security implications of adopting such proposals without a comprehensive approach to

Table 7.6   Proposed military budget cuts

John Lehman, former Navy Secretary, 'A New Blueprint for U.S. Forces', *The New York Times*, 26 March 1989:

$45 billion   A maximum estimate of the defense costs that could be reduced by reshaping the personnel of US Armed Forces to make one third of them 'ready reserves'.

Proposal by Seymour Melman, National Commission for Economic Conversion and Disarmament, Washington, DC for cutting strategic nuclear budget by 75%:

$43 billion   Savings from reductions in nuclear war preparation. The direct costs of procuring and maintaining long-range nuclear weapons, plus the indirect costs of preparing for nuclear war, for 1989 totals $57.5 billion. A 75% reduction in this spending would amount to savings of $43 billion and would leave multiple overkill capacity in place. Calculated from Stan Norris, Table C: Nuclear Weapons: FY 1982–1989, in 'Nuclear Notebook', *Bulletin of the Atomic Scientists*, Vol. 44, no. 10, December 1988.

'Effective Defense for Less Money', News Release 160, Center for Defence Information, Washington, DC, March 15, 1989.

$4.9 billion   Savings in 1990 from termination of the research/development of space-based components of the SDI program. This proposal would continue research only for land-based ABM system consistent with the ABM Treaty.

$3.4 billion   Savings in 1990 from termination of the Stealth bomber program.

$2.9 billion   Savings in 1990 from termination of the C–17 airlift aircraft program.

$2.0 billion   Savings in 1990 from suspension of the MX/Midgetman programs until rational mobile missile requirements are defined.

$1.6 billion   Savings in 1990 from termination of the V–22 Osprey aircraft program.

$1.5 billion   Savings in 1990 from ending overseas military construction and the U.S. contribution to NATO construction projects.

$.4 billion   Savings in 1990 from reduction in DoD civilian employees by 5% per year.

$.3 billion   Savings in 1990 from reduction of troop levels overseas by 5% per year.

$.1 billion   Savings in 1990 from suspension of the manufacture of new chemical weapons.

Congressional Budget Office, *Reducing the Deficit: Spending and Revenue Options* (Washington, DC: US Government Printing Office, February 1989):

$3.2 billion   Savings in 1990 if US allies increased their spending for US forces stationed overseas.

$1.7 billion   Savings in 1990 from cancellation of further development and procurement of the F–15 fighter plane.

$1.4 billion   Savings in 1990 from slowing procurement of DDG–51 Guided-Missile Destroyers.

$1.2 billion   Savings in 1990 from cancellation of the Rail MX basing system.

$.5 billion   Savings in 1990 by retiring the two oldest aircraft carriers.

$.38 billion   Savings in 1990 from cancellation of all future procurement of Phoenix Missiles.

$.12 billion   Savings in 1990 from slowing funding for the National Aerospace plane.

$.1 billion   Savings in 1990 from cancelling all programs for manufacturing binary (nerve gas) munitions.

Estimates by Robert Costello, Assistant Secretary of Defense for Procurement, as cited by Leonard Silk, *The New York Times*, 28 April 1989:

$50 billion   Savings from elimination of waste in Pentagon procurement.

Estimated savings from proposed military cuts: $100–$120 billion.

---

establish a multilateral arms reduction and disarmament process. Therefore, a realistic program of economic conversion must involve a comprehensive approach to security and disarmament.

A COMPREHENSIVE POLICY FOR ECONOMIC CONVERSION, DISARMAMENT AND ECONOMIC RECONSTRUCTION

We have already mentioned that more than 26 million persons are dependent on the military economy, including armed forces personnel, persons in military industry and their families. This dependency has created political and economic barriers to arms reductions, which can, it is argued, be overcome by systematic democratic planning for economic conversion. Economic conversion is the political, economic and technical process for assuring an orderly transformation of public and private economic resources now being used for military-oriented purposes to alternative civilian uses. Conversion planning involves several fundamental changes in the structure of political and economic decision-making and institutions. First and foremost, it involves a fundamental shift in national budgetary priorities to fund social needs. Second, in structuring alternative public spending priorities, state policy must manage aggregate demand so that the alternative set of civilian programs will compensate for the lower level of military spending. Third, the industrial and regional dependency on military production and activities must be addressed through the adoption of a conversion-planning process which involves: prenotification of contract termination or reduction; mandatory funding of alternative-use planning out of defense contractors' revenues; establishment of alternative-use committees within the firm which involve participation and co-decision-making by management and labor and consultation with the affected communities; worker and management retraining programs; and income maintenance and economic redevelopment assistance to impacted regions. Each of these steps is an essential component of a broader democratic planning process in restructuring the control over public capital and resources. Moreover, by providing these constituencies with new civilian jobs, the political and economic resistance to disarmament is likely to decrease. Defense managers, engineers and workers, as well as those seeking opportunities outside the armed forces, could find new opportunities through the social and infrastructure opportunities created by a comprehensive alternative budget.

What would the employment implications be from adopting such an alternative set of budgetary priorities? To establish a benchmark, let us examine the proposals advanced for increased infrastructural investment. David Alexander, a research fellow with the National Commission for Economic Conversion and Disarmament, has developed a conservative estimate of the number of direct jobs which could be generated in construction, and in the manufacture of materials and equipment for the infrastructural projects described by the Joint Economic Committee of Congress (see Table 7.4). He estimates that between 2.1 million and 2.7 million workers would be required annually to produce the materials, equipment and construction services in these types of public capital projects.[68]

Such a large-scale undertaking could more than compensate for much of the decrease in demand and employment brought about by a large-scale reduction in military spending. Yet, at the level of individual industries, firms and occupations, there would be a great deal of economic dislocation which would have to be addressed. It is for these reasons that economic-conversion advocates have identified the need for advance planning and prenotification of contract reductions and termination, as well as a program of alternative-use planning, income maintenance, retraining and relocation allowances. This programmatic approach could help to address the problems which are peculiar to military-serving industries and militarily-dependent regions.

The very organization of military-serving firms acts as an obstacle to conversion and disarmament. For example, military engineers are encouraged to design complicated systems which are not sensitive to costs and therefore limit the application of products to civilian markets. When military engineers have tried to design civilian products, they have often produced trolley cars and buses which don't work.[69] These failures to produce reliable, maintainable and competitively-priced civilian goods illustrates the need to retrain military engineers so that they can function in a civilian design culture. These shortcomings in military conversion experiences are compounded by the lack of familiarity with marketing requirements for civilian markets. To a large extent the military firms' marketing experience simply involves connections with Pentagon bureaucrats and an understanding of arcane bureaucratic regulations.[70]

The largest military-serving firms also lack an economic incentive to diversify into civilian production because profits tend to be higher in defense work and the market is guaranteed. Moreover, the Pentagon subsidizes a large portion of the costs of operating military production plants. Once a contract is won, military firms have often received what amounts to a 'blank check' from the federal government that covers the escalating costs of exorbitant military products.[71] In contrast to the lack of cost constraints in military industry, conversion depends on self-financing from contractors' revenues and an end to all subsidies.

A critical step for achieving this goal is the establishment of Alternative Use Committees to identify new products which can be produced with the existing workforce and productive resources. Such mandatory alternative-use committees would comprise management and labor under an arrangement of co-determination in civilian production decisions. This process of co-determination must be seen as a quid-pro-quo from any contractor when receiving substantial public monies for a federal defense contract. Planning must take place on the facility level to insure proper attention to the detail of regional economic needs and to apply the first-hand knowledge of management and labor in organizing new production. Planning must be decentralized and funded out of facility contracts to insure adequate economic support for advance planning and to avoid the exorbitant cost and planning difficulties in a centralized national planning office.[72]

Contingency plans must be developed in military-serving facilities across the nation before defense layoffs occur. Otherwise, military firms do not have sufficient lead-time to adequately retool factories, retrain workers and develop marketing plans necessary to competently serve civilian markets. Two-years lead-time is needed on average for this purpose. Funding must be in place to maintain workers' benefits while military firms, bases, laboratories and training institutions undertake conversion to civilian work. Without such funding, workers are not given the security that disarmament will not lead to displacement. The provision of two years of worker benefits for displaced defense workers would help maintain the labor pool needed while military plants are reorganized for civilian work.

The Defense Economic Adjustment Act, H.R. 101, introduced by Congressman Ted Weiss (Democrat from New York) contains the mandated alternative-use committees, facility-based planning apparatus, income maintenance and proper funding mechanisms necessary to insure a stable and orderly conversion of military-serving institutions.

In addition to the Weiss Bill, economic alternatives are needed for the millions of armed forces personnel who face unemployment as they are demobilized after any large military reductions, especially in the case of major arms reduction and disarmament treaties. Thus, there needs to be an explicit link between new employment and training legislation and economic conversion for military and civilian Defense Department personnel. Such retraining initiatives would embrace a wide range of occupations and skills within the military and its bureaucracies. This includes officers, non-commissioned officers, enlisted men and women, military engineers, technicians and specialists.

There is also the specific problem of economic conscription, or the process by which the poor and people of color are forced into military service, which has created a contradictory position for black leaders that advocate military cutbacks. Within the black and minority communities it is widely recognized that the military functions as the employer of last resort. As is well known, the unemployment rate of black youths has been around 20 per cent for most of the past decade, which is more than twice the rate for white youths. One estimate has found that 42 per cent of black youths who are eligible for military service actually enlist, as compared with 14 per cent of white youths. Furthermore, the percentage of blacks in active duty forces from the last year of conscription in 1972 to the end of 1986 nearly doubled, increasing from 11.1 per cent to 19.1 per cent.[73]

One proposal which seeks to provide alternatives for communities which have been forced into the armed forces by economic conscription is the 'Future Corps' bill in the Massachusetts legislature, sponsored by Mark Roosevelt in the House of Representatives and Mel King, Boston Rainbow Coalition leader. Such proposals need to be supplemented by national legislation which would provide educational and employment opportunities for the millions now serving in the nation's armed forces. These opportunities should be seen as part and parcel of a national economic conversion program.

DISARMAMENT AND CONVERSION

The fear of other nations' conventional and nuclear arsenals requires the establishment of a comprehensive and multilateral disarmament process in order to carry out major military budget reductions. A comprehensive disarmament treaty can make military reductions between the superpowers and other significant military powers mutually supporting. The historical precedent for such reductions lies in proposals developed in the Kennedy Administration.

Twenty-seven years ago policymakers at the highest levels of the US government were actively engaged in the formulation of plans for general and complete disarmament. They focused on the need for mutually verifiable, phased weapons reductions and strengthening of international institutions for conflict resolution. In 1961, John J. McCloy, President Kennedy's special adviser on disarmament, and Valerian Zorin, special ambassador of the Soviet Union, reached accord on the 'Joint Statement of Agreed Principles on General and Complete Disarmament'. These discussions led to the development of an 'Outline of Basic Provisions on General and Complete Disarmament', presented by the US Government to the Eighteen Nation Disarmament Conference in Geneva in 1962. Today, a revised version of such comprehensive proposals has been drafted by Marcus Raskin, co-founder of the Institute for Policy Studies in his 'Draft

Treaty for a Comprehensive Program for Common Security and Disarmament'. These documents provide a concrete focal point for public debate and organized action in Congress.[74]

CONCLUSION

The comprehensive conversion and disarmament program outlined here offers a viable and realistic political alternative to the current malaise. While some liberal policymakers continue to talk about increased taxes, deficit reduction and modest military budget cuts, they largely ignore the mounting social deficits which must be confronted. On the other hand, progressive social groups remain largely divided, focusing on single issues, rather than forging a common program which could draw together the political constituencies capable of reversing the nation's priorities. Meanwhile, certain elements of the left have focused their analysis on transnationals, failing to provide an alternative program to military hegemony over economic and political institutions – viewing the military economy as 'necessary' for capitalism – thereby ignoring the long-term decay and contradictions induced by militarism.[75] Other progressives have continued to focus on the necessity for changing the tax structure to resolve the fiscal crisis of the state. Yet they have not considered how these proposals fit into an overall program of conversion, disarmament and a realignment of our national priorities.

Expanded taxes are certainly warranted for corporations and the higher income groups that benefitted from Reagan's policies. However, industrial policy advocates like Jeff Faux and Seymour Melman have pointed out that one of the failings of the US economy has been insufficient domestic investment and cultivation of production competence;[76] domestic producers have either taken production elsewhere or opted for speculative financial investments instead. New taxes alone will not lead to the rebuilding of the productive base and the generation of social wealth (although it is necessary to revoke the foreign tax credits which encourage multinationals to take production overseas).

More directly, the revitalization of the economic base is another way to expand tax revenues. As more of the unproductive technological, labor and capital resources are shifted out of the military sector through conversion, the former military enterprises will become significant generators rather than absorbers of real wealth and taxable income. If military firms are able to produce the range of goods now imported, then they will contribute to the reduction of trade deficits and provide a new range of taxable income necessary to fund relatively non-capital-intensive social services and programs.

Conversion is a feasible solution to the nation's budgetary and social deficits. Increasingly, Congressional leaders are looking for new options instead of choosing between cutbacks in military jobs and social programs. Most recently, Richard Gephardt, Democratic House majority leader, and the presidents of six trade unions have each supported plans for national conversion legislation. Their interest corresponds to the 45,000 layoffs of military based and industrial workers which have occurred or are planned for the next several months.[77] Internationally, conversion planning has also been supported by Soviet President Gorbachev, Social Democratic and Green Party leaders in West Germany, the Labour Party in the United Kingdom and major trade-union federations and the government of Italy.[78]

Arms contractors within the United States are also exploring new civilian production options. A major aerospace firm in California has begun to explore the ways and means of expanding civilian production in an exchange program with the Soviet Union. The president of one of the US Navy's major producers, the Bath Iron Works, is an active supporter of economic conversion. President Duane Fitzgerald has made conversion part of the Bath company's strategic planning process.[79] A recent survey of forty-one top defense contractors by the Center for Strategic and International Studies, in Washington, DC, found that 'almost half are planning to switch more of their production effort into civilian goods'.[80] In addition, Grumman, an aerospace firm which has been the target of military cutbacks, has studied the possibilities of developing magnetically-levitated transportation (Maglev).[81]

Increasingly, it is clear that the military budget must be reduced to meet fiscal pressures, relieve the debt burden and provide the means for social, economic and environmental renewal. However, reductions in the military budget in and of themselves will not lead to the development of new productive investments or programs necessary to confront the nation's social deficits. Because of the concentrated political interests that lie behind military spending, support for a national economic conversion and disarmament program is necessary to provide the capital, labor and technological resources for rebuilding the nation. As a result, this program has become the necessary condition for meeting the political agendas of diverse social groups. The alternative is continued economic decay and splintering of the coalitions which have sought to maintain the Democratic Party's support for a progressive social welfare policy. This alternative also involves a basic change in the decision-making process about the control and use of public capital and resources, namely decisions about what is produced, where production is made, and for whose benefit.

Notes

1. Bill Keller, 'Economist's Deficit Figure Is Triple Kremlin's', *The New York Times*, 26 January 1989.
2. See Jonathan Feldman, Robert Krinsky and Seymour Melman, *Criteria for Economic Conversion Legislation* (Washington, DC: National Commission for Economic Conversion and Disarmament, December 1988); hereafter cited as Feldman et al.
3. John L. Palmer, 'Income Security Policies in the United States: The Inevitability and Consequences of Retrenchment', *Journal of Public Policy*, Vol. 7, Part 1, January–March 1987, p. 16.
4. Ibid., p. 18.
5. *A Shift in Military Spending to America's Cities*, US Conference of Mayors, p. 6.
6. Ford Foundation Project on Social Welfare and the American Future, *The Common Good* (New York: Ford Foundation, 1989), p. 6; hereafter cited as Ford Foundation.
7. *Statistical Abstract of the United States, 1989* (109th edition) (Washington, DC: US Bureau of the Census, 1989).
8. William B. Cannon, *New Class Politics*, (Washington, DC: Institute for Policy Studies, 1986), p. 1.
9. Ibid., p. 8.
10. Quote from Ford Foundation, *The Common Good*, op. cit., p. 19; data on child-care program from Nancy Saltford, Employee Benefit Research Institute, calculations as published in Harry Bernstein. 'Child Care a Big Need That U.S. Can't Meet on the Cheap', *The Los Angeles Times*, 10 January 1989.
11. Michael Weisskopf, 'Toxic Air Far Exceeds EPA Limits', *The Washington Post*, 9 June 1989. For an overview of the links between environmental security and military policy, see Michael Renner, 'Enhancing Global Security', in *State of the World, 1989* (New York: W. W. Norton & Co., 1989).
12. Robert O. Boorstin, 'Aging of Water Systems a Northeastern Epidemic', *The New York Times*, 3 August 1986.
13. Richard L. Wentworth, 'Cost and Profit in Cutting Acid Rain', *The Christian Science Monitor*, 17 March 1989.

14. 'Great Lakes Cleanup Costs Tallied', *The Washington Post*, 22 August 1989.
15. Environmental Protection Agency as cited in accompanying table to Barnaby J. Feder, 'Wringing Profits From Clean Air', *The New York Times*, 18 June 1989.
16. Margaret E. Kriz, 'Effluent, Not Affluent', *The National Journal*, 25 March 1989, p. 740 and Robbie Savage as quoted in Kriz, p. 741.
17. Philip Shabecoff, 'Rules on Drinking Water Not Enforced, Study Says', *The New York Times*, 13 December 1988.
18. Michael G. Renner, 'Shaping America's Energy Future', *World Policy Journal*, Summer 1987, pp. 393, 400.
19. Larry Tye, 'Solar Energy: A Technology Whose Time is Coming?', *The Boston Globe*, 11 April 1989.
20. Ibid.
21. Robert Suro, 'Grass-Roots Groups Show Power Battling Pollution Close To Home', *The New York Times*, 2 July 1989.
22. Frederic G. Reamer, 'The Affordable Housing Crisis and Social Work', *Social Work*, Vol. 34, no. 1, January 1989, p. 5.
23. 'Study Warns of Inadequate Housing', *The New York Times*, 18 March 1988.
24. The Institute for Policy Studies Working Group on Housing with Dick Cluster, *The Right to Housing* (Washington, DC: Institute for Policy Studies, 1989), p. 14.
25. Ibid., p. 8.
26. 'Units Reserved and Completed, 1981–1988', Public and Indian Housing Budget Division, Department of Housing and Urban Development, Washington, DC, 21 December 1988.
27. *The Federal Response to the Homeless Crisis*, Third Report by the Committee on Government Operations, 98th Congress, 1st Session, dated 18 April 1985 (Washington, DC: US Government Printing Office, 1985), p. 7.
28. Ibid., p. 3.
29. As cited in Reamer, 'Affordable Housing', op. cit., pp. 6–7.
30. Raymond J. Struyk and Christopher Walker, 'America's Housing Needs to the 21st Century', *The Urban Institute*, Washington, DC, January 1988, pp. 20–21.
31. Table 2 in the Institute for Policy Studies Working Group on Housing, op. cit., p. 11. Reamer, 'Affordable Housing', op. cit., reports that 'during the past 15 years, housing costs have accelerated almost three times faster than incomes', p. 5. Another major factor in the housing crisis is that 'the number of households in the United States is growing at a much faster pace than is the size of the population'. Quoted in Reamer, ibid., p. 63.
32. The housing march involved about 100 national organizations and about 150 or 200 steering committees, local and regional taskforces, and coalitions. See Jim Naureckas, 'HUD versus the huddled masses', *In These Times*, 30 August–5 September 1989.
33. Vincente Navarro, David U. Himmelstein, and Steffie Woolhander, 'The Jackson National Health Program', *International Journal of Health Services*, Vol. 19, no. 1, 1989, p. 19; hereafter Navarro et al.

34. Navarro et al., ibid.; Vicente Navarro, 'A New Health Care System for the United States', in *Winning America*, Marcus Raskin and Chester Hartman, eds (Boston: South End Press, 1988), pp. 216–17.
35. See Tables 3.3 and 6.1 of *Historical Tables, Budget of the United States Government, FY 1989* (Washington, DC: Government Printing Office, 1988).
36. Navarro et al., 'Jackson National Health Program', op. cit., p. 20.
37. Milt Freudenheim, 'Rising Number of Hospitals Forced to Close', *The New York Times*, 23 June 1988.
38. Robert Pear, 'Grants for Medical Research To Be Cut by Administration', *The New York Times*, 21 January 1985.
39. Ford Foundation, *The Common Good*, op. cit., p. 67.
40. Navarro et al., 'Jackson National Health Program', op. cit., pp. 29–31.
41. Martin Tolchin, 'Government Action Urged to Ease Nursing Shortage', *The New York Times*, 13 December 1988.
42. Public Information Division, Center for Disease Control, Atlanta, Georgia, August 1989.
43. Navarro, 'New Health Care System', op. cit., p. 224; Julie Kopsterlitz, 'AIDS Strains the System', *The National Journal*, 27 June 1987, p. 1650.
44. Milt Freudenheim, 'Big Gain Seen for Owner of AZT Maker', *The New York Times*, 19 August 1989; Philip J. Hilts, Major Changes for Health System Seen in Wake of the AIDS Finding', *The New York Times*, 19 August 1989.
45. Navarro, 'New Health Care System', op. cit., pp. 218–19.
46. Glenn Kramon, 'Employees Paying Ever-Bigger Share of Medical Costs', *The New York Times*, 22 November 1988.
47. Amanda Bennett, 'Firms Stunned by Retiree Health Costs', *The Wall Street Journal*, 24 May 1988; Michael Freitag, 'The Battle Over Medical Costs', *The New York Times*, 17 August 1989.
48. Freitag, ibid.
49. Cited in *Children's Defense Fund, A Children's Defense Budget, FY 1989* (Washington, DC: Children's Defense Fund, 1988), p. 135; Ford Foundation, *The Common Good*, op. cit., p. 135.
50. Leon Botstein, 'Education Reform in the Reagan Era: False Paths, Broken Promises', *Social Policy*, Spring 1988.
51. Ford Foundation, *The Common Good*, op. cit., p. 29.
52. 'Survey Finds Urban Schools Lacking Equipment and Staff', *The New York Times*, 29 September 1988.
53. See Ann Bastian et al., 'Restructuring Education', in Raskin and Hartman (eds), *Winning America*, op. cit.
54. 'Campus Buildings are Decaying, Survey Says', *The New York Times*, 18 October 1988.
55. *Historical Tables, Budget of the United States Government, FY 1990*, Executive Office of the President, Office of Management and Budget, Washington, DC, 1989, pp. 250–97, Table 12.3.
56. *The Economic Dislocation and Worker Adjustment Assistance Act of 1987*, Committee on Labor and Human Resources Report, 100th Congress, 1st Session, 2 June 1987, p. 7.
57. 'Is the Public Capital Stock Too Low?' by David Alan Aschauer, in

Chicago Federal Reserve Board Newsletter, October 1987, no. 2.

58. 'To Rebuild America – \$2.5 Trillion Job', *U.S. News & World Report*, 27 September 1982.

59. *Hard Choices: A Report on the Increasing Gap Between America's Infrastructure Needs and Our Ability to Pay for Them*, A Study Prepared for the Use of the Subcommittee on Economic Goals and Intergovernmental Policy of the Joint Economic Committee, Congress of the United States, 98th Congress, 2nd Session, dated 25 February 1984 (Washington, DC: Government Printing Office, 1984), p. 5.

60. David Alan Aschauer, 'Rx for Productivity', *Chicago Federal Reserve Board Newsletter*, September 1988, no. 13.

61. Robert Eisner, *How Real is the Federal Deficit?* (New York: Free Press, 1986), especially Chapter 3, pp. 26–32.

62. Thomas B. Edsall, 'Consensus Builds to Expand Aid for Working Poor', *The Washington Post*, 21 August 1989. Harold Wolman and Fred Teitelbaum, 'Interest Groups and Interests in the Reagan Era', *The Urban Institute*, Washington, DC, September 1983. William Greider, 'The Education of David Stockman', *Atlantic Monthly*, December 1981. See for example, James R. Barron, 'Gay and Minority Groups Compete for AIDS Money', *The New York Times*, 30 March 1989.

63. Peter Grier, 'US Public Wants Slender Pentagon', *The Christian Science Monitor*, 3 May 1989.

64. E. J. Dionne Jr., 'Governors Call for Spending to Prevent Economic Slide', *The New York Times*, 30 July 1989.

65. Jay M. Stein, The Economic Context of the Infrastructure Crisis', in Jay M. Stein (ed.), *Public Infrastructure Planning and Management*, (Newbury Park, CA: Sage Publications, 1988), pp. 26–9; Jonathan Rauch, 'Zero-Sum Budget Game', *National Journal*, 10 May 1986.

66. Ford Foundation, *The Common Good*, op. cit., p. 11.

67. Estimates for each element of the Save America Budget are derived respectively from the following: *Environment, Safety and Health Needs of The U.S. Department of Energy, Volume 2: Site Summaries*, US Department of Energy, Washington, DC, December 1988; 'Toxic Waste Threat Termed Far Greater Than U.S. Estimates' by Philip Shabecoff, *The New York Times*, 10 March 1985, p. 1; 'Enhancing Global Security' by Michael Renner in *State of the World, 1989* (New York: W. W. Norton & Co., 1989); p. 150; *Hard Choices: A Report on the Increasing Gap Between Infrastructure Needs and Our Ability to Pay for Them*, Joint Economic Committee, US Congress, Washington, DC, 1984, p. 5; the estimate for electrifying the nation's railroad was prepared by Professor John Ullmann, of Hostra University, Hempstead, New York; 'Reconstructing Education' by A. Bastian, N. Frucher, and C. Green in *Winning America* edited by Marcus Raskin and Chester Hartman (Boston: South End Press, 1988), p. 11; ibid; 'The Bush Budget' by the Center on Budget and Policy Priorities, 17 February 1989, p. 10; 'The President and the Children' editorial, *The New York Times*, 18 October 1987, p. 26; 'The Bush Budget', op. cit., p. 10; 'Campus Buildings are Decaying, Survey Says', *The New York Times*, 18 October 1988, p. 12; 'More Than a Fifth of School Buses are Unsafe, Agency Says', *The New*

York Times, 29 March 1989, p. 14; 'Decent Affordable Housing for All' by Chester Hartmann, *Winning America*, p. 197. 'A Fair Chance for the Baby', editorial, *The New York Times*, 27 September 1988; *Hard Choices*, op. cit. p. 5; 'The Bush Budget' by the Center on Budget and Policy Priorities, p. 5; ibid; 'Richest Got Richer and Poorest Poorer in 1979–87' by Martin Tolchin, *The New York Times*, 23 March 1988, p. 34.

68. David Alexander, *Peace Without Depression* (Washington, DC: National Commission for Economic Conversion and Disarmament, October 1989).

69. See Suzanne Gordon and Dave McFadden (eds), *Economic Conversion: Revitalizing America's Economy*, (Cambridge, MA: Ballinger, 1984), pp. 15, 133.

70. See Feldman, et al., *Criteria*, op. cit.; Seymour Melman, *Profits Without Production* (New York: Alfred A. Knopf, 1983).

71. Melman, *Profits Without Production*, op. cit.; A. Ernest Fitzgerald, *The Pentagonists*, (Boston: Houghton Mifflin, 1989).

72. Feldman, et al., *Criteria*, op. cit.

73. Alvin J. Schhexnider and Edwin Dorn, Chapter 5, 'Statistical Trends' in *Who Defends America?* (Washington, DC: Joint Center for Political Studies Press, 1989), p. 42. See also Jonathan Feldman, *Universities in the Business of Repression*, (Boston: South End Press, 1989). Also see the discussion in Thomas Byrne Edsall, *The New Politics of Inequality* (New York: W. W. Norton, 1984).

74. See Robert Krinsky, *An Introduction to Disarmament* (Washington, DC: National Commission for Economic Conversion and Disarmament, May 1988).

75. For example, see the comments in an interview conducted by Alexander Cockburn of James O' Conner in *Zeta Magazine*, February 1989, p. 20; also see the subsequent exchange of views on conversion in the letter by Jonathan Feldman, *Zeta*, May 1989, pp. 4–5, O'Conner's response in *Zeta*, July–August 1989, p. 6 and Feldman's rejoinder in *Zeta*, September 1989, p. 6–7.

76. See Jeff Faux, 'The Austerity Trap and the Growth Alternative', *World Policy Journal*, Summer 1988; also see Melman, *Profits Without Production*, op. cit., Chapters 13 and 14.

77. Laurie Essig and James Raffel, 'Conversion Gets A Hearing', *The New Economy*, National Commission for Economic Conversion and Disarmament, Washington, DC, Vol. 1, no. 1, August–September 1989.

78. See *The New Economy*, Vol. 1, no. 2, October–November 1989; Diana Johnstone, 'But Just How Big is the Market for Plowshares?', *In These Times*, 30 August–5 September 1989.

79. Donald M. Kreis, 'The Ploughshares Option', *Maine Times*, 28 July 1989.

80. *The Wall Street Journal*, 31 August 1989. See also, for example, 'Honeywell Announces Program to Enhance Shareholder Value', press release, Minneapolis, Minnesota, 24 July 1989. This release notes that the company intends to reduce its dependency on its weapons business. A report in *Business Week* describes pressures in addition to defense cuts that face

defense contractors. It notes that 'by the end of 1991 a huge chunk of the defense industry's unpaid taxes will come due. The 10 aerospace contractors . . . must come up with perhaps $6 billion between them . . .'. See Eric Schine et al., 'Incoming! Incoming! Arms Contractors Head for the Bunkers', *Business Week*, 11 September 1989.

81. The Maglev Technology Advisory Committee, 'Benefits of Magnetically Levitated High-Speed Transportation for the United States,' Vol 1. – Executive Report, Grumman Corporation, Bethpage, New York, June 1989. Also see Paul Kemezis, 'Department of Energy Proposes Maglev Network', *New Technology Week*, published by King Communications Group, Inc., Washington, DC, Vol. 3, no. 22, 30 May 1989. This form of rapid transit system could answer some of the pressing transportation problems in the United States, by enhancing mobility, reducing congestion on the roadways and airports, and by increasing energy efficiency and lowering transport costs. The Maglev system requires technologies traditionally associated with airplane manufacturing. A recent study by the Department of Energy's Argonne National Laboratory found that a $30 billion, 2000-mile magnetic levitation train system connecting large US cities to regional hub airports could pay for itself in twenty years.

Index